FIRM IN THE FAITH

For George John Bruce

Firm in the Faith

STEVE BRUCE

Department of Social Studies,
The Queen's University of Belfast

Gower

Published by
Gower Publishing Company Limited,
Gower House, Croft Road, Aldershot, Hants GU11 3HR,
England.

Gower Publishing Company,
Old Post Road,
Brookfield,
Vermont 05036,
U.S.A.

 British Library Cataloguing in Publication Data

Bruce,Steve
    Firm in the faith.
    1.Evangelicalism——Great Britain
    I.Title
    306'.6   BX4838   84- 5964

    ISBN 0-566-00705-3

Printed in Great Britain by
Antony Rowe Ltd.
Chippenham

Contents

Preface

This book is the product of about seven years of research. My interest in conservative Protestantism began when, as an undergraduate doing a degree in sociology and religious studies, I was obliged to undertake a small research project in the sociology of religion. A friend suggested that the campus Christian Union - a small group of evangelical students - might be interesting. The members of the Christian Union agreed to be the objects of research and I produced a report on the problems of proselytising and maintaining the faith in a hostile secular environment. My subsequent doctoral work was concerned with the history and development of the national organisation to which the Christian Union was affiliated. An interest in the rise of the Christian Unions involved me in explaining the decline of the once large, liberal Student Christian movement. I quickly realised that the rise of the Christian Unions and the decline of the Student Christian Movement simply represented in the universities a major change in the general popularity of liberal and conservative Protestantism. Thus my interest in a small group of student evangelicals became an interest in the fortunes of evangelical Protestantism.

Early on in my research one of the people who later turned out to be a great source of assistance confronted me with the problem of the difference between 'knowing' and 'knowing about'. He suggested that I could not really understand conservative Protestants until I shared their beliefs. If that were true then there would be no possibility of communication across boundaries. There would simply be closed worlds of believers who could only comprehend other inhabitants of the same belief world. I recognise that it is very easy to fail to understand people who share beliefs that are different to one's own and I also appreciate that there is a qualitative difference between 'knowing' and 'living' but I do not accept that these two observations prevent the outsider from a useful comprehension of worlds that are alien to him. After all, every sport attracts the devoted supporter who understands all the rules, tactics and stratagems of play, who is well acquainted with the history, traditions and folk-lore of the game and yet who has never played. To continue the twee metaphor, I feel that my relationship to conservative Protestantism is similar to that of the well-informed fan who, despite having never played, can claim to understand the game.

I might add that I have no desire to play. To be clear about my own values, I have consistently sought to understand the world of convervative Protestants, but I remain an atheist. However, I do not share the belief, common to many social scientists and journalistic commentators, that conservative Protestantism yet poses any major danger to the culture and institutions of pluralistic liberal democracies. I cannot equate pentecostalist meetings with the Nuremburg rallies nor can I believe that a desire to turn the moral clock back twenty years is comparable with the witch trials of Puritan New England.

The methods of the research have been many and varied. The first Christian Union study combined participant observation with the use of a questionnaire and long interviews. The doctoral research relied heavily on an examination of the records and documents of the Student Christian Movement, and on interviews with those involved in the Student Christian Movement and the Inter-Varsity Fellowship. Again, I tried to participate as much as possible in the Student Christian Movement. The subsequent work on conservative Protestantism has relied on documentary evidence, interviews, correspondence with leaders of various organisations, and my own observations from participating in activities such as evangelical crusades.

Although this book is written by a sociologist, it is not intended directly for other sociologists. It has little to say about specific debates within sociology even when the material presented could clearly have been used to illuminate such debates. I have chosen instead to keep the purely sociological to the minimum. I believe that conservative Protestantism is of sufficient importance and interest to require a treatment that is accessible to any reader of serious books.

Any work of this nature involves the accumulation of an enormous number of debts and I can only acknowledge these briefly. In the first place I am indebted to all of those people who participated in my work by giving me access to their records and their memories, and by introducing me to their activities and enterprises. It is invidious to single out any particular individual but Dr Douglas Johnson, who organised the Inter-Varsity Fellowship for thirty years, does deserve special mention as his support was instrumental in arranging contacts with other evangelicals. As well as access, one requires funding, and I wish to acknowledge a debt to the University of Stirling and the Social Science Research Council who each supported a year of my doctoral research, and to the Queen's University of Belfast and the British Academy, who have since assisted with small grants.

My main intellectual debt is to Professor Roy Wallis of Queen's University who first took an interest in my work when I was an undergraduate and who, as supervisor of my doctoral research, dispensed an ideal combination of encouragement and criticism. It is only fair to add that he has been consistent in opposing my tendency to abandon sociological rigour in favour of popular journalism. Failings in that direction are a product of my predelictions and not his guidance.

Earlier formulations of parts of chapters 4 and 5 have previously been published as 'The Student Christian Movement: a nineteenth century new religious movement and its vicissitudes' in the International Journal of Sociology and Social Policy, 2 (1), 1982, and 'Born again: crusades, conversions and brainwashing' in the Scottish Journal of Religious Studies, 3, 1982. Part of chapter 3 appeared in 'The Persistence of Religion: conservative Protestantism in the UK', Sociological Review 31 (3). I am obliged to the editors and publishers of these periodicals for their permission to re-use this material.

I would like to record my gratitude to a number of people who have become close friends since my arrival in Belfast and who have, with my wife, been instrumental in encouraging me through the doldrums of a long project. They would be embarrassed to be named but they know who they are.

Finally, I would like to thank the Queen's University Secretarial Centre for the excellent and expeditious production of this camera-ready copy.

1 Identifying conservative Protestantism

Writing about an organisation is relatively easy. It has edges. It has boundaries and one can decide that things inside those boundaries are one's concern while things outside are not. Writing about a tendency, a set of beliefs and practices that are constantly changing and shifting, which take different forms and shapes in different circumstances, presents a particular problem of selection. This book is concerned with the Ku Klux Klan in Texas, tent crusades in Belfast, sabbath observation on the island of Lewis, the innumberable splits in the Scottish Church, and the holy roller evangelists of the electronic church. Given this range of material, it is necessary to find some organising principle for this study, and I have decided to employ a question. This book is directed to answering the question: 'Why has this particular form of religion persisted as well as it has, and where it has?" At the end of the last century, it was commonplace for supposedly well-informed commentators to predict the rapid decline of old-fashioned supernaturalist religion. On all sides, religious practioners and atheists alike bowed down to the new God of secular culture. Man had come of age and no longer needed the old superstitions. The cognoscenti were agreed that the survival of religion depended on it finding a new modernised form, stripped of supernaturalism and made relevant to modern man. Making religion acceptable to secular reason and culture was recognised as the path to success.

From our vantage, such views seem naive. While religion may have been prepared to strike a bargain with the secular world, the secular world did not fight fair. The liberal churches with their modern faith have declined rapidly. The ecumenical movement has failed to produce either a united Christian presence or a halt in the decline of the fortunes of the cooperating churches. In contrast, the conservative variety of Protestantism has survived and, in some guises actually prospered, in this period of general decline of religion. Detailed evidence of this will be presented later but, as illustrations of this trend, one might point to the disappearance of the once dominant Student Christian Movement and its replacement in British universities and colleges by the conservative Christian Unions; the success of creationists in persuading school boards in some American states to down-grade evolution from an orthodoxy into simply one hypothesis among others; the success of the Moral Majority in displacing a number of leading liberal Senators and Congressmen in America and the rise of Ian Paisley's Free Presbyterian Church in Ulster. If conservative Protestantism is the dinosaur that the turn of the century liberals painted it to be, then it is a beast that has continued to survive in a hostile climate, and which, far from becoming extinct, shows signs of revival and growth. This book intends both to document and explain that reality.

WHAT IS CONSERVATIVE PROTESTANTISM?

Fundamentalist, reformed, orthodox, conservative evangelical, pentecostal; all of these adjectives and many more have been applied to the various groups and individuals who feature in this study. Naming is always difficult because it is not just a matter of identifying but also of judging. Naming is also complimenting and insulting. To make matters worse, some groups compete with each other for sole possession of some titles while other groups go to great lengths to avoid being given any of the above names. In this part of the introduction I want to advance a simple and, I believe, useful method for dividing up and distinguishing the various strands of Christian tradition in a way that makes clear the distinctive nature of conservative Protestantism.

Although the word 'epistemology' is rarely uttered outside philosophy departments, epistemology - the study of the grounds of knowledge - plays a large part in our lives. We all have to face the question of how we distinguish truth from error, of how we secure knowledge. It is this fundamental question which lies at the heart of the various conflicts within Christianity. What separates Protestant and

Catholic, liberal and conservative, is the problem of revelation. I will now depict four positions, four answers to the question of how one gains reliable salvational knowledge.

Liberal Protestantism

Being Protestant, the first feature of this position is its insistence on the superiority of the Bible over the traditions of the Church as a source of reliable knowledge. The second feature concerns the way in which the message of the Bible is to be discovered: 'the Bible has presented a changing face to changing circumstances. It is not as permanent as might appear at first ... The Bible belongs to its world and we belong to our world and the gap between the two amounts to a great chasm' (Bowden, 1970:91-2). The key to the liberal position is interpretation. Every culture has its own language, culture and circumstances. The Bible, although it contains the core of the transcendent teaching, is a product of particular culture. Thus to know what God expects of us, we must strip away the accretions of Greek, Hebrew and Aramaic worldviews and translate the core into our own culture. Only then have we correctly interpreted it. In its refined, intellectual form, this exercise is Bultmann's 'demythologising'. In its more popular form it is secularisation by separation of event and significance. Such a separation can be seen in the following remarks of Ruth Robinson about teaching a child the Gospel:

> We tell him: "Jesus was born in Bethlehem", and we tell him also "God sent his son into the world". The first of these statements is about what actually happened and the second is the interpretation we put upon it ... To confuse the two is to risk reducing the event together with its interpretation to incredible fantasy (Robinson, 1965:126).

The advantage of this distinction between the event and its significance is that it allows one to shift the creation of significance from God to man. It thus opens the way for believing that significance can change, without having to believe in a capricious God who changes his mind. The same event can be given different meaning and significance by the early Church Fathers, the Reformers, and ourselves. This is the 'new light' aspect of liberal Protestantism. Liberals do not believe that God's revelation was a once and for all act, the meaning of which is fixed and known. Revelation is seen as more of a progressive process. Hence no creedal statement can be complete; there may always be 'new light'. In practice, this method produces a 'secularised' gospel. Because the reason and culture of our secular society no longer accepts miracles, the miracles have to be removed from the Bible. The secular world no longer believes in the supernatural so the liberal removes the supernatural and turns away from an idea of a God 'out there' to a psychological idea of a 'God' 'in here', inside each of us.

Conservative Protestantism

Like the liberal, the conservative position asserts the primacy of the Bible but in contrast to the liberal treatment of interpretation and 'new light', the conservative position maintains that one can take the Bible at something close to face value. The Bible is seen as literally true (although certain stories may be taken as myths), as inspired by God, and as being penetrable by the same routine methods of reading that we use for any other sort of book. The conservative position then denies that there is any great chasm between the world of the Bible writers and our world. The only problems of understanding the Bible are those caused by bad translation, or the wrong attitude on the part of the reader. The evangelical position is captured in this quotation:

> Without entering into the irrefutable argument for the complete authority of the Bible in matters pertaining to God and His redemption of sinful man, I would criticise in the strongest terms the folly of those who, however scholarly they may be, have made it their business to tamper with the apostolic witness to Jesus in the days of his flesh. That witness is single, unmistakable and consistent ... We must linger upon this note, for it is futile to proceed until we are satisfied about the source upon which we must draw for our knowledge of the Word of God. If the apostolic witness is not our source, what is the alternative? (Lamont, 1946:7).

What Lamont calls 'the apostolic witness to Jesus in the days of his flesh' is, of course, for Lamont, known only through the words of the books of the New Testament.

Catholicism and Pentecostalism

If reason and culture, and the Bible, are the sources of reliable knowledge for the liberal and conservative Protestant respectively, one can, for the sake of completeness, mention the other two sources of authoritative revelation: the Church and the Spirit. In the Roman Catholic Church and the various Orthodox Churches, the traditions of the church are the main source of knowledge. In the pentecostalist churches and the charismatic movement, it is supposed that the Holy Spirit can speak to believers, either directly or through some piece of scripture.

There are thus four main sources of knowledge available in the mainstream Christian traditions; a reliance on one source rather than another neatly identifies the main groupings within modern Christianity. Hence one can introduce an element of rigour and consistency into the use of terms such as 'conservative Protestant'. The system of categorisation is summarised in the following diagram.

Sources of Salvational Knowledge

1 Reason/Culture	2 Bible
Liberal Protestant	Conservative Protestant
3 Church	4 Spirit
Catholic and Orthodox	Charismatic and Pentecostal

As always with an exercise like this, there are a number of points of likely misunderstanding which should be clarified. Firstly, this system is concerned only with the proximate source of authoritative revelation; with the part of the process nearest to the believer. It does not matter that the people who would fit into each of the four cells would claim that their revelation was not from the Bible, the Church or the Spirit but rather from God. Although each group believes that God is speaking, each has different notions about how that voice is heard. A second point to be made is that many Christians claim that they possess the 'right' mixture of all four elements. In some cases this is

5

just good politics (after all, most parties claim to be the centre party) but in other cases it is true that mixtures are offered. David Watson of York, for example, is an Anglican minister (hence he has some reliance on the authority of the Church), an evangelical who insists on the primacy of the Bible and he has the Pentecostalist's belief in the present-day availability of 'the gifts of the Spirit'. This sort of combination does not, however, reduce the value of the typology. One can still see that Watson gives less authority to the Church than does the high church Anglican or the Roman Catholic and his views on the Spirit are tempered by his evangelicalism. Thus, in my typology, I can locate his beliefs as being predominantly in cell 2, with elements of 3 and 4.

A further point to notice is that the system of classification is static while the beliefs of any identifiable group of people may well be changing. Again the value of the typology is that one can depict the direction of change. For example, the recent history of the Roman Catholic church shows moves of significant numbers from the traditional position in cell 3 towards cell 4 (Catholic Charismatics), cell 2 (the 'Biblical theologians') and cell 1 (the Catholoc modernists like Kung and Schillebeeckx).

The final point to be made about this system is that I am not personally committed to any of the epistemologies offered by the competing traditions. It is of no interest to me, as a sociologist trying to sort out his material, whether the Spirit really does talk to Pentecostalists, or whether the teachings of the Catholic Church really do embody the true essence of the Gospels. This system describes the foundations of the views that believers themselves have about the source of their revelation. I intend to use the believers' views as the basis for distinguishing between them, but this does not commit me to endorsing all, or any, of those views.

In terms of the typology, this book is concerned with the fortunes of the beliefs located in cell 2; conservative Protestantism. In places, time will be given to making points about liberal Protestantism in order to use the contrast to make clear some aspects of the conservative faith and fortune. There will also be references to Pentecostalism in discussions of some movements that would be placed in a grey area on the borders of cells 2 and 4. However, it is the cell 2 which is the main focus of this study, and the final section of this introduction will attempt to show some of the major divisions within the conservative Protestant tradition.

Fundamentalists, Evangelicals and the Reformed

The conservatives divide into a number of camps built round the fires of controversy about man's role in salvation, the way the world will end, and the nature of prophecy.

An important part of religious thinking concerns the relative power and autonomy of God and man. In many religions there are arguments about the degree to which humans can do anything to improve their chances of salvation. In the Protestant tradition, this controversy takes the form of an argument between those who call themselves Calvinists, and those whose position is called Arminian (after Jacobus Arminius, a seventeenth century Dutch divine, and not the country of Armenia). People such as Pastor Jack Glass of Glasgow, who would describe themselves as 'five point Calvinists', believe that men can do nothing at all to improve their chances of being saved. God decides (in advance) who will form part of the small 'elect'. Christ died not to atone for the sins of all of us, but for the sins of the elect alone. If one is part of the elect, that position cannot be lost. The cardinal doctrines of this view are often called by the acronym TULIP which is made from the first letters of the following phrases: total depravity of man, unconditional election, limited atonement, irresistible grace, and the perseverance of the Saints. Arminius argued against this highly deterministic view of man's position, and attempted to show that one could believe in an all-powerful sovereign God and still believe that men had real free will. American fundamentalists have always been Arminian; almost certainly as a result of the popularity of revivalism. While Calvinists protest that they have been misunderstood if one argues that revivalism and Calvinism are incompatible, it must be the case that it is hard to be enthusiastic about mass evangelism if one believes that only a predetermined elect will be saved anyway. Furthermore, there is always a distrust among Calvinists of revivals and crusades for the onus they put on the individual's 'decision for Christ', as if the individual sinner had any power to choose salvation or damnation. The views of the Highland Calvinist, John Kennedy, are well expressed in the following critique of crusades and revivalism:

> By means of sensational addresses a blind alarm is excited, those who are thus afflicted are treated as enquirers, they are plied with propositions about grace till a rational faith is produced, which has neither the Spirit as its author nor Christ as its object, and he who thus believes is called a convert, and the

result is ascribed to the Spirit of God
(Bulwark, October, 1971:120).

While the American fundamentalists are Arminian, the Scottish
and Ulster conservatives tend to be Calvinist and are often
called 'reformed' because of their claims to be the carriers
of the teachings of great Reformation divines. In fact, all
the Presbyterian Churches are still nominally Calvinist,
claiming as they do to support the Westminster Confession;
the fulsome statement of Calvinist Presybterianism that was
accepted by the Church of Scotland in 1647. In reality, most
Presbyterian church members are ignorant of the nature of the
Confession and most churches have passed later Acts which
were presented as modern principles for interpreting the
Confession, while actually denying its main teachings.

English conservatives are a mixture of Calvinists and
Arminians (Charles Simeon of Holy Trinity, Cambridge, was
reported to have described himself as a Calvinist when
praying and an Arminian when preaching). The arguments
between the fundamentalists and the evangelicals on the one
hand, and the reformed on the other, tend to focus on the
'altar calls' and doctrinal teaching. The fundamentalist
practice of asking people to make decisions for Christ, to
let the Lord into their hearts, and so on, is condemned by
the reformed as giving too much weight to man's part in the
process of getting saved. This revivalist practice is also
condemned for a lack of systematic doctrinal teaching. Where
the fundamentalist emphasises preaching, the reformed
emphasise teaching.

The precise order of events at the end of the world is
another focus of controversy. All are agreed that there will
be a millennium, a period of a thousand years of blessedness,
but there is much argument about whether this will occur
before the Second Coming of Christ (post-millennialism) or
after it (pre-millennialism). There are other disagreements
about who will enjoy this millennium and where it will be (in
heaven or on earth), but it is the timing issue that is
important in understanding conservative Protestantism because
of the different consequences that pre- and
post-millennialism have for politics and social reform.
Those people who believe that the millennium will come before
the day of Judgement tend to an optimism in social and
political matters. Those who expect the Judgement to come
before the millennium are usually very pessimistic about
man's ability to improve his fortunes on this earth.
American fundamentalists are pre-millennialists. In
contrast, the British reformed tradition is
post-millennialist or uncommitted on the question.

The final main area of difference between the
fundamentalists and the reformed concerns prophecy. The

fundamentalist tradition is very keen on the idea that the prophecies of the Bible (especially those of the books of Daniel and Revelations) are to be interpreted as applying to our present and future. While other traditions have either ignored these prophecies or have seen them as applying to some time that was in the future of the writer but which is now in our past, the fundamentalists continue to look to the prophecies of Daniel and John for the meanings of present-day events. Ian Paisley (who, although he sees his position as 'reformed', is far nearer to the fundamentalism of the American Bob Jones than he is to the Calvinism of Jack Glass) regards the European Economic Community as a body whose existence was prophesied by Daniel. Evangelicals tend to an undecided position on the prophecy question.

These various distinctions will hopefully become clearer in the historical review that follows this introduction, when particular people, organisations and issues will be presented to embody these abstract systems of belief.

2 Conservative Protestantism: recent history

This chapter has two purposes. It aims to put flesh and blood around the rather abstract bones of the introduction. It also aims to introduce the organisations whose fortunes will be compared in the next chapter, which presents detailed evidence on the survival and revival of conservative Protestantism. I will begin this brief review with an account of American revivalism and fundamentalism. I will then describe the development of Scottish and of Ulster Presbyterianism, and look at the position of conservative Protestantism in England. The situation in other countries, South Africa for example, will be referred to at various points in other parts of the book. I have chosen to focus on America and the United Kingdom for two reasons. In the first place, the nature of conservative Protestantism in other parts of the English-speaking world is largely a product of British and American influences. Where there are important variations, such as in the role of the Dutch Reformed Churches in South Africa's apartheid policy, these will be brought out. In the second place, this arena provides enough variety of forms of conservative Protestantism for one to be able to make worthwhile generalisations.

REVIVALISM IN AMERICA

Revivalism has always been American. It is not unfair to say that little has been contributed by Britain to this

10

phenomenon; with the exception of Methodism, British revivals have been sparked either by the example of a preceeding revival in America or by the direct action of visiting American evangelists. The first 'Great Awakening' of religious enthusiasm was led by Jonathan Edwards in the 1740's but of more significance was the outburst of revival feeling on the Kentucky frontiers between 1798 and 1810. In Tennessee, West Virginia and the Carolinas, large numbers of people, isolated by the rough pioneering existence from their traditional cultures, were caught up in an outburst of religious activity that was more than frenzied. Camp meetings ran for days on end with thousands of people listening, not to one preacher, but to scores of preachers and lay individuals, standing on wagons and sitting in trees, proclaiming the message of sin, damnation, salvation and redemption. Fainting was common, as were trances and cases of catalepsy. As Weisberger (1958) puts it, this emotionalism was the natural reaction of a people who spent the rest of their lives controlling their emotions and feelings in order to channel their energy into a sometimes desperate, but always hard battle with their harsh environment[1].

Like all novelty, these revivals received differing reactions from different Protestant churchmen. The long-established Presbyterianism of New England and the mid-Atlantic states, the grandson of seventeenth century Puritanism, had become sophisticated. It was now the faith of the successful classes with its intellectual base in the prestigious colleges of Princeton and Yale. Weisberger describes the preaching of this Presbyterianism in the following way: 'the established method in the East was to choose a text, deduce a doctrine from it, and lead the doctrine through an hour or two of "application" honeycombed with theological pits and snares' (1958:39). In contrast, the frontier preacher was committed to making the word 'quick and powerful'. Thus one source of conflict between the Frontier revival and the old Eastern religion was the nature of religious teaching and the use of untrained ministers. In the camp meeting, vigour and enthusiasm counted for more than erudition. Another axis of argument was the Calvinism/Arminianism conflict. For those people who believed in the doctrines of grace, in predestination and in a small body of the elect, the religious enthusiasm of the frontier revivals, with their implication that any sinner could be saved by 'being converted', was anathema.

These two things, the learned ministry and basic Calvinism, hindered the Presbyterians (and to a lesser degree, the Congregationalists) from profiting from the Frontier revivals. The Methodists were mainly Arminian, however, and had no problems with the practice of 'saving souls'. Revivals were not immediately accepted by the Eastern churches and even after the Presbyterians had come to live with 'experimental religion', revivals were often talked of as producing 'reported conversions' rather than simple 'conversions', in order to make it clear that someone claiming to have been converted was not itself enough, and did not guarantee salvation except to the elect. Only God knew if that person was really saved and so one used the 'new methods' but reserved judgement as to the validity of the conversions of any particular individual.

The next major stage in the development of revivalism was its 'return' to the East. In order to make the new measures palatable to the New England urban audiences, the wild antics of the Frontier had to be tamed and routinised, and this task was well performed by Charles Finney. Finney was mid-way between the old circuit-riders of the West and the intellectual pastors of the cities. He had trained as a lawyer and tempered his post-conversion enthusiasm with some theological training, but he still retained the melodramatics of the earlier form. Preaching on hell he said:

> Look! Look! ... see the millions of wretches,
> biting and gnawing their tongues, as they lift
> their scalding heads from the burning lake
> ... See! See! how they are tossed, and how
> they howl ... Hear them groan, amidst the
> fiery billows, as they lash! and lash! and
> lash! their burning skins (Weisberger,
> 1958:115).

Finney not only moderated the style of revivals, he also participated in the erosion of Calvinism. He agreed with Beecher and Taylor (the leading exponents of what was called "New Haven' theology) that man was a reasoning moral agent capable of responding to the threats and promises of the scriptures.

Revivalism and Social Reform

A common mistake is to transfer the features of a phenomenon of one period back into its past. Revivalism is today firmly connected with conservative social and political positions but this was not always the case. Finney's revivalism was far from being conservative in its social implications. In the period from 1830 to 1880 conversion and reform were twin waves. There is the example of the theology students who walked out of their college because the trustees were pro-Slavery. They took with them one member of the faculty, Asa Mahon, and founded Oberlin College. Finney accepted

Oberlin's theology chair and his first act was to erect a large tent for prayer meetings with a banner reading 'Holiness to the Lord' streaming from its top. Oberlin, unlike most colleges of that period, was open to negroes and women.

The revivalists of this period could be associated with movements for social reform because they were for the most part post-millennialists. They believed that the millennium would precede judgement and that it could be created here on earth by the conversion of everyone. Holiness and reform were both laying the foundation for the Kingdom of God on earth; holiness by converting the people, and reform by channelling the energies and finances of converts into works that would make it easier to convert others. Because social problems were seen as caused by the sinfulness of the individual there was no conflict in viewing conversion as the solution to the problems of the modernising world. Poverty, alcoholism, bad housing, were all laid at the door of sin, and conversion was their cure.

Thus the serious division in American religious life of this period was not between conservatives who believed in conversion and crusades, and the liberals who did not (as is the case in this century). Rather the major division was between the very conservative (such as the Princeton theologians) who were reluctant to become involved either in 'the new measures' or in the new theology, and the revivalists. Revivalism was radical.

Another error of historical naivete would be to suppose that revivalism was always associated with sectarianism and doctrinal conservatism. Dwight L. Moody was the next great evangelist after Charles Finney. Raised in 'poor but honest' rural circumstances, Moody went to Chicago and quickly showed himself to be a very promising salesman. He got involved in minor religious works during his spare time (such as renting a church pew and then going out into the streets to find strangers to fill it) and gradually became a full-time evangelist making his first mark by building up a very large Sunday school. Although he was soon quite well-known locally, he did not achieve national status until he swept through Great Britain in 1872 and 1873. Moody's innovation (apart from the use of a professional singer, Ira D. Sankey, as his co-evangelist) was in the preparation of an area for a revival. He normally refused to hold meetings in a town until most of the clergy of the major denominations had jointly sponsored the mission and invited him. In this way he avoided the error of Finney who, on his Scottish tour, had allowed himself to be promoted by the Evangelical Union. The Union had broken away from the Kirk in order to reject the traditional conservative Calvinism of mainstream Scottish Presbyterianism. By allowing himself to be sponsored by this small movement, Finney guaranteed a cold reception from the rest of Scottish Protestants. Moody's own personality and theology made inter-denominational co-operation possible. He was the archetypal 'simple man', who had no interest in the finer points of doctrine and theology, and who was so disregardful of the popular controversies as to promote harmony among all who met him. In his British mission he gained the co-operation of Horatius Bonar (a leading Scottish Calvinist), the Brethren, low and high Church Anglicans, and dissenters of every variety. Significantly, his strongest supporters in Scotland were not in the Church of Scotland but in the Free Church. The Glasgow and Edinburgh Free Churchmen were becoming progressively more liberal. For example, the man who was probably Moody's closest friend in Scotland was Henry Drummond, a Free Church college teacher and the author of The Ascent of Man, a work that affirmed man's own capacity for improvement and which reeked of Darwinism, and The Spiritual Law in the Natural World, which was heavily rationalistic. Moody straddled two worlds, as did the Free Churchmen who could combine an appreciation for higher criticism, evolutionism and natural science and a social gospel with a belief in the necessity of conversion and personal piety.

A modern fundamentalist historian, George Dollar, has tried to claim Moody for the fundamentalist stance of separation from more liberal Protestants by showing that toward the end of his life he bowed to pressure from colleagues, and refused to invite his old friend Drummond to speak at his annual Northfield Conferences (1973:80). This story is, however, suspect. Drummond himself reports that he did give a series of addresses at Northfield in 1893, and that he 'felt rather out of it' (Smith, 1902:421). But, whatever the audience reception it is clear that he was there. He never returned to the States, and was an invalid from 1895 until his death in 1897. But although there is no evidence for any final break between the two men, the cultures they represented were moving apart. J.W. White (1963: Chapter 3) expressed the development very clearly in noting that after Moody's death the two institutions he had created parted company. The Chicago Bible Institute (now the Moody Bible Institute), under the leadership of Reuben A. Torrey, became a stronghold of separatist fundamentalism and the Northfield Conferences, under the influence of John R. Mott, became the spawning ground for the rising ecumenical movement[2].

AN EXCURSUS INTO SOCIOLOGICAL EXPLANATION

Leaving aside for a moment the development of revivalism and
the attendant changes in belief and practice, there is the
fascinating question of why these revivals occurred when, and
where, they did. The Christian might explain them as being
simply the working of the Holy Spirit, but even most
believers would want to go beyond the idea that the Lord acts
in a totally random way, and offer reasons for the revival
being in, for example, 1859 rather than 1860. When such
reasons are given they are normally sociological or
quasi-sociological. Features of the social or material world
are identified as things that brought large numbers of people
under 'conviction of sin', and the influence of social
pressure on the sinner is often mentioned. McLoughlin argues
that there is no meaningful correlation between the 'Great
Awakenings' and periods of political or economic crises.
Sizer (1979:87) disagrees and argues that episodes of
revivalism coincide with periods of major political change.
Lyman Beecher came to the fore when Federalism was in decline
and America was witnessing the rise of Jeffersonian
Democracy. Finney's best work coincides with the rise of
Andrew Jackson. The revivals of 1857-58 coincided with the
anti-slavery crisis, and the rise of republicanism, and the
Moody revival of 1875-77 followed on the failure of
post-civil war reconstruction and the resurgence of the
Democratic Party. The 1857-58 revival also followed a
financial crisis and was built on lunchtime prayer meetings
filled by businessmen and their clerks whose anxiety about
their souls was probably related to anxiety about their
wealth.

One of the best arguments for a casual relationship
between social change and religious enthusiasm is Norman
Cohn's The Pursuit of the Millennium (1970). He is concerned
with the genesis of the curious, often violent, movements of
revolutionary millenarianism that occurred in medieval
Europe. His thesis is that economic and social change was
destroying the stability of peasant life. Early
industrialisation produced new desires while the
precariousness of the economies and the large fluctuations in
markets prevented these desires being regularly met. He
argues that it was not hardship as such that produced the
flagellants and the crusades of the poor. Hardship was the
norm, the accepted mundane reality for most peasants. Rather
it was the disruption of the traditional economy that
produced disruptions in society and culture:

> Journeymen and unskilled workers, peasants
> without land or with too little land to
> support them, beggars and vagabonds, the

> unemployed and those threatened with
> unemployment, the many who for one reason or
> another could find no assured and recognised
> place - such people, living in a state of
> chronic frustration and anxiety, formed the
> most impulsive and unstable elements in
> medieval society (Cohn, 1970:59).

At its most general the argument is that major social,
political or economic change disrupts people's worlds and
causes them to react irrationally and inappropriately. Where
the 'real' problem is economic disruption, the flagellants
reacted in an inappropriate religious manner. Where the
'real' problem was the failure of post-Civil War
reconstruction in America, Moody's 1877 audiences responded
with religious conversions.

There are a number of difficulties with using crises or
rapid social changes as explanations of behaviour. In the
first place there is no surety that what appears _in
retrospect_ to be a 'crisis' actually felt like that to those
who were there at the time. Before one could use tension
associated with some event or set of circumstances to explain
anything, one would have to be convinced that the people
whose behaviour one was explaining, themselves regarded that
event or those circumstances as a 'crisis'. My own
experience of living in Belfast suggests that one can live in
a time and place that is regarded from outside as 'in crisis'
(and will be recorded that way in history), and yet feel no
particular tension or fear. One has to be careful of
generalising from one's own supposed reactions to a
re-creation of 'what it must have been like', to the
reactions of either all the people involved or to unspecified
groups of people involved. To continue the Belfast example,
it seems clear to me that the staff of Queen's University who
lived in the south of the city were far more concerned about
the effects of government cuts in university budgets than
they were about the political climate of Ulster.

The second problem with this type of explanation is that
even when one chooses events which few people would regard as
anything other than a massive upheaval and crisis, one
sometimes finds no religious revivals and no outbreaks of
collective behaviour or social movements. The two world wars
were notable for producing little or nothing by way of new
religious movements (Wuthnow, 1980:57-58) nor any increased
commitment to the existing forms of religious practice. One
of the most extensive studies of the impact of war on
religious belief, the YMCA's study of the British Army in the
First World War (Cairns, 1919) contains no suggestion that
the war caused any increase in interest in religion.

But even if one allows the identification of the supposed crisis, and finds that it does actually coincide with some outburst of collective behaviour, one still has to be clear about the nature of the connection between the two things. In most explanations that take the form of some objective reality being related to the behaviour being accounted for, the objective reality is given as the 'cause' of the behaviour. That is, there is a mechanical cause and effect model in which human behaviour is seen as an automatic response to some objective stimulus. In some cases such an implication is not intended and is only there because the author is less than specific about the connection between the supposed stimulus and the behaviour being explained. In other cases, however, the implication is intended and it follows from an initial distinction between rational action and irrational behaviour. Certain types of activity are seen as rational and purposive and these are explained by pointing to the actors' beliefs and intentions. Other types of behaviour are regarded as irrational and are explained, not in terms of beliefs and intentions but in terms of anxiety and compensation. Some social change worries people. They become anxious and they resolve their anxiety, not by rationally solving their original problem, but by engaging in some compensatory activity. In such a view, religious revivals are seen as compensatory rather than purposive. They are to be understood, not in terms of the stated purposes of those involved (who may say that they are whipping themselves in order to hasten the end of the world and the arrival of the Millennium), but in terms of whatever objective factor is thought to have caused the anxiety for which the activity compensates.

This type of explanation involves a basic misunder-standing about the nature of human action. It supposes that people respond automatically to stimuli. Such a model has been effectively criticised by Chomsky (1973) and Blumer (1969) among others. Unlike some other species of animals we do not possess a well-developed set of instincts that tell us how to behave in any given situation. Like it or not, we have to construct our own action, and we have to <u>interpret</u> the circumstances in which we find ourselves. Objective circumstances do not mechanically produce responses from us. Rather they provide the basic material which we have to deal with in constructing our own plans of action. What we make of those circumstances is determined, not by the circumstances themselves, but by our reaction to them, by our interests, aspirations and existing beliefs. Thus any satisfactory account that uses objective circumstances (such as the financial crash of 1856) as an explanation of religious revivals cannot take the form of 'reality-anxiety-compensation'. It has to be deployed in a more circumspect fashion. For example, one could suggest that there were in New York in 1857 a large number of people who shared a vague belief in the basic doctrines of Christianity. There were also people steeped in the millennial tradition that interpreted every major event as a sign of the 'end times'. For such people the crash could be easily been seen as divine judgement. If the crash was a sign from the Lord, then showing deference to the Almighty and getting some religion would be quite a sensible course of action. Thus there were a number of people in New York in 1857 who possessed a worldview in which a revival was quite an appropriate reaction to economic problems. In addition, the preachers and purveyors of revivalism offered their product as a solution to problems of every sort, including financial ones. Given such a combination, engaging in a revival, far from being irrational and compensatory behaviour, appears quite sensible and purposive. For those doing it, revivalism was a solution to problems; it had a purpose which would be realised in the first place by getting saved oneself and then by saving the rest of the world. The Lord would right the financial institutions (if he did not return before their chaos became a serious nuisance).

In a later discussion of conversion, I will pursue some of these ideas. At this stage all I want to argue is that if objective circumstances are going to be used to explain why people behaved as they did, then they must be viewed as circumstances which create problems for actors, which create new opportunities, and which perhaps set limits on what actors can and cannot achieve. That is, the role of the human consciousness must be preserved. It cannot be neglected in favour of a mechanical causal story. In the particular case of religious revivals, it is clear that the search for some single objective cause of revivals has led many analysts to miss the obvious. Revivals occurred where and when they did because those were places and times in which people wanted revivals. It is said of an Ulster preacher in 1859, that: 'news of revival in America stirred him to seek to promote a revival among his own people. He often preached on this subject and read accounts of great revivals of the past to his congregation. The idea of having a revival began to grip the people and it became the subject of much prayer' (Allen, n.d.:27). Prayer may well be talking to God but it is firstly talking to oneself and to other's engaged in communal prayer. Given that those who prayed for the revival were the same people who first claimed the effects of the revival, there is no need to go beyond the proposition that these people had a religious revival because they wanted one. Those who were not initially involved then became drawn in; in some cases attracted by what was on offer, in other cases forced in by the pressure to conform.

Good marketing played its part. Reality is socially constructed. Most of what we know and believe about the world is acquired from others and kept in place because others continue to support that view of 'how things are'. For this reason, new movements can acquire legitimacy simply by virtue of their popularity. If enough people are doing it, it must be correct. If enough people believe it, then it must be true. Good marketing techniques can thus produce legitimacy for a new movement by creating the impression that the movement is already popular. Marketing, even in its pre-electronic media days, required financing, and a vital part in the spread of the 1858 revival from America to Ulster (where it became the 1859 revival) was played by a sum of $70,000 which was raised in America to finance the Ulster work (Carwardine, 1978:405).

The parting of the ways; revivals become conservative

> Who does not see that, with the termination of
> injustice and oppression, of cruelty and
> deceit; with the establishment of
> righteousness in every statute book, and in
> every provision of human legislation and human
> jurisprudence; with art and science sanctified
> by the truth of God, and holiness to the Lord
> graven upon the walls of our high places, and
> the whole earth dwelling in the rain of
> righteousness, this world will be renovated by
> the power of holiness ... Oh, this is the
> reign of Jesus (Smith, 1965:221).

Thus wrote a Dutch Reformed Church pastor in the 1850's. By 1900, such a fusion of personal and social righteousness was an anachronism. The two streams had separated, with revivals becoming the preserve of the conservatives, and the social gospel becoming a specialist creed associated with modernism and liberalism. The explanation of this requires an understanding of a number of changes. Firstly, the population which provided the audience for evangelistic rallies has to be identified. The people who went to hear the revivalists in this period were not the old established bourgeoisie of the towns and cities; they were the white Anglo-Saxon Protestants moving in from the countryside. 'It meant nothing to them if the preacher talked of social responsibility, or the mutual duties of classes, or the uselessness of struggle for gain. They wanted to hear, rather, that the ancient virtues still paid. They wanted to be told that the only obstacles in their way were those of character' (Weisberger, 1958:159). The social reforming gospel had no appeal for this large constituency who were concerned with 'getting on'. Secondly, the traditional evangelical analysis of social problems as the result of individual moral failings became patently inadequate for the new problems of massive urban decay, cycles of trade depression and poverty, industrial unrest, and 'robber baronism' in business. As Weisberger suggests, the traditional crusades against drinking, gambling, smoking and dancing, which had once seemed noble efforts, now looked petty and mean.

Thirdly, even if the social analysis of the evangelicals had been capable of explaining and suggesting reasonable solutions for these new problems, there were large vested interests which would have opposed such a move. Apart from the interests of the audience - which I have already mentioned - there were also the class interests of the men who were taking an ever larger part in sponsoring evangelistic work. Moody was heavily financed by leading American tycoons and robber barons as were later evangelists, and, even today when much of the successful evangelist's income derives from a very large number of small donations, such sponsorship is important[3]. Without accusing Moody or others of hypocrisy, one can appreciate how such indebtness could reinforce the individualistic nature of evangelical social thought.

Twentieth Century Fundamentalism

Dollar (1973) has summarised the essence of liberalism as a respect for science, a belief in scepticism as the basis of knowledge, confidence in man and his future, a replacement of the Bible by 'the religious life' as the centre of the faith, and a desire to emphasise similarity and likeness rather than dissimilarity. This description is certainly more to the point than the normal focus on the Darwinian controversy. It was against these tendencies, rather than against Darwin, that fundamentalists defined themselves. From the turn of the century onwards, all the major denominations were racked with controversy between liberals and conservatives. By 1930, the major denominations were solidly liberal, and the conservatives were to be found in small breakaway churches. By and large conservatism was given its organisational base, not by any one church, but by Bible Institutes and Colleges. Moody's Chicago Bible Institute was one such establishment. The Northwestern Schools, founded by W.B. Riley, was another location of fundamentalism. Riley himself refused to leave the liberal Northern Baptist Convention until 1947, hanging on in the hope of bringing the Convention back to its traditional faith, even though every motion he supported at the Convention was overwhelmingly rejected. It was some time before the doctrine of total separation from apostasy became established among fundamentalists. The Bible Baptist Union, a short-lived body formed in the late 1920's to give coherence to the fundamentalists' opposition to liberalism, allowed dual membership and Riley was prominent in that fellowship while remaining within the Northern Baptist Convention.

Modern American Fundamentalism and the Rise of Billy Graham

As the theology of the liberals developed into modernism, so the concept of individual conversion came to have little or no meaning for them, and 'revivals' and 'crusades' in the traditional sense were left in the hands of the conservatives. The liberals had won the battles within the churches, and the conservatives formed their own parallel organisations. As is normally the case, the conflict with the liberals produced a sense of cohesion and consensus within the conservative group that blinded many to differences which were later to emerge.

Even as Carl McIntire, a notorious conservative figure, was forming the American Council of Christian Churches (ACCC) to oppose the liberal and ecumenical Federal Council of Churches, the basis was being laid for an alternative organisation – the National Association of Evangelicals – which came to stand for the 'neo-evangelical' position. The most famous neo-evangelical is Billy Graham[4]. Graham was born in South Carolina and raised in a conservative church-going environment. He was converted after being brought under conviction of sin by Mordecai Ham. After school he went for a brief period to the Bob Jones University (described by one writer (King, 1966) as 'the buckle on the Bible Belt'), but found the discipline and seriousness a little too narrow and constraining for him. After completing his education at Florida Bible College, Graham ran a small Lutheran ministry for a short time before embarking on a career as an evangelist. His entry into big league evangelism was made possible by Torrey Johnson. Johnson organised a series of special revivals for young people (which grew into the Youth for Christ International organisation), and he was impressed by Graham's success with this audience. Johnson also passed over to Graham a television slot that was to prove his forte (Larson, 1945).

Soon Graham was organising ever larger campaigns in bigger tents. More television slots were hired and more money raised to pay for them. William Randolph Hearst, the American newspaper magnate, (who provided the model for Wells' Citizen Kane) is reputed to have instructed his editors to 'Puff Graham'. Certainly he got a great deal of media attention, in no small part due to his own flair for self-promotion. An important part of Graham's work was built on advertising the conversion of celebrities. One such case was Jim Vaus who was advertised as a serious gangster but who in reality was only the electronic bugging specialist for Mickey Cohen, a rather small time operator (Vaus, 1961). Like Moody, Graham soon sensed the need for a broad base of denominational support, and he very quickly lost whatever qualms he had about cooperating with liberals, and even Catholics. Again, like Moody, fine points of doctrine were never Graham's concern, and 'soul-saving' became the sole criterion for evaluating the work. McIntire, Bob Jones and other leading fundamentalists were quick to perceive and denounce the 'middle-of-the-roadism' (as Jones called it) of Graham's position. A major focus for the 'neo-evangelical' view, apart from the National Association of Evangelicals (NAE), is the magazine <u>Christianity Today</u>.

A common sociological phenomenon is the intensity of conflict <u>within</u> apparently similar cultures of belief. In my own research I have found that most shades of conservative can communicate with me because I pose no threat to them. I make no claims to the territory they want to hold, and I am in no position to claim that I am 'the true Christian'. Fundamentalists seem to spend more of their time attacking other people who call themselves Christians (such as liberals, ecumenists and modernists) than they do arguing against the heathen. And they spend more time arguing their possession of the one true faith with neo-evangelicals than with liberals. The fundamentalists can usually live with the reformed provided the issues of prophecy and millennialism do not come up. They are reluctant to accept the Holiness movement of the British Keswick tradition, with its argument for a 'higher spiritual life', because of its lack of doctrine and the willingness of Keswick evangelicals to work with churches such as the Church of England which have modernists, liberals and ritualists within their ranks. But fundamentalists dislike Billy Graham intensely. Dollar of Bob Jones University clearly expresses the fundamentalist position (1973:193) in attacking the NAE's interest in social issues, its soft line on the ecumenical movement and its permissive attitude towards separation.

The secretary of the British Evangelical Council, a 'reformed' body which has among its members the Free Church of Scotland, the Evangelical Presbyterian Church of Ireland and various Strict Baptist Churches, enthusiastically attacked the neo-evangelicals who - at the invitation of Billy Graham - attended a Conference on World Evangelism in Lausanne in 1975:

I want to pinpoint the extraordinary double
thinking evidenced by so many evangelicals in
that congress (at least half of whom are said
to be still in doctrinally mixed denominations
that support the WCC) when they seriously
considered setting up a rival evangelical
world organisation. How could they reconcile
staying within denominatins supporting the WCC
with the suggestion that they should set up
something in opposition to it? (Lamb, 1975:12).

This brief survey of the conservative Protestant field
in America has been used to introduce some idea of the main
differences between conservatives and liberals. The last few
points should remind us that there are also serious divisions
within the conservative camp.

CONSERVATIVE PROTESTANTISM IN SCOTLAND

Although there have been (and still are) Congregationalists,
Baptists, Episcopalians, Methodists and Quakers in Scotland,
to all intents and purposes the history of Protestantism in
Scotland is the history of the Church of Scotland and its
attendant offshoots; and the history of the Church of
Scotland is a story of schism and reunion. Even before the
1733 split which led to the formation of the small Associate
Presbytery, a small group existed outside the Kirk. The
Covenanters, or "Cameronians', did not join the Church of
Scotland in 1690, because they could not accept the proposed
relationship between church and state[5]. The Reformed
Presbyterians, as the Cameronians are formally known, have
always refused to co-operate with the political power until
the State recognises its obligations to maintain 'the true
religion'. The first split from the national Church was over
the right of certain patrons to appoint or veto the
appointment of a minister. The Presbyterians have for most
of the time jealously guarded the right of the Presbyters
(full members of the Church) to call their minister.
Although this principle was enshrined in the 1690 Revolution
Settlement, the monarchy, at various times, attempted to
introduce a patronage principle akin to the right of certain
individuals in England to give 'the living' to the person of
their choice even against the will of the church members.
Within fourteen years of its departure from the National
Church, the organisation produced by the first patronage
dispute had divided again; this time over a question of the
application of oaths. The Burgher Oath was required to be
sworn by any 'burgess', a town dweller of certain wealth and
status. The oath involved a declaration of support for 'the

23

true religion professed within this realm' (Drummond and Bulloch, 1973:110) and the argument was over whether this statement was compatible with the most orthodox Calvinism. The moderates, men who were already having trouble with Calvinism, were expelled. Less than fifty years later, the two Secession Synods that came from this controversy each themselves split in two over the interpretation of the Westminster Confession! The 'New Licht' School had modified their beliefs while the 'Auld Licht' stuck to a rigid Calvinism. One of the charms of Scots church history is that the process of schism produced bodies with names like 'the Auld Licht Anti-Burgers'!

The patronage argument was responsible for another departure from the national Church. In the 1760's a handful of congregations left to form the Relief Presbytery which stood for religious liberty from civil interference. They could not, however, join the Seceders because they held to a liberal position on Calvinism. What makes the subsequent period of Scottish church history so confusing is the fact that each reunion of churches <u>increased</u> the total number. When the majority in two churches decided to come together, a minority in each church would stay out; where once there were two churches, now there were three.

The largest division within the Scottish Church occurred in 1843 when, in what was called 'The Disruption', Thomas Chalmers led one third of the clergy into the Church of Scotland Free or the Free Church. This split was composed of the same elements as the others: church and state, and the patronage question and Calvinism. For over a decade before the division the conservatives had been strengthening their position. They were not opposed to the establishment principle whereby the state supported the church; they simply objected to an establishment wherein the state only intervened in the church's affairs in a negative way, seeking to control the church without abiding by its side of the bargain, and supporting true religion by supressing heresies. The controversy was also theological, with the majority of the Calvinists going into the Free Church.

The Free Church

On its foundation the Free Church was mostly Calvinist and conservative. Its two colleges, New College in Edinburgh and Trinity College in Glasgow, were established to defend the verbal inspiration of the Scriptures. But while the Colleges were Calvinist in teaching, these sentiments were not shared by all of the students. In 1856, Professor James Gibson charged some of his students with 'virtually denying the doctrine of human depravity and attributing to the reason of fallen man abilities which it did not possess' (Drummond and

Bulloch, 1975:18). Just how the Calvinism of the Free Church was altered and moderated is not clear. Maclaren's study of Aberdeen (1974) suggests that the answer may lie in the gradual growth of a feeling of security among the rising new business class which made up the active eldership of the Free Church. As they came to feel more established and less 'arriviste' they ceased to battle against the more established business families of Aberdeen who had stayed with the National Church.

This is an interesting example of the common sociological observation that religious divisions tend to parallel class divisions. However, one would need further evidence before one could conclude that the Disruption was simply an expression of class conflict; or that Calvinism was abandoned once the new class had established itself because it was no longer 'needed' to claim moral superiority over the old bourgeoise and had become a hindrance. One would also have to consider the problems involved in generalising from Aberdeen to other parts of Scotland. Whatever its roots, the movement to displace the Calvinism of the conservatives reached the point in 1892 when a 'Declaratory Act' was passed which, although advertised as containing the principles by which the Westminster Confession was to be interpreted, actually denied and rejected many of the fundamental points of Calvinism. The Declaratory Act carried most of the Free Church but met determined opposition from the Highlanders.

Before the Disruption, Highland divinity candidates had been recruited from the well-to-do tenant farmers. The famine of 1846 and subsequent population changes had reduced this stratum and the Free Church had then to draw its Highland ministers from poor but pious families. This created one social division between the men from above the Caledonian Canal and those below it. A further division was that of language; the Highlanders were mostly Gaelic speakers. The isolation resulting from those two social divisions, coupled with the physical isolation of that part of the world, left traditional Calvinism intact in the north and the west and in 1893, in protest at the Declaratory Act, two Highland ministers and an elder left the Free Church and constituted themselves as the Free Presbyterian Church.

Reunion

Outside of the Highlands there was little or nothing in theology that now separated the three main churches; the National Church, the Free Church and the smaller United Presbyterian Church (which had been formed by the fusion of the New Licht parts of the Secession Church and the Relief Presbytery). The end of patronage in 1874 had removed one of the main sources of division, and union was only a matter of time. In 1900, the Free Church and the united Presbyterians merged to form the United Free Church, and in 1929, this body joined the Church of Scotland. One hundred and fifty years after the process of schism had begun in earnest, Scotland once more had a genuinely national Church (although the proportion of the population that it could speak for and its influence, had declined markedly). There were, however, small groups left behind at each stage in the process of reunion,; some of them, like the Free Presbyterians, were out on matters of doctrine, while others such as the United Free Church (those who did not go into the National Church in 1929) remained out on the church and state question.

Tortuous though it may be, some understanding of the nature of these splits and reunions is essential for an evaluation of the present state of the Presbyterian Churches in Scotland. I now intend to summarise briefly the origins and principles of the Presbyterian churches that exist today. The Church of Scotland is by far and away the largest of these Churches. Its organisation is democratic, being based on the local presbytery which elects representatives to the higher courts and which has the right to veto the legislation of higher courts. In addition the presbytery chooses its minister. The Church is broad in doctrine, containing within it some conservatives, but its centre is liberal and ecumenical.

The Reformed Presbyterian Church was described in 1870, as 'perhaps the most orthodox body in Great Britain, or even Christendom' (Wallace, 1870). It adheres to the Westminster Confession, practises 'closed Communion', maintains that the state must respect the Word of God in all its laws and refuses to regard the state as valid until this condition is met. It is this 'civil disobedience', exhibited in a refusal to vote, which separates the Reformed Presbyterian Church from some other very conservative bodies. Reformed Presbyterians also reject 'human invention' in worship, and sing only unaccompanied metrical psalms and paraphrases.

The Free Presbyterian Church claims that it, and not the Free Church is, the true descendant of the Chalmers Free Church, having left that body after the 1892 Declaratory Act modified the Free Church's commitment to the Westminster Confession. This very conservative body is committed to the inerrancy and verbal inspiration of Scripture, and in worship it – like the Reformed Presbyterian Church – uses only unaccompanied psalms. It has hardly broadened its base since its formation, and is strongest in the Highlands and Islands of Scotland. The Free Church is the best known of the smaller Scottish Churches and is usually what people mean when they talk about 'the Wee Frees' (although sometimes it is the Free Presbyterians that are actually being referred to). To the outsider little, if anything, separates this body from the Free Presbyterians.

This brief run-through the schism-riddled history of the Presbyterian Church in Scotland paves the way for a discussion of the history of Presbyterianism in Ulster. The Ulster divisions mirror those of Scotland to the point of actually having some of the products of divisions (the Secession Church for example) where the initial cause of the Scottish argument (in this case the Patronage Act) did not apply to Ulster.

PRESBYTERIANISM IN ULSTER

The position of Presbyterians in Ulster was, until the latter part of the last century, an insecure one[6]. For most of their history they have been the targets of both Catholic nationalists and English landlords. Being at odds with both the established Church of Ireland and the other major persecuted group - the Catholics - the status of Presbyterianism has fluctuated, with some periods of being supported by the state because they were Protestant, and others of being persecuted by the state because they were too protestant.

The first recorded Presyterians in Ulster were actually admitted to the parishes of the established Episcopalian Church without any re-ordination and they remained within the Anglican Church until Laud re-established rule by Bishop, and expelled the Presbyterians in 1636 for refusing to accept prelacy. In 1638 and 1639, the anti-monarchist Black Oath was used by the state to suppress the Scots Presbyterians, because it required them to reject their committment, made in the Scots Covenant, to the monarchy. 1640 was a good year for them with the Long Parliament redressing their grievances, but the Rebellion of 1641 involved serious attacks on Protestants. Ironically the Presbyterians suffered less than other Protestants in these massacres because many were still in Scotland, hiding from the last round of persecution.

The arrival of Presbyterian chaplains with the Scots Army (sent to put down the rebellion) gave a boost to Presbyterian fortunes, but the arrival of Cromwell in Ireland, and the execution of Charles Stewart, offered no comfort to them. The majority of the roundheads were Independents and Puritans who had little liking for Presbyterianism. John Milton referred to 'this unchristian synagogue in Belfast' (McConnell, 1912:5). The Presbyterians refusal to take the Engagement Oath (another anti-monarchist oath) and their support for the Stewarts led once again to persecution and expulsion. 1654-1660 was a period of relative prosperity when under the protection of Henry Cromwell they were exempted from the Oath and even given a government grant, but with the restoration of the monarchy the tide once again turned against them. Since 1646, the Established Church in all three kingdoms had been Presbyterian in government. Charles restored the Bishops, and once more the Presbyterian ministers in Ulster were out in the cold. When James came out in support of Catholicism they felt that, although they had no reason to love the Episcopalians, they had less to fear from that source than they did from the Catholics, and they joined in the invitation to William of Orange.

The irony of the fortunes of the Ulster Presbyters continued. They were hardly any better off under William than they had been with the Stewarts. Although a Toleration Act that allowed a certain freedom of belief and worship was passed in England, the strong Episcopal party in the Irish Parliament blocked the Act's application to Ireland. Presbyterian marriages were judged to be invalid, and any Presbyterian calling himself a clergyman was liable to trial and punishment.

Controversy and Division

Until 1825, the Presbyterians in Ulster were part of the Scottish Church and governed by the acts of the Scottish General Assembly. Some ministers in Belfast had formed themselves into a society and this group developed a liberality in doctrine that had them accused of Unitarianism: a set of doctrines that deny the triune nature of the Divinity and emphasise the human nature of Jesus Christ. The solution to this growing Old Light - New Light controversy was to rearrange the distribution of congregations in Presbyteries so that the liberal non-subscribing ministers (so called because they refused to sign the Westminster Confesion) were organisationally distanced from the conservatives who supported compulsory subscription.

The Reformed Presbyterians came to Ulster in 1757, and formed their own Presbytery in 1763. This bridgehead died out and it was another 50 years before the Cameronians re-established themselves. The Patronage Act and the Burger Oath were both unknown in Ulster but this did not stop the arrival, rooting and spreading of the schismatic Scottish Churches that had been formed out of controversies concerning those measures. The Secession Church prospered in Ulster by creating congregations in new areas of population that were not being cultivated by the existing Presbyterians. One explanation of the Presybterians' reluctance to expand is that to do so would have meant splitting the small state bounty into even smaller units. Whatever the reason, the lack of expansion left open the field to the Secessionists, and in many cases the creation of a Secession congregation had less to do with doctrinal or ecclesiastical disagreement, than with other - more secular - quarrels. One congregation of Presbyterians invited in the Secession Church in a fit of pique over the sale of some local land. However irrelevant the original Scottish source of the first Secession, the arrival of the Secession Church in Ulster led to considerable church extension. In less than 100 years the Secessionists established 140 new congregations, and spurred on by competition, the Synod of Ulster Presbyterians planted 130.

In 1818, the Burgher and Anti-Burgher Synods united to form one Secession Synod based on subscription to the Westminster Confession, the Longer and Shorter Catechism, and the forms of worship of the Scottish Church. Twenty-two years later, this body joined the Presbyterian Synod of Ulster to produce the present Presbyterian Church in Ireland. This Union was made possible by the work of Henry Cooke in leading the Synod of Ulster in a more conservative direction. Since the formation of the Belfast Society, influential men in the Synod had been committed to eradicating the Society's theology by making subscription to the Westminster Confession mandatory. The first non-subscribing controversy was about Unitarianism (a belief that Christ was a man adopted to the office of Son of God); this second controversy was about Arianism (a belief that Christ, while being the Son of God, was created and was not of the same substance as the Father). Seventeen ministers led by Henry Montgomery withdrew, and formed their own Synod which later became the Non-Subscribing Presbyterian Church in Ireland.

United Irishmen, the Orange Order and the Social "Arrival" of Presbyterianism

The political situation began to turn in the favour of the Presbyterians in 1778. When English troops were withdrawn from Ireland to fight in the American War of Independence, a volunteer force was raised to counter the threat of French invasion. A large part of this armed but in the event, unnecessary, force was Presbyterian, and the Parliament's preception of the potential strength of armed Presbyterianism was enough to produce a number of reforms, and to lay the foundations for a Protestant alliance. But for all this liberality easing some tensions between Presbyterians and the English Episcopalian landlords, there was still the possibility of another alliance. After the abolition of the Test Acts in 1870 and 1871, the Presbyterian Convention passed a motion rejoicing in their new freedom for both themselves and their 'Roman Catholic fellow subjects' (Barkley, 1960:35).

The nationalist and republican United Irishmen movement contained many Presbyterians; 12 of the proprietors of the Belfast-based <u>Northern Star</u> are known to have been Presbyterian. Although financially better off than the Catholics, in some matters related to status and culture, the Presbyterians did worse in this period. For example, in 1795 the Government gave permission for a Catholic seminary at Maynooth, but refused to allow the Presbyterians a university. Although Trinity was opened to Presbyterians in 1793, it was so Episcopalian in tone that they continued to cross to Scotland for a university education. Even when Queen's College was established in Belfast it was designated non-sectarian, and the Presbyterians had to establish their own religious university at Magee College in Londonderry; an institution, which, unlike Maynooth, was not subsidised by the government.

Thus there were grounds for alliance with the Catholic nationalists, and, for a period, the Presbyterians were influenced by a liberal republicanism. The strength of this should not, however, be exaggerated. Although some ministers took part in the 1798 rebellion, the Synod as a whole, while recognising the existence of real grievances, condemned armed insurrection and subscribed £500 to the Government (Moody n.d.). Nor was it simply the machinations of wily Tory landlords that turned the tide among Presbyterians. The Scullabogue massacre of a large number of Protestants reminded the Presbyterians that they might be swopping the devil they knew for one they knew not. It is against that background that one has to set the work of first Henry Cooke and then 'Roaring' Hugh Hanna. Cooke strengthened conservatism in doctrine by making subscription to the Confession mandatory and thus driving out Montgomery and the non-Subscribers, who were more liberal than the rest of the Synod. Supported by wealthy Tory landlords, Cooke forged the celebrated marriage between the Orange Order, which was largely Episcopalian, and Presbyterianism. Hanna's congregation by 1857 was '90% Conservative' (Brown, n.d.:13) and he helped to cement the Protestant alliance by supporting the Episcopal Church against its disestablishment. Hanna, and many other Presbyterians, argued that it was better to have the state support some Protestant Church (even if it were the wrong one), than to support none at all.

The increasing conservatism of the Presbyterians has to be set against the attitude of the Catholic hierarchy. In this period the doctrine of papal infallibility was promulgated. The decree <u>Ne Temere</u> was issued restating the Catholic position on mixed marriages, which was that such marriages were not binding unless solemnised in a Catholic ceremony. A scandal was caused by the McCann case in which a Catholic father, having been told by his priest that his Presbyterian marriage was not recognised, removed his chidren from their Presbyterian mother (see Corkey, 1962:151-158). This was in 1910, but already by the end of the previous century the Presbyterians had totally abandoned any republican sympathies and allied themselves firmly in a class alliance with the landed gentry and the capitalists. Before Cooke and Hanna there was considerable flux in the political implications of Presbyterianism, and there was considerable flux in the theological position of the mainstream of Presbyterianism. By the last third of the nineteenth century the Presbyterians had chosen the conservative theology and the Orange road.

There are two reasons why I have concentrated on the history of Presbyterianism in Ulster. In the first place, it is the dominant expression of Ulster Protestantism. There are Baptists, Methodists, Congregationalists, Episcopalians, varieties of old Pentecostalism, and the Brethren, but it is Presbyterianism that is, be far and away, numerically superior. Moreover, it has a second attraction for this study. Ulster possesses a variety of Presbyterian churches, which share a common history and form of organisation co-existing in the same society. There is thus more hope of worthwhile comparison between the fortunes of theologically conservative and liberal churches since the differences between them are not compounded by differences of social context or of culture. The main Presbyterian Church of Ireland and the small liberal Non-Subscribing Presbyterian Church have already been mentioned. The small and very conservative Reformed Presbyterian Church has retained a fairly constant presence in this century. Another small conservative church, the Evangelical Presbyterian Church, is of more recent origin. Although the Presbyterian Church made subscription to the Westminster Confession a requirement for elders, this did not prevent the gradual encroachment of modernist and liberal theology (any more than it did in the other churches that accepted the Confession). New movements of rationalism began to be heard in the colleges and pulpits. Controversy broke out when W.J. Grier returned in 1925 from two years of study at the Princeton Theological Seminary. Princeton was still conservative and reformed; Machen had not yet led the conservatives off to found the rival Westminster College. Grier entered Assemblies College in Belfast and was unhappy with Professor Davey's teaching. He reported his disquiet to James Hunter[7]. Hunter formed the Bible Standards League to rally the faithful against Davey and his like, but the Presbyterian Church Assemblies consistently supported Davey and other like-minded people against Hunter. Hunter withdrew from the Church, and in

1927, he and a group of fellow dissenters decided to form
what was initially the Irish Evangelical Church and is now
called the Evangelical Presbyterian Church. Although this
group was born out of controversy it did not immediately
define itself in the characteristically fulsome detail that
most schismatic groups summon in order to clarify their
doctrinal position. Eight articles of faith which were
clearly anti-modernist were drawn up, but these gave no
specific position on the millennial question. Dissent
developed around two 'modern dispensationalists', who
withdrew from the Church, and to make the doctrinal basis
more specific, the Westminster Confession and the Longer and
Shorter Catechisms were adopted. This brought the EPC into
conformity with the practice of the Free Church in Scotland
and the Free Church now acts as a channel for EPC missionary
interest, trains EPC ministeral candidates, and joins the EPC
on the British Evangelical Council. The EPC is on fraternal
terms with the Reformed Presbyterians and it is essentially
only the latter's refusal to exercise certain civil rights
(such as voting) and to employ mechanical music and
non-scriptural songs in worship, that separate the two bodies.
    The largest and most significant of the churches founded
in this century is Ian Paisley's Free Presbyterian Church,
which has nothing whatsoever to do with the Scottish church
of the same name. Furthermore, it is not especially
presbyterian in structure. While the form is similar to that
of the other Presbyterian Churches, there is no annual
election of a moderator and Dr Paisley has filled this office
since the church's foundation. There is sufficient in its
nature to make the ordinary Presbyterian feel at home
however, and many members were recruited from the main
Presbyterian Church. Ian Paisley was educated at a Baptist
Bible College in Wales and the Reformed Presbyterian
theological hall in Belfast before being called in 1946 to
pastor a small congregation that had split from the Ravenhill
Road Presbyterian Church. In 1956 a split in the Crossgar
Presbyterian Church added a second congregation and the Free
Presbyterian Church grew from those two groups. The main
growth in the Church came in the late sixties and early
seventies as Dr Paisley was building his schismatic political
movement.

ENGLAND

The recent history of Protestantism in England is
considerably more complex than that of Scotland and Ulster
for the simple reason that there is a far greater variety of
numerically significant churches in England.
Congregationalists, Presbyterians, Baptists, Quakers,

Unitarians and Methodists, and more recently the pentecostal churches, have all offered alternatives to the established Church of England. These alternatives, although they are to be found in Ulster and Scotland, have never been on remotely the same scale as the dominant Presbyterianism.

England is also unique in that the major Protestant church is not entirely Protestant. The Episcopal Church is a curious combination of Protestantism and Catholicism. Its creeds are Protestant but it retains Bishops and rituals and ceremonies that are not 'reformed'. The partially reformed character of the Church of England is a direct consequence of radical changes of government from Catholic to Protestant and back again. With one change of government Catholics were suppressed and episcopacy outlawed. With the next change, the Catholic element was restored and the Protestants outlawed. For the last 200 years, this mixed character hs been surprisingly stable; a condition promoted by the structure of the Church with its autonomy of Bishops and the legal security of the parson's freehold. From time to time, the mixture has reached critical temperature and one faction has either left or been ejected. John Wesley and his supporters were defectors to a purer Protestantism. At the other end of the spectrum one has the defection to Rome that occurred during the revival of 'high' anglicanism known as the Oxford Movement. John Henry Newman became so attracted by the importance of the continuity of the church since the time of Christ, that he left the Church of England for the Church of Rome.

Since the departure of Wesley there has been no concerted move out of the church by the evangelicals. Rather they have claimed that the Church is their church and that it is the anglo-catholics who are in the wrong place. At times they have tried to substantiate this claim by prosecuting ritualists in various church courts. They have also tried to prosecute modernists and liberals and ironically have been joined in this effort by the ritualists, who were equally opposed to modernism; but by and large the evangelicals have uneasily co-existed with both ritualists and modernists. They have maintained their evangelical identities through participation in various evangelical associations within the Church (the Evangelical Fellowship in the Anglican Communion, for example) or across church boundaries (for example, the Keswick Convention and the Inter-Varsity Fellowship). Such associations also exist for the other parties: liberals may be members of the William Temple Association, and ritualists of various sorts might be members of such bodies as the Society of King Charles the Martyr, or the Anglican and Old Catholic Society of St. Willibrod.

The other major Protestant churches do not have 'high' or 'catholic' wings but they do display the divergence between liberals and conservatives. At times these divergences develop into wholesale movements of people from one organisation to another. In the nineteenth century a number of leading Quaker families left the Society of Friends for the Church of England. Gurneys, Barclays and Buxtons found the evangelicalism of the Anglicans with whom they associated more attractive than the Quaker 'inner light' doctrines. The Unitarian and Free Christian Churches were formed in the main from liberal English Presbyterian congregations. There is little value in rehearsing the many schisms from the English churches. The main point for this book is that the dominant trend of the last 100 years has been one of increasing liberalism in the main churches. This has been associated with an increasing ecumenism. The main fruit of the ecumenical movement has been the merger of the Congregationalists and Presbyterians in the United Reformed Church. Discussions between the Church of England, the Methodists and the United Reformed Church have made little progress in recent years and one doubts whether there is any possibility of unions between the Church of England and other churches given that there are within the Anglican Church some who want to see closer cooperation with the Roman Catholic and Orthodox Churches, and some who want reunion with other Protestants such as Methodists and the United Reformed Church. But although the ecumenical movement has not produced any major mergers in the last decade, it has produced a climate in which local ventures, such as joint ministries and shared church buildings, are becoming increasingly common. The ecumenical movement, whether in this form, or in the form of the World Council of Churches (WCC) and the British Council of Churches (BCC), is the key to conservative identity. Conservative Protestants do not like the ecumenical movement. The expression of the dislike varies; some people feel impelled to leave a denomination that is in the BCC while others confine themselves to attacking the ecumenical movement when they have the opportunity. Evangelical conservatives prefer to support the Evangelical Alliance and conservatives of a Calvinist tendency tend to be members of small churches (such as the Strict Baptists) or independent congregations associated with the British Evangelical Council.

The basic pattern of Protestant church history in the last quarter of the last century and in this century has been a trend to liberalism. There has been a gradual 'secularisation' of the Christian tradition. Supernatural elements of faith have been replaced by existential themes so that the old creator God 'out there' becomes the 'spirit of true humanity' or some such notion. This has been accompanied by ecumenism; a gradual erosion of denomination identities and increased cooperation between denominations.

This was certainly the case for the large Protestant denominations. In each country there were small conservative alternatives which were not influenced by these tendencies but until recently they seemed insignificant and fated to disappear. The next chapter considers the recent fortunes of conservative and liberal Protestantism and documents what appears to be a reversal of the earlier success of the liberals.

Notes

1. Other major works on American revivalism are McLoughlin (1959), Smith (1965), White (1963), Hanke (1977), Dike (1909), and Ahlstrom (1972). Marsden (1980) is a valuable internalist history of American fundamentalism which contains many insights I would have been happy to use had the book been available when the bulk of this was written.

2. The story of Mott, Northfield, Wilder and the student movement is told in Bruce (1980), Tatlow (1933), Mackie (1965), and Matthews (1934).

3. Moody was sponsored by John Wanamaker, Phillip Armour, Cornelius Vanderbilt III, and J.P. Morgan. Billy Sunday was backed by John D. Rockefeller and John Studebaker (Pierard, 1970:30). Mordecai Ham was supported by Henry Ford (Frady, 1979:80).

4. There are many biographies of Graham. The Pollock books (1966;1979) are detailed but sycophantic. Frady (1979) is far from sycophantic but his work is marred by excessive imagination. In the style of the 'new journalism' of Tom Wolfe, Frady constantly pretends to an insight into the minds of those he writes about that is only possible for the novelist. With Pollock one wonders about what has been left out; with Frady one has to try and identify what should have been left out. Other works on Graham are Target (1968), Ashma (1977), and Bestic (1971).

5. The standard history of the Reformed Presbyterian Church is Hutchinson (1893). Drummond and Bulloch (1973;1975;1978) include the Church in their general history of the Church of Scotland.

6. The material for this section has been drawn from, among other sources, Gray (1972), Barkley (1960), McConnell (1912), Redmond (1962), Corkey (1962) and Miller (1978).

7. The liberals' account of the controversy can be found in Fulton (1970), and the schismatic conservatives' version is given by W.J. Grier (1945).

3 Conservative Protestantism: present strength

Patterns of change in religious belief and practice have been the focus of a great deal of attention in America where there has been far more analysis of church membership statistics, and of opinion polls on questions of religion, than there has been in this country. Hoge and Roozen (1979), Kelley (1972) and Carrol et al (1979) all present detailed evidence about the state of religion in the United States. From 1955 until 1965, almost all the denominations showed patterns of growth. The greatest percentage increases were registered by the more conservative churches such as the Assemblies of God, the Missouri Synod Lutherans, the Southern Baptists, and the Church of the Nazarene. In the five years from 1960 one of the liberal denominations - the United Church of Christ - recorded a decline in membership, part of which was due to conservatives leaving the bodies which united in this denomination.

> In the other major liberal denominations the rate of growth slowed, while the conservative bodies, large and small, continued to grow at a more rapid rate. It was in the latter half of the 1960's, continuing into the middle 1970's, that all of the theologically liberal denominations began to experience membership decline (Carroll and Roozen, 1979:13).

While the American scene is well documented, there is little material which allows a similar analysis of Britain. Currie et al (1977) is a useful resource, but apart from that there has been very little statistical analysis of changes in religion. This chapter presents various sorts of evidence, from church membership figures to magazine circulations, to support the argument that conservative Protestantism has survived the last quarter century of secularisation in better shape that liberal Protestantism. Further, I will suggest that, while those conservative churches which try hard to convert the heathen are in better health than those which tend to become introverted and concerned with maintaining their own purity, this improved health is not the result of converting the heathen. Those churches which try hard to convert outsiders are not very successful at drawing in the heathen but they have a better record of holding their own children than have those conservative churches that are not so actively conversionist. This apparent paradox will be pursued later; first I will demonstrate the conservative resilience to secularisation.

CONSERVATIVE RESILIENCE

Church membership figures are notoriously unreliable. This is sometimes forgotten by those who use them and it is instructive to list some of the weaknesses of this form of data. In the first place, the totals are only as reliable as the original figures sent in by local ministers and clerks to the central bureaucracy and it is not unknown for mistakes to be made, especially when the return forms offer different categories for recording members[1]. In the second place, what counts as a member may well be very different from one denomination to another, and may vary within the same denomination from time to time and place to place. One cannot assume a great deal of consistency. As a general rule of thumb it is usually the case that the more conservative the theology of the denomination, the more strict the notion of membership and the greater likelihood that such figures under-represent the support that the church has. The Free Presbyterian and Free Churches have very few full communicating members because their supporters hold the communion service in great awe and are reluctant to sit at the Lord's Table in case they are not truly saved. This may produce life-long adherents who have been raised in the church, attended faithfully and regularly, know their catechism perfectly, and yet are still reluctant to put themselves forward for full membership. It seems likely, given this attitude, that even combined totals for membership and adherents may underestimate the total support. At the other extreme one has the liberal denominations which have always been loath to remove individuals from the rolls of membership. When such revisions are carried out, it is often found that as much as a third or half of the roll is fictitious. One Church of Scotland parish church had a membership that had apparently shrunk from 500 in 1963 to 233 in 1972, but in that year only 82 people took communion. The following year the roll was revised and only 116 members were recorded (Osborne, 1980).

There are other sorts of problems among those churches that support congregational autonomy and independence. Any figure for the Christian Brethren has to be a wild guess because the Brethren are not organised under any central authority, and even the Christian Brethren Research Fellowship could not persuade all the Brethren meetings it approached in the course of its survey to allow themselves to be numbered. The same lack of formal membership of any central organisation also makes estimating the scale of the new pentecostal movement a hazardous enterprise.

The relationship between the central organisation and some of its regional or national divisions may also change. In this century the Irish Baptists have been outside the Baptist Union, inside the Baptist Union of Great Britain and Ireland, and now, once more, outside. Thus, one has the problem of knowing whether Irish Baptist totals should be added to those for England, Scotland and Wales. Equally, it is not always clear whether or not figures compiled by others include the Irish totals. Similar uncertainties arise with any denomination that has national or regional subdivisions[2].

Finally one comes to the problem of the 'meaning' of church membership figures. They are compiled by assuming that every member is equal, that ten members is the equivalent of two lots of five members, and so on. Once one tries to go beyond the very basic idea of 'membership' to some more useful idea about commitment and belief, one realises the mistake in such an assumption. Some members are more committed than others, are 'worth more' than others. However, the statistics do exist and for that reason are worth consideration. I do not propose to review the statistics for every Protestant church. Rather, I intend to select figures that throw light on the contrast between conservative and liberal theologies.

Scotland and Ulster both offer good arenas for observing the influence of doctrine on church survival. As I have already noted, both possess a variety of churches of various sizes, with similar organisations and a shared history but differing markedly in doctrine. I have abstracted the membership trends of the various Presbyterian churches in Scotland for the last 25 years[3].

Table 1   Scottish Presbyterianism (1956-80)

Church	Overall Membership Trend
Reformed Presbyterian Church	- 50%
Free Presbyterian Church	+ 48%
Free Church	- 12%
Church of Scotland	- 26%
United Free Church	- 56%

While the Church of Scotland and the United Free Church compile and publish detailed membership statistics, the other three churches do not, and the figures from which these trends are inferred can only be treated as informed estimates. Information on the number of ministers is more reliable and shows a similar pattern[4]. The Reformed Presbyterian Church now has only four ministers when it had five, and two of these were recruited from other Reformed Presbyterian churches abroad. The Free Presbyterian Church has been able to launch a new church in Aberdeen, while the Free Church has seen a slight decline in its clergy from about 110 to about 95. The Church of Scotland and the United Free Church[5] have both seen major decreases in the number of their clergy. In the terms of the typology given in the introduction, the first three Churches, the Reformed and the two Free Churches, are conservative while the last two, the Church of Scotland and the United Free Church, are mainly liberal Protestant. The patterns suggest that, with the exception of the Reformed Presbyterian case, there is some connection between rate of decline and liberalism.

Like Scotland, Ulster offers a range of Presbyterian churches with differing theologies, and their membership trends are shown in Table 2.

Table 2   Ulster Presbyterianism (1956-80)

Church	Overall Membership Trend
Reformed Presbyterian Church	0%
Evangelical Presbyterian Church	0%
Free Presbyterian (Paisleyite)	+ 3000%
Presbyterian Church of Ireland	- 1%
Non-Subscribing Presbyterian Church	- 30%

The general pattern here follows that of the Scottish churches. The three conservative Churches, the Reformed, the Evangelical and the Free, have either remained stable, or increased. The broad Presbyterian Church has declined slightly (after a slight rise between 1956 and 1967) and the liberal Non-Subscribing Presbyterian Church[6] has declined rapidly. The rapid rise of Dr Paisley's Free Presbyterian Church from its foundation in 1951 to a membership of about 10,000 today, obviously owes a lot to the political situation in Ulster, but its removal from the table leaves the pattern unaltered.

The decline of the liberal churches in England is nowhere more evident than in the fortunes of the United Reformed church. This church was created as a practical exercise in ecumenism with the merger in 1972 of the Congregational Churches in England and the English and Welsh Presbyterians. Peter Berger (1963) sees ecumenism as a reaction to decline. Unions reduce the amount of church 'plant' and the number of clergy that are required to service the membership. Unfortunately they also reduce the membership. Far from halting the decline, the merger has been followed by an increase in the rate of decline. This should not have been surprising. The administrative advantages of merger have to be weighed against two major costs. In the first place, many church members are sentimentally attached to their own buildings, modes of worship, and so on. Integrating what were once two congregations of different denominations makes it unlikely that the resultant body will, for a long time, draw the sort of loyalty that the two bodies did before the union. In the second place, such dislocations cause people to think anew about their commitment. This in turn provides them with an opportunity to find good reason to withhold it. A good part of human activity is habitual. While we once had a good reason to do one thing rather than another, we very often continue in that pattern for no better rason than that it is 'something we always did'. Major upheavals give us occasions to reconsider and to change our habits. The membership totals for both Presbyterians and Congregationalists declined by 12% between 1956 and 1966, while the membership of the combined Church fell by 22% in the eight years between 1972 and 1980. The rethinking of members' commitment led not only to losses to the secular world as people stopped going to church. There were also defections in the direction of a more conservative Protestantism. The doctrinally conservative churches who had been ill at ease in the Congregational Union for some time before the merger, used that occasion to found their own Evangelical Fellowship of Congregational Churches, which has grown slightly in the last eight years[7].

The Unitarian churches, which are extremely liberal in theology, have shown severe decline, and have lost members and clergy at a rate that exceeds that of the broad churches. In 1956, there were about 28,000 Unitarians served by 222 ministers (Currie and Gilbert, 1974:431). The 1981 Directory of Unitarian and Free Christian Churches gives no figures for membership, but records only 84 full-time ministers. This produces a decline rate of 62% for the period from 1956.

The National Initiative in Evangelism survey of churches in 1979 (NIE, 1980), showed that the fastest growing group of churches were the West Indian and African organisations. The second most successful were the 'independents'; the Brethren, the Fellowship of Independent Evangelical Churches (FIEC), the Union of Evangelical Churches (UEC) and the 'house churches'. The estimated total membership of these bodies has risen from some 134,000 in 1970, to 137,000 in 1975, and 169,000 in 1979. A more reliable statistic which suggests a similar pattern, is that of the number of congregations affiliated to the Fellowship of Independent Evangelical Churches; there were 244 in 1955, 319 in 1965, 415 in 1975 and 434 in 1980. This of course tells us nothing about membership size, but there seems no reason to suppose that there has been a serious reduction in the size of the average congregation. More spectacular than the rise of the FIEC has been the growth in the 'house church' movement. The Evangelical Alliance (Brierley, 1978) guesses that some 20,000 people were involved in these small fellowships in 1975. Thurman (1979) puts the figure nearer 50,000. What we can be sure of is that there are more than 20,000 involved, and that this movement has been growing steadily. Restoration, the magazine that links together the Harvestime Fellowship Churches, now has a UK circulation of 8,000 copies. To infer anything about readers from that, one has

42

to make guesses about how many people read each copy, and how many copies are given away to people who are not supporters. Given that the same considerations probably figure in the circulations of other religious periodicals, we can compare Restoration with, for example, the Methodist Recorder (33,3000 in 1980), and see that the magazine of the Harvestime Fellowship already has a circulation a quarter of that of the main paper for one of the major liberal denominations.

But far more important than growth itself is what growth implies for the future. New movements usually recruit from people who are younger rather than older. The older we get, the less we are available for some new perspective or experience. The Harvestime Fellowship, in contrast to most of the liberal denominations, has a young membership. I was surprised myself at the high percentage of young people at the Dales Bible Week in Harrogate. Three of us who were observing the main worship made guesses about the age distribution, and agreed that no less than half, and more likely about two-thirds of the 7,000 people in the hall were under 30. This age distribution, combined with their traditional views on importance of the family, means that the Fellowship will shortly have a large number of adolescents. As I will demonstrate shortly, most recruitment to conservative Protestantism results from childhood socialisation, from keeping the members' children in the faith. The age profile means that this movement, if it is reasonable successful in keeping its children, will soon see its membership grow even more dramatically than it has done in the last ten years.

Not all of this growth can be laid at the door of conservative Protestantism (as defined in my typology; cell 2). The 'house church' movement (this is usually a misnomer, as most of the groups quickly grow to the size where they either hire or buy a large building of some sort for their meetings) has an ideology that combines many of the features of conservative Protestant belief with the old Victorian holiness emphasis on spiritual gifts and the new charismatic practice of speaking in tongues. It thus occupies an area overlapping cells 2 and 4 in my typology. However, it seems likely that a full explanation of the success of conservative Protestantism will involve factors that it shares with the new Pentecostal movement. For example, both require significant separation from the secular permissive world in matters of moral and social behaviour. Both tend to be built on an infrastructure of small prayer groups and fellowships which provide a more intimate focus for the individual's membership than does the full congregation.

Changes Within Churches

The material presented above compares the fortunes of different churches. I think that it does enough to justify my proposition that the conservative churchs have been more resilient to secularisation than have the liberal and broad churches. There is one further point to make here, and that concerns the asymmetry of liberal or broad and conservative churches. By their nature, liberal churches tend to <u>include</u> some conservatives. They are tolerant and cannot be dogmatic about tolerance. Hence for long periods conservatives may remain in fellowship with such churches, and it usually requires some major occasion (such as the formation of the United Reformed Church) to break the traditional commitment of the conservatives and force them into schism. For this reason one can suppose that the statistics for liberal churches include conservatives. Conservative churches, on the other hand, tend to be exclusivist. They operate strict membership requirements based on an agreed narrow body of doctrine that ensures that there will be very few (if any) liberals in such churches. Put in political terms, there are people within broad churches (such as the Church of England) who share more in common with the Fellowship of Independent Evangelical Churches in matters of theology, than they do with their fellow Anglicans. Were such people to leave the broad churches one would see a dramatic fall in membership figures. Thus in going from thinking about the fortunes of churches <u>as organisations</u>, to considering the popularity of a certain type of <u>religious belief</u>, one can suppose that the figures presented above flatter liberal Protestantism.

One way to demonstrate this is to bring forward evidence about shifts <u>within</u> churches. There are two recent studies of Baptist congregations. One surveyed some 100 congregations and found that 'the smaller churches, by and large, are growing while the larger ones are declining' (Briggs, 1979:15). The report goes on to note that these smaller congregations are predominantly conservative in theology. A second survey of Baptist congregations controls to some extent for size, by comparing only those with more than 50 members. It also identifies a relationship between church growth and the theology of the minister. Radical and 'middle of the road' ministers tended to have declining churches, while conservative evangelical ministers had growing congregations. The most successful ministers were those who offered a combination of evangelicalism and support of the charismatic movement (Murray and Wilkinson, 1981:36).

Towler and Coxon's study of Anglican ordinands concludes that, 'at least in the short term, the future of the Church will be with the conservatives' (1978:205). Those involved in the teaching of prospective ministers in the Methodist

Church and in the Church of Scotland are likewise convinced that the last decade has seen an increasing proportion of students supporting conservative theological positions.

Conservative members of mixed churches tend to display their commitment to conservative theology by their membership of some association or 'fellowship'. One can thus gauge the popularity of the conservative position by examining the fortunes of such groupings. The Methodist Revival Fellowship has shown a steady rise since its foundation in 1952, and the membership of the more recently formed Conservative Evangelicals in Methodism has risen from 192 in 1974, to 437 in 1980[8].

There are three main groupings in the Church of Scotland. The National Church Association (NCA) was founded in 1932 to suport a theologically conservative Presbyterianism. The Scottish Church Society (SCS) is the nearest thing the Church has to a 'high' church presence. Its members are concerned with liturgy, church architecture and ritual, and especially with arguing that the Church of Scotland is in 'visible continuity' with the early church. Thus for the members of the SCS, it is the Roman Catholic Church in Scotland that is the newcomer, the interloper; the Kirk is the continuing Christian Chruch and not some dissenting or 'Protestant' sect. The third grouping within the Kirk is an annual meeting of theologically conservative ministers, brought together at the invitation of Reverend William Still of Aberdeen. It first met in 1971 in Crieff (thus its title of Crieff Brotherhood), and has met every year since with a growing membership. The growing fortunes of these groupings can be represented in the following table:

Table 3   Church of Scotland Associations

	1958	1971	1981
NCA	94	--	203
SCS	108	--	128
CB	--	19	170

At its simplest, these figures could be interpreted as showing conservative resilience. All three groupings are conservative in theology and all three have been stable or growing in a period when the numbers in the ministry have declined from 2113 to 1424[10]. Such an interpretation would, however, be more convincing if there were comparable statistics for the support of liberal associations within the Church of Scotland. For reasons I take up in Chapter 4, liberals do not normally band themselves into associations, even of the form as loose as Still's Crieff Brotherhood. In a very crude survey of the membership statistics of denominational associations I found only two theologically liberal or mixed bodies. The material gathered in the survey is of such a nature as to make interpretation highly dangerous. Breaking the results down by the theological tone of the association and the main trend of its membership since either 1956, the nearest date to that for which data is available, or the foundation of the association produces the following:

Table 4   Denominational Associations

Theological tone

Membership	CP	LP	AC	PC
Rising	5	0	2	3
Stable	0	0	2	0
Falling	1	2	1	0

KEY   CP = Conservative Protestant
           LP = Liberal/Broad Protestant
           AC = Anglo-Catholic
           PC = Pentecostal/Charismatic

Again one has to be very cautious about making anything of these figures, but they are the best that are presently available.

What is, in my own view, considerably more convincing than these hardly sophisticated statistics is the anecdotal evidence of conservative church growth. It cannot be accidental that there are no stories of liberal ministers rescuing decaying congregations and turning them into thriving churches, that can be laid alongside stories of evangelicals (such as David Watson of St. Michael-le-belfry, York) presiding over growing congregations[11].

Inter-denominational Associations

Conservatives not only form groups within their churches to witness to their faith; they also participate in a wide variety of organisations that are inter-denominational. The most important of these, both as an indicator of conservative health and as a cause of conservative growth, is the Universities and Colleges Christian Fellowship (UCCF; formerly known as the Inter-Varsity Fellowship). UCCF grew out of a number of schisms from the liberal Student Christian Movement (see Chapter 4). Since the nineteen thirties, UCCF has grown from being a minority organisation, to having a branch in every university and major college in the United Kingdom. In the same period the Student Christian Movement has declined to the point where it has almost no student members and it remains in existence only because a small staff can be supported on the interest from capital invested in the nineteen thirties and forties, when the movement was popular. In many colleges, the conservative Christian Union (as the local branches of UCCF are known) is the largest student society.

Although organisationally separate, the Scripture Union shares a symbiotic relationship with the Christian Unions. The Scripture Union organises Bible study groups in schools and evangelistic summer camps for children. Scripture Union group leaders channel their children who are going to university into the Christian Unions. Graduating Christian Union members who go into teaching then lead Scripture Union groups. Although officers of the Scripture Union report some fall in membership and in funding in the last few years, any decline has been considerably less than the rate of decline for the churches at large.

The evangelical milieu contains a number of professional associations, some of which are offshoots of UCCF. One such body is the Christian Medical Fellowship (CMF). Although now organisationally independent, the CMF still uses the UCCF basis of faith as its doctrinal statement. It has grown in size from the 100 or so who joined when it was launched in 1949, to a position of having some 3,000 members[12]. Another UCCF product, the Research Scientists' Christian Fellowship (RSCF), was launched during the second World War with about 20 members, and it now has around 800. RSCF has grown steadily with the gradual addition of new members and little loss through death and retirement, although it is now beginning to lose members in these ways. Recruitment for the last four years shows a fairly stable picture and this is confirmed by the circulation of the UCCF journal, Christian Graduate, which has varied little in the last 15 years.

Periodical Circulations

The most common form of linkage in any milieu is the printed word. People who see themselves as sharing common interests and beliefs tend to express this by subscribing to a periodical that promotes whatever it is that they support.

This would suggest that an obvious way of measuring the popularity of different varieties of Protestantism would be to collect and compare data on the circulation of periodicals with a clear theological identity[13]. I have done this, and I will shortly present the results of such a survey but, to continue the pattern established above, I will first mention some of the difficulties one has in interpreting such results.

In the first place there may be reasons why people read, or do not read, any particular periodical, which are not related to the acceptance or rejection of the theology of the publications. There are various characteristics such as availability, presentation, style, and price which affect consumption, and there are characteristics of the public (such as the popularity of reading) which are relevant. A second problem concerns the different ways in which a reader may be committed to a particular periodical. Different people may read the same periodical in different ways, paying attention to different features and 'meaning' something different by their readership. Can one assume that all of the readers of the Christian Herald similarly assent to those beliefs that the observer thinks are typical of the paper? This observation raises the third problem, and that concerns the correctness of my judgement of the theology of any particular paper or magazine. Some periodicals such as Watching and Waiting need no great insight to identify their theology, nor need one doubt that the readership is fundamentally agreed with that theology (because there is little other reason to read it). But the same is not the case for the popular conservative evangelical papers such as the Christian Herald and Crusade, which have sections (such as general Christian news features) that do more than simply expound a theology. One can suppose that no one who consciously thought of himself as a liberal or radical Protestant would buy either of these publications, but the letters columns testify to a range of opinion.

A further difficulty with reasoning from the size of a publication's circulation to support for its beliefs is caused by the employment of subsidies. An extreme case is provided by H.W. Armstrong's Plain Truth which is given away free by the Worldwide Church of God[14]. Its circulation then depends not on what the market will bear, but on the extent to which the organisation can afford to subsidise it. On a lesser scale, many conservative periodicals are brought by believers in quantity for distribution to unbelievers. However, one might note that in such cases there is still a roundabout connection between circulation and support for the theology; Armstrong can only afford to give away copies of Plain Truth because he attracts committed support from believers. Subsidised publishing required funding, and such funding is usually evidence of popular support. (Although this need not be the case; it could be that popularity in some _previous_ time provided capital which keeps a presently unpopular enterprise in business; that a particular enterprise has the backing of a very small number of wealthy people; or that money is raised by fraud, deceit, and the use of 'fronts').

For all these problems I would still maintain that there is truth in the commonsense notion that the circulation of periodicals _reflects_ (albeit in a distorted fashion) the popularity of the ideas expressed in them. In assembling data on circulation I have followed much the same procedure as for denominational associations. The periodicals are arranged into four theological categories, and the dominant pattern of the circulation since 1956; the year nearest to that date for which the information is available; or the year of foundation, is described as rising, stable or falling. Table 5 summarises the data for all of the periodicals surveyed. Table 6 summarises the data on those periodicals that are not 'house' journals for a denomination. The _Baptist Times_, for example, is widely read by Baptist clergy who also read other things and who would not agree with its theology, because it is the carrier of information about what is going on in the Baptist Union. As one would expect, the circulation of 'house' journals is loosely related to the membership patterns of the denomination. I have supposed that the figures for those periodicals that do not have the character of being the news organ for a denomination will be more illuminating for changes in theological preference.

Table 5   Periodical Circulations

Theological Tone

Circulation Pattern	CP	LP	AC	PC
Rising	10	3	1	3
Stable	5	0	0	2
Falling	11	6	0	0
Totals	26	9	1	5

Table 6   'Non-house' Periodical Circulations

Theological tone

Circulation Pattern	CP	LP	AC	PC
Rising	10	2	1	1
Stable	1	0	0	0
Falling	9	3	0	0
Totals	20	5	1	1

A number of observations can be made about these figures. In the first place, there are very few liberal journals that are not 'house' journals. This follows from the liberal emphasis on reducing barriers between the believer and the non-believer, and confirms my earlier observation about the lack of liberal Protestant associations. The second point is that proportionately more of the liberal periodicals are in decline. The one surveyed anglo-catholic periodical - the Church Observer - has undergone a recent revival, and added to other observations suggests that some of the movement away from the liberal position in the Church of England has been in the 'high church' direction. The major difference between conservative and liberal fortunes is not actually visible in these two tables, and that concerns the age of the conservative periodicals. The last decade has seen no new major liberal publication, but in that time there have been a number of significant conservative launches and, perhaps more importantly, conservative periodicals in decline have been bought over, 'modernised' and re-launched. Peter Meadows began Buzz in 1964 with a print run of 200 copies. It was an evangelical 'comic' with a light Amrican style. It grew steadily; in 1976 it sold 13,000 copies and in June 1981 the circulation was still rising at 30,500 copies. Life of Faith was a conservative paper founded in the last century which had declined rapidly, changed to a glossy monthly format in 1977, and continued to lose readers until it was taken over by Meadows and re-launched as Family. The circulation had dropped from 1978's 12,000 to only 8,000 in 1980, but by December 1981 the circulation of Family had reached 20,000. Crusade is another evangelical publication that was declining in its old newspaper format and was successfully changed into a glossy monthly.

Missions, Crusades and Tract Distributors

Three other strands of the conservative Protestant milieu are missions, crusade organisations and literature distributors. There are 13 city missions in Great Britain, the oldest of which trace their origins to David Naismith's nineteenth century attempts to christianise the inner cities. These organisations combine evangelistic activity with welfare work in a manner similar to that of the Salvation Army. The typical city mission will operate a number of small gospel halls in run down areas, organise door-to-door visitation, distribute tracts, run a hostel for homeless people, arrange Christmas parties for the elderly, distribute food parcels to the poor, and have a member of staff preaching in the open air in some crowded part of the city centre. Some missions also act as crusade organisations, providing evangelistic preachers for special 'outreach' efforts. Most of the city missions are working at a level similar to that of ten years ago, despite the problems of inflation eroding the value of contributions. Glasgow City Mission, for example, while having constant budget problems, is supporting much the same amount of work as it has done in previous years. Two mission halls have been shut because the damage done by vandals was making them a serious liability, but the door-to-door visitation continues. Birmingham City Mission has expanded its work over the last six years and, making allowance for inflation, its income increased by 50% between 1974 and 1979. Birmingham is able to do a great deal of evangelistic work on a very small budget because the full-time staff is augmented by a number of students who are given experience of missionary work and very little help with their expenses.

There are a large number of crusade organisations operating in the United Kingdom, and it would be impossible to do more than mention a few of the best known. These agencies are usually organised around a central evangelist who has gradually established himself as a popular preacher. The career of Dick Saunders is in many ways typical. He began his preaching with the Open Air Mission, and after 'learning the trade' and developing a network of contacts and sponsors, he went solo. He progressed gradually from speaking in churches and mission halls to owning his own tent. As his reputation grew, he was invited by larger churches and by greater numbers of local church leaders, to run crusades in their area. His team was gradually increased with the addition of a soloist and an organist. The major break-through for evangelists is the step into radio. The fact that British radio and television companies do not sell airtime has prevented the development of an 'electronic church' on the scale of the American model, but time can be bought on Radio Monte Carlo (TransWorld Radio) which broadcasts on medium and short wave to Europe and Britain. Reception on medium wave is not good outside the south of England but most of the major British evangelists use this outlet. Airtime is usually also purchased from various stations that broadcast to Africa, the Phillipines, the Caribbean and the United States (although the latter sounds like a case of transporting coals to Newcastle!). In the case of Saunders, his tent crusades complement his broadcasts, providing both the funds (from collections) and the material (the tent services are recorded and edited into programmes of the right length).

Don Summers is another itinerant evangelist who buys time on Radio Monte Carlo. In recent years he has specialised in bringing well-known American evangelicals to Britain for a tour. Nicky Cruz and Rick Stanley (Elvis Presley's brother-in-law) have both toured under Summers' direction. Summers' holds the exclusive rights to the film of Wilkerson's The Cross and the Switchblade (the story of Wilkerson's evangelistic work with hoodlums in New York slums), which has proved to be successful both in attracting crowds and in stimulating some conversions.

Cassette recordings are becoming increasingly popular in the evangelical milieu. In many churches it is customary for members to record meetings so that sick friends and relatives may listen to them at home. Some ministers, Ian Paisley for example, have recording and duplicating facilities built into their churches, and routinely record and distribute copies of their services. But cassettes are not only used for preserving 'live' events. More and more evangelists and missions are offering recordings of talks of a 'how to' nature. The Harvestime Fellowship sells a set of cassettes which offer 'Bible-based' instruction in parenthood. Crusade for World Revival (CWR) produces cassettes on 'family life', 'health and wholeness', 'managing your finances', 'six areas of spiritual growth', 'why children misbehave', and similar topics. Paisley offers a boxed six cassette 'life and times' set. Cassette recordings have two major advantages over books as a means of communication. In the first place they are faster and cheaper to produce, and hence should produce a larger profit (as an example, cassettes which probably cost about 20p blank were being sold for £2 once they had been turned into recordings of Luis Palau's 1981 Kelvinhall meetings). In the second place they allow doctrinal instruction and teaching to an audience that does not have a cultural tradition of serious reading. Nonetheless, the evangelical milieu still consumes a large amount of literature. Closely associated with the missions and crusade organisations are the literature producers and distributors. Although the term 'colportage' is no longer common currency, the activity referred to - the selling of Christian literature - is still a major element of evangelistic activity. In this area, as in other parts of the milieu, there appears to have been stabilty and growth. In the last 17 years, Send the Light Trust has grown to the point where it has five profitable bookshops, and a distribution centre for Christian literature large enough to warrant an IBM computer for stock handling. Another publishing success has been the Banner of Truth house, which reprints Calvinist and Puritan writers, and has seen a steady increase in its turnover since its foundation in the nineteen fiftes. Christian Focus Publications, the literature arm of the Scottish Free Presbyterian Church, has also shown a steady increase in its volume of business. The Canadian based Evangelical Tract Distributors claims a threefold increase in their output of tracts in the last ten years.

So far I have presented various sorts of material which I believe illustrate and demonstrate a significant change in the nature of Protestantism in the United Kingdom. I have looked at church membership, movements within churches, membership of inter-denominational associations, the circulation of periodicals, and the health of various allied organisations. There are very good reasons to be careful about making inferences from the statistics and other material presented. Extensive research on the way in which crime rates are produced makes it clear that even such sophisticated statistics cannot be taken as realistic reflections of the actual frequency of the 'criminal events' they are supposed to represent. Each item in my collection of data is weak and open to a large number of interpretations other than the ones I wish to offer. Agencies are obviously loath to record and publicise their failures. Enterprises that are total disasters usually sink without trace. There is an obvious danger that the research, no matter how committed to 'de-bunking', will observe and record only the survivals. It is in order to reduce that danger that I have surveyed so many different areas of conservative Protestant life. My conclusion is that, although individual observations and interpretations may be suspect, the overall impression is reliable. Furthermore, my view of conservative resilience and growth is shared by almost all of the many church leaders, evangelists, theologians and others to whom I have talked in the course of my research, and that extends to those who would call themselves liberal Protestants.

There is one notable exception to my general picture of conservative Protestant resilience and that is the Scottish Reformed Presbyterian Church. This small body of conservatives, which has been outside the national Church since 1690, has shown a recent rate of decline which is in marked contrast not only to other conservative churches but also to the stability of its sister church in Ulster. The membership has fallen from 600 to 300 since the nineteen fifties, and it is certain to collapse in the next few years as a result of the very high age profile of the remaining members. One minister estimated that the average age of the members of one congregation was 60. The same church in Ulster is maintaining its membership, has a normal age profile, pays its clergy as well as any other church, and has sufficient ministers to be able to spare one for missionary work in Eire. In part the difference in fortunes is the difference between the place of religion in Ulster and in Scotland, but the Reformed Presbyterian Church has also fared significantly worse than the other two conservative churches in Scotland.

To explain this one must consider the relationship between religion and culture. The Reformed Presbyterians were strongest in the Lowlands of Scotland. The seventeenth century Highlands were mainly Roman Catholic and Episcopalian with large elements of paganism and folk religion. Because the Reformed Presbyterian Church did not accept the Revolution Settlement it remained excluded from the mainstream of Scottish religious culture. When evangelical Protestantism spread through the Highlands and Islands, it did so through the agency of the National Church and its later offshoots; the Reformed Presbyterians were not involved in the conversion of the Highlands, and no additions came to their organisation. The Reformed Presbyterians continued to be confined to Fife, Ayrshire and parts of the Lothians. This was not a problem until the spread of industrialisation began to alter the composition of these areas. Ayrshire was much affected by the growth of Glasgow. The Reformed Presbyterian churches lost members as people moved into Glasgow, and as the sort of society from which it had recruited was undermined by the movement of industry into Ayrshire, and by the attendant creation of new towns.

For two reasons, similar movements of population have not yet undermined the two Free Churches. In the first place, there is a size below which organisations cannot readily reproduce themselves. The Free Presbyterian Church is small, but it is sufficiently large to produce enough ministers and enough capital so that, when it became clear that many Free Presbyterians were moving to the east coast of

Scotland from places like Kinlochbervie, the Church could afford to plant a new congregation in Aberdeen. The Reformed Presbyterians have for a century been at the sort of size where such brave ventures could not easily be funded or manned. In an extensive analysis of patterns of secularisation, David Martin (1978:79) makes the point that where a society has a centre and a periphery, religion is usually associated especially strongly with one or the other. In the case of the United Kingdom one finds a secular centre (London and South East England) and a number of peripheries (Wales, Scotland and Ulster) in which religion plays an important part in identifying the peripheries against the centre. If one looks only at Scotland, one can regard the rural Lowlands and the Highlands and Islands as peripheries with Glasgow, Edinburgh and central Scotland as the more secular centre. As a periphery, the Highlands and Islands, the home of the two Free Churches, has two distinct advantages; it is geographically more isolated, and it has its own language. The Lowlands has no physical protection against penetration nor any great cultural insulation. The Highland culture (and the Glaswegians reaction to it; ridiculing Highlanders as country bumpkins) gives the Free Churches a greater ability to keep their members even when they have moved to Glasgow. The Glasgow congregations with their Gaelic services offer social support and identity to the immigrants and for this reason have a special attraction to Free Church members who may feel isolated and alienated in the 'centre'. There is no longer any comparable Lowland culture (not even the efforts of Hugh McDiarmid could revive the Lallans language), and hence no reasons other than denominational loyalty to persuade Reformed Presbyterians who moved to Glasgow to continue in church membership.

The Reformed Presbyterian Church in Scotland has declined because it was traditionally tied to a particular population base which was itself being eroded. It was always a small church and thus unable, due to its limited resources, to move with its population. Being a very conservative church, whose raison d'etre was its refusal to accommodate to prevailing norms, it could not change to attract members from new populations. This example makes the point that talk of conservative Protestant growth need not imply that everything that is conservative Protestant is growing, only that the overall trend is in that direction.

THE SOURCES OF STABILITY AND GROWTH

In his own answer to the question of why it is that the conservative churches are growing, Kelley (1972) attributes the success to the greater ability of conservative beliefs to provide solutions for the problems that confront us, and to provide greater meaning and significance. This may well be the case, but it would be a mistake to suppose that there was a pool of heathen, out there in the secular world, looking for meaning and suddenly finding it in conservative Protestant beliefs. Bibby and Brikerhoff (1973) demonstrate that very little of the recruitment to Canadian conservative churches is due to converting the heathen. Most of those joining conservative churches were either moving from one such church to another, had grown up in that church or one similar, or were accommodating themselves to the faith of their spouses. This later category might include a number of atheists, but this is unlikely given the strong views that conservatives have about not being yoked in marriage to unbelievers. It seems fair to suppose that those people who marry members of conservative churches are already fairly close to believer status. The Canadian data matches my own impressions in the British case. Evangelicals are produced by efficient childhood socialisation and adolescent social control. They are cultivated and propogated by evangelical parents and relatives, Sunday schools and youth fellowships, school Bible classes and summer camps. They acquire their view of the world from their parents and from those with whom they associate when young. Undoubtedly there are dramatic sinners to saints conversions. In her autobiography, Doreen Irvine (1973) tells of her career as a drug-taking prostitute engaged in witchcraft, which was ended by her conversion through the ministry of the late Eric Hutchings; but the prominence given to such accounts shows the rarity of this pattern.

Evidence on the background and conversion of evangelical Protestants is available in the results of a large survey organised by the Evangelical Alliance (1968). Some 4,000 Christians were interviewed by volunteers drawn from the ranks of Evangelical Alliance supporters. The Alliance is a conservative evangelical organisation, less liberal than the British Council of Churches, and less conservative than the British Evangelical Council (which is distinctly Calvinist). Its theological tone would be similar to that of the National Association of Evangelicals in America. Its members would believe in the necessity of a personal saving faith in Christ. Thus the people whose experiences were surveyed would probably have been predominantly conservative evangelical with possibly a few Calvinists.

The main result of the survey was a demonstration of the importance of a Christian home background and early influences. In the first place, the age of conversion is significant. Seventeen percent of the sample had their conversion before the age of 12. More than half were converted between the ages of 12 and 20, and fewer than a quarter recorded an adult conversion. Asked about the main background influence on their conversion, half the sample gave either 'home' or 'personal witness outside the home'. The first category, with about a quarter of the sample, shows direct parental influence. The second category does not point directly at the convert having Christian parents but is, in many cases probably allied, in that parents are important in determining a child's friends. Furthermore, the alternative categories are of such a nature that they might well include some early childhood elements. When asked directly whether they had come from a Christian home, the sample divided in the middle. In interpreting this report one must bear in mind the special and limited usage of 'Christian' that is common among evangelicals. One often finds the distinction between conformist religion and a 'real' faith being made, 'churchianity' and Christianity, and many evangelical children would not describe their non-evangelical, but nonetheless regular churchgoing parents as 'Christian'. This narrow and exclusive use of the term sometimes leads to unconscious humour. One couple, in reporting to Life of Faith (Special issue, 1978:21) on their evangelising experiences on the Island of Arran mentioned that 'another Christian couple' had recently settled there, as if all the Arran Free Church members were not Christian! In view of the minimalist way in which the term 'Christian' is used by evangelicals, I think one might suppose that perhaps 60 or 70% of the sample had been raised in a home that had a more than nominal connection with a Christian tradition, and had been either socialised into their faith or had had enough 'anticipatory' socialisation to lay the foundations for their later conversion. Where this has not been the case, personal witness – personal relationships between the convert and an existing believer – seems to be central. This accords with what is known of recruitment into other sorts of religious organisations and will be pursued in the later discussion of conversions and crusades in Chapter 5.

The Secondary Consequences of Evangelistic Activity

Consideration of the biographies of new members of conservative Protestant groups suggests that the conversionist activity of such bodies is not the key to their success. They are not recruiting members through their presentation of the gospel message to the great unchurched masses. In hard economic terms, missionary work seems to be unproductive. Luis Palau's six week crusade in Glasgow in 1981 cost at least £100,000, and if one makes an allowance for the enormous amount of unpaid voluntary work that was done one could estimate a total cost of about £200,000. The returns in terms of 'souls saved' seem small in the light of such expenditure. This is the criticism that liberal Protestants routinely make of crusade evangelism. In the last section of this chapter, I want to argue for the paradox that the proselytising of some conservative churches while not being a major source of direct recruitment, is nonetheless a major part of their success. That is, there are important secondary consequences that are of value to the group even when the primary aim of evangelising is not attained.

In theory almost all conservative Protestants are committed to saving souls but, as Bryan Wilson demonstrated (1970), the notions of salvation, and the ways to attain this state, may vary considerably. Wilson offers a typology of different sectarian reponses to the world, two of which are relevant to this study: the conversionist and the introversionist. The conversionist response argues that neither religious ritual nor social improvement can purchase salvation and that only a radical individual change of heart will do. The result is usually the devotion of a lot of energy to trying to convert people. Many Protestant sects and movements - Methodism, for example - were conversionist. The introversionist response is to retreat from the impurity of the world, to withdraw into fellowship with only the pure in the hope of maintaining one's own pure condition. Examples of this sort of view can be found in the communitarian sects; the Hutterites, Doukhobors and Old Order Amish, all of which deliberately keep themselves separated from the surrounding secular world[15]. In making a distinction between conversionist and introversionist groups, it is important to bear in mind that the rhetoric and the reality of the group may well be different. This was the case with an evangelical student group who found that their surroundings caused problems (Bruce 1978). They wanted to evangelise, and yet they were in an hostile environment; a secular permissive, radical campus in the nineteen seventies. They could best have maintained their own faith by having as little as possible to do with other students and by withdrawing into a 'holy huddle', but then they would have been unable to evangelise. What they actually did was to produce a working combination of the two positions. They engaged in what I call 'routine proselytisation'. That is, they went through the motions of having missions but organised their evangelism in such a way as to minimise the contact between themselves and the secular world, and hence to reduce the humilation and embarassment that the rejection - found in much of that contact - caused. They advertised meetings which could be attended by the interested student but they avoided any activity that was not part of the accepted routine of student clubs and societies; hence the term 'routine preselytisation'. The young evangelical students then reacted to the failure of this evangelism by arguing that their own lives were a 'witness', and that their behaviour and demeanour was the most useful part of their evangelising. In practise, however, the term 'witness' figured most often in talk about internal social control. If a member was seen smoking, or taking a drink, or was known to be dating a non-Christian, then other members would talk of that person not keeping up a 'good witness'. 'Witnessing' seemed to be used as a means of keeping each other on the straight and narrow rather than as a means of impressing the secular world, especially as the closed friendship patterns of the group meant that most members were hardly visible to any members of the secular world. The conclusion of the study was an awareness that groups with a conversionist ideology may well in practice be quite introversionist.

This is a distinction that was suggested to me by a number of people to whom I talked in the course of my research on conservative church growth. They agreed with my basic thesis on the strength of the conservative churches but added that there was a difference between active and dormant conservative churches. A Baptist historian made the following comment: 'The bulk of (a certain Calvinist sect) form a type of "fossilised" culture, conservative in theology, yes, but not activist in seeking new members ... it is not conservatism per se that determines its growth in contemporary society'.

This insider's view and my own research both suggest that the distinction between conversionist and introversionist responses to the world should be augmented by the awareness that there may be 'active conversionism' and 'rhetorical conversionism'. Yet even rhetorical conversionist conservative Protestantism has a number of advantages over non-conversionist faiths such as liberal Preotestantism in terms of keeping control over existing members and building consensus around a set of dogmatic beliefs (this will be taken up in Chapter 4). However, 'active conversionist' groups seem to be more successful in recruiting new members (albeit the children of existing members). My main evidence for this view is the frequency with which well informed observers of the evangelical world have made such a point to me in correspondence and conversation. There is, in addition, one recent piece of research which suggests a similar conclusion. The Christian Brethren Research Fellowship recently completed a survey of Brethren congregations in England and Wales (Brown and Mills 1980). Firstly, the report confirmed that missions were basically unproductive. While three quarters of the congregations displayed a conversionist response by giving 'conversion' as one of the three main aims of the Brethren, 40% of the groups had seen no adult conversions in the previous year. Almost all of the congregations had meetings supposedly designed to attract the heathen, but 4% of the groups had not attracted one outsider to a year of such meetings, a third had drawn in between one and five outsiders, and less than one third had attracted ten or more non-members. To try and explain why some congregations should succeed where others fail, the report compared two extreme types of Brethren meetings: those that reported no adult baptisms in the past year and those that had ten or more such baptisms.

The 'ten plus' group of congregations did more by way of outreach. They also did more to improve socialisation and commitment. They more often had youth fellowships to bridge the gap between Sunday school and adult activities. They more often had an organised 'teaching ministry' with pre-arranged speakers, and they had more small house meetings for 'building up the faith of the membership' There were also significant differences in attitudes. The 'ten plus' group were more likely to allow women to pray audibly in meetings, were more in favour of united campaigns with other local evangelistic churches, were liable to regard 'soundness' as more important than denominational allegiance, and were less likely to insist on new comeers producing letters of commendation. There is a problem with attributing causal primacy to any of these differences. The groups that had more in the way of youth fellowships also had more young children, and it is by no means clear which is the cause and which the effect.

The Brethren study is not sufficiently detailed to support sophisticated explanations but, coupled with impressions gained from many interviews with conservative Protestants of various denominations, it does suggest that the basic level of activity is an important factor in survival and growth. The successful churches do more than those that are not growing. They are also more willing to innovate, which itself is likely to be a result of an increased commitment to evaluate critically and to improve conversionist activity. Too much innovation, of course, means that the church, rather than growing, changes and, as can be seen in the case of the churches most involved in ecumenism, such changes undermine the membership's commitment. The Brethren Report says: 'Missions had been conducted by about two-thirds of all churches in the previous five years, but results were not very heartening in terms of outreach of numbers converted. The most common response was that the mission had brought the church members closer together' (Brown and Mills, 1980:16-17). This is the point of the apparent paradox. The successful churches did more proselytising but owed their success, not directly to that activity, but rather to the secondary benefits of increased cohesion and commitment. As a source of recruitment, missions and crusades are not very efficient, but the enthusiasm and hard work generated in the organising of such events has the effect of making the individual, 'personal witness' of the activist more positive, and making the socialisation processes of the group more effective. This is thus an important secondary effect. While active conversionism is not itself the cause of the success of the conservative churches, it is, indirectly, the source of much resilience to secularisation.

Notes

1. For example, the Church of Scotland's <u>Life and Work</u>
    (June 1981:31) prints a letter from one minister who had
    inadvertently confused his Presbytery's survey of youth
    work by misunderstanding the age categories.

2. A similar problem arises frequently where a number of
    different groupings could be, and sometimes are, treated
    under the same heading. Although they are well aware of
    this problem and try to avoid it, Currie <u>et al</u>
    (1977:151) still make mistakes. They give some figures
    which purport to be about Particular Baptists but which,
    being drawn from the Baptist Union records, actually
    include lots of General Baptists. I am grateful to John
    Briggs of Keele University and David Bebbington of
    Stirling University for making me aware of these
    difficulties and for warning me off comparisons between
    the Baptist Union and the Strict Baptists.

3. The figures in Tables 1 and 2 were compiled from Currie
    <u>et al</u> (1977), Brierley (1978), Highet (1950;1960), and
    from material supplied by officials of the various
    churches. The overall percentages were arrived at by
    using the year nearest to 1956 for which reliable
    figures were available. In no case is it likely that
    the substitution of, say 1955 for 1956, significantly
    effects the outcome.

4. The figures for Church of Scotland ministers in charges
    are as follows:
    1956 - 2113; 1966 - 1876; 1976 - 1588; 1981 - 1424. The
    ministry has thus contracted by 33%. The United Free
    Church now has 43 ministers in charges where it had
    about 76 in 1956 (it is difficult to know what
    proportion of the 1956 figure represents retired
    ministers as the Year-book did not then distinguish
    active and non-active clergy).

5. The United Free Church is the rump of the combined Free
    Church and United Presbyterian body (formed in 1900)
    which did not join the Kirk in 1929. The congregations
    that continued in the United Free Church did so on the
    principle of autonomy from the state. It is this rather
    than any theological argument that keeps the UFC out of
    the Church of Scotland.

6. The Non-Subscribing Presbyterian Churches are listed in
    the hand-book of Unitarian and Free Christian Churches.

7. In May 1972 there were 2,370 Congregational churches. 1,815 joined the United Reformed Church, 300 joined the Congregational Federation, and 110 joined the Evangelical Fellowship of Congregational Churches. 140 remained independent. Since then 12 have left the URC for either the Federation or the EFCC, 5 have left the Federation for the EFCC, and 5 new churches have been formed and affiliated to the EFCC.

8. For a detailed study of changes within Methodism in the last 25 years, see Kitching (1976).

9. The NCA and SCS do not confine their membership to ministers although most of their members are ordained. However, the total Church membership would provide a similar yardstick for comparison.

10. The data on associations was collected by the rather ad hoc method of asking people what bodies they belonged to and noting mentions in the religious press and the Evangelical Alliances handbooks. I wrote to all the associations thus identified and received replies from most of them. Some were unable to supply sufficiently detailed and accurate membership figures and were therefore omitted from the survey. It is entirely possible that some important associations were overlooked and that some of the data is misleading but poor information is better than no information.

11. Watson went to York in 1965 with one year in which to prevent the closure of his first church. His congregation grew so fast that he had to be moved to a larger church and his congregation is now in the thousands, with a full-time staff of 31.

12. Another evangelical occupational association is the Christian Police Association which was not able to supply detailed membership figures but reports a general increase in membership and activity over the last 15 years. Again, however, there is no similar liberal Protestant police association to provide a basis for comparison.

13. The method of data collection used here was similar to that used to survey associations. I collected titles from Willing's Press Guide, the Evangelical Alliance handbooks, and advertisements in the religious press. Editors and publishers were asked to provide circulation figures for selected years. Of 76 publications identified, 55 responded to my request for information.

Fourteen of these were later deleted because they were either not Protestant or did not provide sufficient data to allow even the roughest computation of circulation pattern. Of particular importance was the failure of the Christian Weekly Newspaper group (which publishes the main evangelical Anglican papers) to respond. This prevented me from making a separate comparison of the fortunes of the various Anglican periodicals. A further obstacle to detailed analysis was the frequent changes in the format and frequency of certain periodicals. It was thus not possible to compare weekly and monthly productions, which would have been illuminating given the possibility that the patterns might really represent the success of the monthlies and the failure of the weeklies rather than theological tone. It might have been possible to collect enough information to allow such a comparison but there are too many difficulties in the interpretation of even accurate circulation figures to justify the expense and time needed for such data collection.

14. Armstrong and his Worldwide Church of God are mentioned here simply because they offer the extreme case of entirely subsidised publishing. Whether or not Armstrong should be regarded as a conservative Protestant is another matter. In style, organisation and rhetoric, Armstrong appears to be a fundamentalist but his beliefs include some rather curious combinations of British Israelism (the belief that Anglo-Saxons are the lost tribes of Israel) and Seventh-Day Adventist beliefs.

15. On the Hutterites, see Peters (1971); on the Amish, see Hostetler (1963); and on the Doukhobers, see Hawthorn (1980).

4 The form of beliefs and the form of organisation

However discomforting it may be for the analyst trying to explain and understand social phenomena, there is little in the social world that is simple. Reality is complex and different types of analysis must be used to penetrate the different levels of reality. Unlike some physical scientists the sociologist can rarely, if ever, use artificial experiments to hold certain factors constant and unchanged while he looks at the influence of some other feature. Generally one has to grub around in historical and comparative material to find some circumstances where the principle one is now interested in stands out and where one can, without betraying the material, talk as if all other things were equal. One way of comparing liberal and conservative Protestantism is to focus on specific organisations that embody conservative and liberal Protestant beliefs. In this chapter, I intend to compare the nature and fortunes of the Student Christian Movement (SCM) and the Inter-Varsity Fellowship (IVF)[1].

As will become clear in a short history of these two movements, they operated at the same time, in the same culture, and in the same market. Both recruited students in universities and colleges and hence both shared the problem of building an organisation in an environment which changed one third of its members every three years. IVF, which grew from defections from the SCM, developed an organisational structure that was identical to that of the SCM, and with the exception of certain activities (such as evangelistic missions) that were in tune with the ideology of IVF but not that of the later SCM, the two movements did similar things. SCM and IVF can be regarded as similar in everything except their ideologies, and their different fortunes can be examined for what they tell us about the role of ideology and in particular, the problems of liberalism and the strengths of conservatism.

THE STUDENT CHRISTIAN MOVEMENT

For most of the nineteenth century missions were staffed by members of the lower classes (Potter, 1975). While the bourgeoisie and the aristocracy provided the funds and occasionally a younger son or daughter for missionary work, there was little active interest in missions among the people who went to British Universities. Small and mainly local groups had begun to make in-roads into this field. Livingstone's address to the University of Cambridge Senate House in 1857 had led to the founding of the Universities' Mission to Central Africa. Cambridge also had a Church Missionary Union, the Jesus Lane Sunday School and the student run Daily Prayer Meeting. The growth of the holiness movement, centred on the Keswick Convention, affected the universities as it did the rest of the country and in 1877 some 250 men in Cambridge formed the Cambridge Inter-Collegiate Christian Union to provide a central evangelical fellowship for students. The decision of seven Cambridge students to volunteer for service with the China Inland Mission gave a national focus to this movement. One of the students, C.T. Studd, had played cricket for England and his two brothers were also well-known sportsmen. Two of the seven were military men. All of them were rich, well connected and well thought of, and their 'sacrifice' (which in the case of C.T. Studd involved giving away an enormous amount of money) attracted a great deal of attention and public interest. The Cambridge Seven, as they were popularly known, signified the growth in prestige and status of pious evangelicalism in Victorian Britain. The Lord Lieutenant of a Midlands county remarked that when he came of age there were only two houses in the county that had family prayers; now there were only two that did not (Bradley, 1976:38). In the eighteen forties evangelical students at Cambridge had been despised. The 'Sims' (the nickname for followers of Charles Simeon) were often scholarship students who lacked status or wealth and who were only at the University to study. While the campaigns of Wilberforce and his colleagues had not entirely removed depravity and drunken licentiousness from public life, they had altered the public tone enough for such behaviour to be less openly flaunted, and as a result evangelical piety was less the object of scorn in 1877 than it had been in 1840.

In their mission campaign of 1873, Moody and Sankey had devoted some attention to the universities. In Edinburgh in particular the students had been heavily involved in the organisation of the crusade, and even in preaching. Before the Cambridge Seven sailed for China, they spent a few months touring the Univeristy towns and speaking to student rallies. The result of this activity was an increase in the size and the morale of the student evangelical groups but as yet they remained localised and fragmented. One early attempt to create a national organisation failed and it was not until the arrival of Robert P. Wilder from America in 1891 that the movement gained a centre. Wilder had founded a student missionary organisation in the United States. He arrived in Britain with letters of introduction to leading evangelicals and he quickly persuaded them of the need for a similar organisation in this country. With the support of Stock of the Church Missionary Society; F.B. Meyer, a leading Baptist evangelical; Lord Kinnaird, the successor to Williams as President of the YMCA; and the Reverend C.J. Chavasse, a leading Anglican evangelical, Wilder toured the colleges and persuaded the student leaders to meet. On March 23rd 1892 representatives of the student groups in London, Cambridge, Oxford, Glasgow, Aberdeen, Edinburgh and Dublin met in Edinburgh and formed the Student Volunteer Missionary Union, with the signing of the statement 'I am willing and desirous, God permitting, to become a foreign missionary' as the criterion for membership. Arthur Polhill-Turner, one of the original Cambridge Seven, now returned after seven years in China, was appointed as the first full-time 'travelling secretary' of the Movement.

The SVMU held its first national conference at Keswick, one week before the main Keswick Convention. This arrangement allowed the students to attend both events and made it easy for them to invite prominent evangelicals to speak at their meetings. Keswick speakers like Prebendary H.W. Webb-Peploe were happy to support the movement and this arrangement allowed them to do so with the minimum of inconvenience simply by arriving at Keswick a few days earlier than they would normally have done.

It became clear from the first year of operation that it was difficult to recruit students for missions in colleges where there was no organised evangelical student presence. Donald Fraser (Fraser, 1934) followed his year as traveller for the Volunteer Movement by spending a year as travelling secretary for the British Colleges Christian Union. This body was a national union of local student fellowships such as the Cambridge Inter-Collegiate Christian Union (CICCU), and it was in theory distinct from the SVMU but in practice it shared the same office, the same staff and the same membership. In 1898 the whole student movement (as SVMU and BCCU were always collectively known) was brought into one organisation called the Student Christian Movement (SCM) under the general secretaryship of Tissington Tatlow, a Dublin episcopalian who then managed the movement for the following 30 years.

Although the evangelicals who later broke away from the SCM tend to talk of the movement as having been at this point thoroughly conservative and later led astry, the reality of the movement's composition is more complex. The movement was a product of that short period in which both liberals (as they later became) and conservatives cooperated around evangelism and outreach. The potency of the missionary appeal and the novelty of cooperation between people of different traditions that had made the Moody missions such a success created a short period of alliance in which doctrinal differences were suppressed in the common pursuit of mission. The movement's early platform was certainly evangelical; there were no high churchmen and for the first three years there was no opposition to the strong links with the Keswick Convention, but the Scottish presence was largely a Free Church presence and the Free Church students were already heavily influenced by the rationalistic higher criticism of German theologians. In a Bible reading, Maclean, one of the Free Church student leaders, reminded the audience that they were to love God 'with our mind as wells our heart and soul'; a proposition that many fundamentalists would violently oppose. The 1894 summer conference had speeches from Professor Snape who thought they had occasion 'to thank God for the higher criticism' and from Canon Taylor Smith, a keen Keswick evangelical who would not have thanked anyone for it. In his history of the SCM, Tatlow (1933) makes the point that the speakers at early conferences were not representative of the students. Various speakers who were not in the pious evangelical mould of Keswick were invited but they did not at that stage think the movement important enough to accept. The SCM leaders could use their contacts in the Keswick world to persuade men like Webb-Peploe to support them but they then had few other contacts. Hence the platform suggests a more conservative evangelicalism than the students, especially the Scots Free Church supporters, would have liked.

The most accurate picture of the beliefs of the SCM can be gained from the inability of the students to agree on a basis of doctrine that did any more than simply exclude the Unitarians. The SVMU had no doctrinal statement and the BCCU was open to any union 'the aims and work of which are in full harmony with a belief in Jesus Christ as God the Son and only Saviour of the world'. This statement was sufficent to keep

the Keswick evangelicals happy but general enough to be
acceptable to almost anyone else as well. It is further the
case that even when the SCM did draft and accept a more
detailed statement of faith, many local branches of the
movement refused to use the statement as a test for
membership. Thus while it is true to say that the early
movement was evangelical and largely did accept such ideas as
the Bible being the directly inspired word of God, nothing
was done to make such a position essential for membership and
nothing was done to curb the increasing liberalism of the
Scottish members.

From the International Missionary Conference of 1896,
which brought 2,000 students from Britain and other parts of
the world together in Liverpool, the movement grew in size
and stature. It also moved away from Keswick, both
spiritually and geographically. Inroads were made into the
theological colleges and that brought broad and high church
Anglicans into the movement. The SCM became established in
the newly opened university colleges in the industrial north
of England. More women joined the movement. These changes
not only expanded the movement, they also altered it. The
interests and problems of the northern college students and
the women were different from those of the CICCU members.
Both groups were new to higher education. They were not at
college to play cricket or because their parents had been.
Where they had problems with their faith (or problems with
their fellow students' lack of it) these were intellectual
problems and they sought intellectual solutions. Under
pressure from these new groups the movement gradually
developed a theological position that was clearly liberal.
The view of the Bible was influenced by the rationalistic
thinking of higher criticism. Emphasis was shifted from
making a taken-for-granted faith 'come alive' to making their
faith 'reasonable' and intellectually defensible in the
modern world.

Another key element in the change of the SCM was the
successful wooing of the anglo-catholics. This powerful
section of the Anglican Church had given the SCM, with its
Keswick background, a very wide berth and their suspicions of
this Protestant movement were difficult to lay to rest.
Anglo-catholics distrusted 'ecumenical' movements because
they were 'undenominational'; that is, they were based on the
acceptance by participants of a common core of belief and
practice, and neglect of all other differences as trivial and
of no consequence. The SCM developed an alternative basis
for co-operation in 'interdenominationalism':

> While the SCM unites persons of different
> religious denominations in a single
> organisation for certain definite aims and

activities it recognises their allegiance to
any of the various Christian bodies into which
the Body of Christ is divided. It believes
that loyalty to their denomination is the
first duty of Christian students, and welcomes
them into the fellowship of the Movement as
those whose privilege it is to bring into it
as their own contribution all that they as
members of their own religious body, have
discovered or will discover of Christian truth
(Tatlow, 1933:400).

The report goes on to emphasise this position:

when at Summer Conferences ... a member of any
religious body addresses the Student Movement
he should be expected to give his full message
and not to seek to modify it in view of the
fact that there may be some in his audience
who, because they are members of other
Christian bodies ... may not agree with him
(in Tatlow, 1933:400).

This position, that everyone is both right and wrong,
provided an acceptable basis for anglo-catholic participation
and leading high churchmen such as Charles Gore and Edward
and Neville Talbot became central in both the SCM and the
developing ecumenical movement.

The Evangelical Schisms

With every broadening of the base and interests of the SCM,
the evangelicals grew more concerned. As early as 1900 we
find Lord Kinnaird, a leading evangelical layman, complaining
about the SVMU's invitation to 'a ritualist like the Bishop
of London' to address the London Conference. On this
occasion Tatlow could defend himself by arguing that he was
simply following the traditional courtesies of inviting the
leading church dignatories to meetings in their areas. In
the same year The Record (an evangelical Anglican paper)
accused the movement of intellectualism. Four years later a
group of Cambridge students criticised the SCM summer
conference for the lack of a strong spiritual tone. Three of
them were invited to a meeting of the General Committee to
make their views known, and they found little support. The
women members of the committee were particularly opposed to
any return to a 'Keswick' platform. This same conference was
also a source of disquiet to Gerald Manley and three other
ex-SVMU missionaries home on furlough who asked for a

restoration of the evangelical emphasis in the conferences.
In 1904 E.S. Woods and other senior supporters of the
movement wrote in similar vein.

The evangelicals were themselves divided in their
reactions to these changes. Eugene Stock was a little
concerned at the direction of the movement but was prepared
to give it his tentative support in these experiments.
Prebendary Webb-Peploe was not. Having heard that 'higher
critics' were to speak at a SCM conference to which he had
also been invited, he threatened to withdraw: 'I have been
twice informed to my astonishment and distress that at your
Conishead Conference I shall not only find present brethren
of the Protestant Evangelical and Keswick school of thought
but higher critics from many parts' (Tatlow, 1933:274). On
this occasion Tatlow persuaded him not to withdraw, but it
was the last time a noted conservative evangelical leader
addressed an SCM conference.

The first significant publicising of disagreement came
through the medium of <u>The English Churchman and St. James
Chronicle</u> in late 1908 and 1909. The first blow was an
editorial which commented on the attempts to get the high
church Anglicans to the Edinburgh 1910 Missionary Conference
and the SCM's connections with such machinations. This was
followed by a letter from 'Puzzled' voicing concern about
high churchmen in the SCM:

> Has this anything to with the similar tendency
> by which the Student Movement has of late been
> giving prominence to high churchmen rather
> than to evangelicals? I observed that at
> Mr Mott's recent meeting at the Albert Hall
> the chief speakers were High-Church Bishops
> and well-known nonconformists. So far as I
> can gather from the report, no prominent
> Evangelical Churchman took a leading part in
> the gathering ... and yet I shrewdly suspect
> that when the leaders of the Student Movement
> need the 'sinews of war' they are apt to fall
> back privately for financial support on
> old-fashioned evangelicals, both Churchmen and
> nonconformists (1st February, 1909).

Tatlow replied at length to 'Puzzled'. He argued that
'head-counting' was not a valid method of evaluating the
Movement's theological preferences. For the particular
conference mentioned by 'Puzzled' special invitations had
been sent to Lord Kinnaird, Prebendary Fox and Bishop
Taylor-Smith. None of these had been able to attend. Tatlow
then surveys the list of speakers for the last few

conferences and notes that there are no high churchmen, two or three of the broad church and the rest all evangelicals.

In conclusion he defends the inclusive nature of the SCM: 'The Student Movement is prepared to accept into its ranks all who have this personal saving faith in Christ as their Saviour, Lord and God, whether they be High Churchmen, Low Churchmen or Nonconformists'. 'Puzzled' offers a rejoinder in which he perversely argues that the very fact that Tatlow had replied at length means that there must be 'something in it' (23rd February, 1909).

Another feature of this controvery was the readiness of the evangelicals to believe rumours which painted in dramatic black-and-white what they sensed in grey. Their uncertain disquiet at what they heard in SCM was amplified and given body in certain rumours that were current and popular. Thus in December of 1907 we find Tatlow writing to a Reverend Griffith Thomas denying that the movement had any plans to get rid of Robert Wilder (in fact they were at that point negotiating a longer contract with him). The Movement's attempts to restore the balance by offering the high churchmen similar recognition to that of the low - having liturgical prayer as well as extempore prayer - was built up into a rumour that: 'Our executive has decided to have a special marquee set aside next year at our summer conference for High Churchmen where they could have an altar ... I need hardly say that there was not a word of truth in it' (Tatlow to Thomas, 9th December, 1907). Secretly disturbed but not yet ready to condemn, one old senior friend of the movement had formed a private prayer circle to pray for the SCM's return to soundness. By 1909, Tatlow was sufficiently disturbed by rumours that John Mott, the leader of the international movement, was worried about the health of the SCM to write to him asking for a letter expressing confidence which Tatlow could circulate to those who looked to Mott for guidance.

The first actual break in the SCM came with the withdrawal of the Cambridge students. The CICCU had always been very conservative and it had not been affected by the changes in the interests of the rest of the SCM. Cambridge, the home of Simeon, was always the most evangelical of the Universities. In addition the strength of the college family tradition - many of the leading Victorian families sent generation after generation to Trinity, and often to the same rooms - provided another powerful reminder of the faith of the fathers and thus another powerful obstacle to experimentation. Finally, the organisational structure of the CICCU, with the committee members selecting their own successors, also acted to discourage change. After three years of argument and negotiation, the CICCU disaffiliated from the national SCM, and as if enacting a symbolic return to purity, the first event they organised was a summer camp at Keswick[2].

The Cambridge split of 1910 was followed by similar divisions in other universities and colleges. The War interrupted the development of the schism but with the return to the colleges in 1919, the controversy was resumed with new vigour and vitality. A national conference of evangelicals was held at the Egypt General Mission's offices in London and a controversy in The Christian provided the students with an opportunity to make a public declaration of their existence and intention. The Christian (20th November, 1919) had published an article highly critical of the SCM on its front page. Called 'Towards what?', it was an editorial comment on a recent SCM publication, God and the Struggle for Existence, which expounded Christ's teachings within a perspective drawn from the German 'sitz im leben' school of criticism[3]. The article also drew attention to the various changes in the SCM's basis of faith statement, especially those of 1913. The main offences in the revised version were the omission of any specific mention of the deity of Christ and the absence of words favoured by evangelicals such as 'sin', 'regeneration', 'forgiveness' and 'salvation'. The tone of the book and the basic changes were enough for the writer to say that 'it is very clearly evident that the Movement does not even stand where its earliest members stood'. This was followed by a number of letters (4th December, 1919). The first, from a Scottish Minister, asked for patience with the SCM. The next, from Colin Kerr, the Vicar of Norwood, called for more 'definiteness' and vital Christianity. As an aside, it is interesting to note that by the end of the War, Norwood had become the equivalent of Clapham in Wilberforce's day. Mrs Studd and her family lived there; Godfrey Buxton had his missionary training camp there; Mrs Howard Guinness moved there with her family after the death of her husband (the son of Grattan Guinness and Director of the Regions Beyond Missionary Union). Kerr seems to have been the chaplain to many of London's leading evangelicals and he would certainly have been known by many of the evangelical students at the conference. Kerr's letter drew a reply from Edward Woods, who was then Chairman of SCM's General Committee, in which he argued the case for the value of translating the Christian concerns into a new language which students would understand. He defended one chapter in the book that had been particularly harshly dealt with:

> Whatever the views of your paper about Evolution and Higher Criticism, these are, as a matter of fact, accepted as true by a vast majority of students and a large number of

genuine Christians ... It is not written to propogate Evolution or Higher Criticism, but to show students that even if they accept these views, Christianity is still true. The book is addressed, not to convinced believers, but to doubters.

This correspondence was published while the evangelical students were still meeting at Drayton Park and they there composed a reply to Wood's letter, in which they claimed that a number of students were going back to conservative views. The letter, as well as advertising the existence of the conference, was essentially a manifesto of the students:

> We are witnessing term by term in the universities, through the preaching of Christ crucified and risen, such radical changes in the lives of men of various temperaments, abilities and types of thought as are evidence that this Gospel is still 'the power of God unto Salvation' and that the blood of the Lord Jesus Christ is still the only remedy for the sin and evil in the human heart ... We write this in our confident expectation of our Lord's Return for His people and desiring thereby 'to give a reason of the hope that is in us with meekness and fear' fully realising our own short experience in His service. (The Christian, 18th December, 1919).

This 'Inter-Varsity' conference was repeated in 1920 and 1921 and at the fourth meeting it was formally made an annual event. A constitution for the Conference was accepted in 1923 and in it, the following doctrines were presented as a basis of faith:

(a) The divine inspiration and infallibility of Scripture as originally given, and its supreme authority in all matters of faith and conduct ...
(b) The Unity of the Father, the Son and the Holy Spirit in the Godhead ...
(c) The universal sinfulness and guilt of human nature since the Fall, rendering man subject to God's wrath and condemnation ...
(d) Redemption from the guilt, penalty and power of sin only through the sacrificial death (as our representative and substitute) of Jesus Christ, the Incarnate Son of God ...
(e) The Resurrection of Jesus Christ from the dead ...

(f)   The necessity of the work of the Holy Spirit to make the Death of Christ effective to the individual sinner ...

(g)   The indwelling and work of the Holy Spirit in the believer ...

(h)   The expectation of the personal return of the Lord Jesus Christ ...   (IVC Constitution, 1923-24).

In addition to stating what it was they believed, they also incorporated the lessons they had learnt from 'the decline' of the SCM. To prevent the gradual erosion of evangelical identity, they insisted that all office holders subscribe to the basis of faith. Only those speakers 'whose views were known to be in accordance with the truths stated in the constitution' were to be invited to speak. The Conference was to refrain from organising any cooperative activity with any organisation not substantially in agreement with the Conference basis. As a final safeguard of orthodoxy it was stated that this constitution could only be changed with the agreement of three-quarters of the attending members at a Conference General Committee meeting.

The existence of the Inter-Varsity Conference provided a source of encouragement for small groups of students in SCM branches throughout the country to 'come out' and some leading student evangelicals toured the colleges encouraging the schismatics. In April 1928, the movement was further consolidated with the transformation of the Conference, which had begun as an ad hoc event, into a full 'Fellowship of Evangelical Unions'. There now existed in the universities two rival organisations. The SCM was completely identified with liberalism, modernism and the ecumenical movement while the IVF stood for 'old paths in perilous times'; a full conservative evangelicalism.

THE DISINTEGRATION OF SCM

It is impossible to compress the history of 50 years of a national organisation into a few hundred words without doing damage to detail but one can convey the essence of the changes by talking of growth, diversification and fragmentation. The SCM established itself not only in all the universities and major colleges (although it had a presence in the teacher training colleges it could not be called strong there) but also in the religious life of the country at large through its provision of ex-staff and students who became major leaders of the ecumenical movement, both in their own churches and in the central bureaucracy of the World Council of Churches. Its publishing arm, the SCM Press, became famous for major works of theology (especially the work of German theologians such as Barth, Bultmann and

Tillich) and for its Religious Book Club which produced cheap editions of theological and more general interest religious works. An Auxiliary Movement for ex-SCM graduates was created and the student movement expanded into schools with the SCM in Schools organisation. The careful investment of funds allowed a large full-time staff to be supported (in the fifties this was often 40 strong) and superficially the story of the SCM from the schism to the nineteen sixties is one of growth.

Each element of growth, however, also contained an element of fragmentation. The SCM Press, created to serve the movement, became to all intents and purposes an independent company and the relationship with the movement became one of company and shareholder. At one point in the nineteen fifties the board of the press seriously considered changing its name to lessen the association with the student movement. The First Conference Estate Co. was another venture, created by Tatlow to provide residential accommodation for the movement's annual summer conferences, which gradually began to follow its own commercial interests at the expense of those of the movement. It is ironic that in the late nineteen sixties and seventies, the Company's best customer was not the SCM, which by then no longer required that scale of accommodation, but the IVF. The Schools work had been started to promote the SCM among school children so that recruitment would be easier when those children came to university. This work also developed its own interests. Instead of servicing the SCM, it offered general educational material for religious studies teachers in schools and drew most of its finances from local educational authorities for just that work. The Auxiliary Movement soon ceased to confine its membership to ex-SCM members and began to enroll anyone who shared its interests until it was taken over by the British Council of Churches as an ecumenical fellowship.

With the radical changes in thought and behaviour among students in the later part of the nineteen sixties, the SCM shifted from being a liberal and sometimes socialist movement of ecumenically minded Protestants to being an outright radical organisation that numbered some Roman Catholics among its membership and staff. Its activities began to alienate even its staunchest supporters. As someone active in the SCM at the time later said:

> The SCM of the late sixties and seventies ...
> rejected the divisions between students and
> others as being a capitulation to the norm of
> capitalist society; it regarded both the
> clerically dominated church and the
> universities as dying institutions which would

not be produced in the same form in the new
society; it fantasized itself as a
revolutionary apocalyptic movement whose
priority was to 'live the truth' rather than
make it survive as a growing institution. But
this image of the SCM as a 'remnant' again
encountered the fundamental contradiction,
that its radicalism was being financed from
capital accumulated in the past and was
therefore accountable not only to God but to
some very earthly institutions (Condren,
1979:4).

One of the earthly institutions was the Trust Association.
This body was a legal entity created by Tatlow to hold funds
on behalf of the Movement. It was made up of senior staff of
the SCM and a number of old ex-SCM staff members. Until 1975
it had acted only as a 'rubber stamp' for financial decisions
made by the SCM's General Committee. By 1975 however, there
was so much disquiet among the ex-members of previous
generations about the policies being pursued by the Movement,
that the arrival of a number of complaints from students
about financial misdealings within the SCM was enough for the
Trust Association to refer the SCM to the Charity
Commissioners for investigation and to try to sack the SCM
staff and freeze the Movement's assets. The Trust dispute
continued for four years and it was not until 1979 that
agreement was reached between the students and the senior
supporters. This agreement was made possible by the decline
of the idealism of the nineteen sixties and early seventies
among the students. By 1978 most of the student members of
SCM shared the Trust Association's distrust of a radicalism
that insisted that all of the staff (General Secretary as
well as bookkeeper) should do their own typing, filing, and
cleaning. This new generation did not share the vision of
the radicals who had moved the SCM's headquarters from an
office in London to a crumbling old manor house in the
country in the hope that a commune might give a spiritual
centre to the ailing movement. But by this point it hardly
mattered. The membership had dwindled to the level where it
was less than 200. This is in contrast to a figure of over
7,000 in 1957 and has to be read in the context of the
massive increase in the numbers of students in higher
education. With no income at all from current members, the
SCM continues to exist because income from capital invested
in the nineteen fifties allows the employment of about eight
full-time staff who spend their time trying to build support.

THE UNIVERSITIES AND COLLEGES CHRISTIAN FELLOWSHIP (UCCF)

From its slow but steady start the IVF continued to grow to first rival and then dwarf the SCM. In 1974 the name was changed to the Universities and Colleges Christian Fellowship (UCCF) in order to give recognition to its strong presence in the smaller colleges. Like the SCM, UCCF has shown growth and diversification but unlike SCM, it has not suffered from fragmentation. What is interesting is the degree to which IVF/UCCF has duplicated the Tatlow era SCM. There is the same two-tier staff system with a small core of senior staff members who serve for long periods and a larger group of young staff who serve the movement for a short period between graduating and moving on to their careers. Annual conferences are held at Swanwick, the centre created by Tatlow. Travelling secretaries service the branches. The Inter-Varsity Press publishes material both for the organisation and for a wider audience of evangelicals. There are special interest offshoots such at the Theological Students Fellowship and the Graduates Fellowship. In brief, IVF/UCCF has grown to the size and complexity of requiring and being able to support a staff of 50 and yet shows little sign of breaking up and declining in the way that SCM did. This brief history and survey serves to make the point that in most things SCM and IVF were very similar. In only two things, ideology and fortune, did they differ markedly and I now want to consider the relationship of the former to the latter.

THE FORM OF THE IDEOLOGY

There are many ways in which systems of belief can be examined. One simple division would emphasise three important features of ideology; specific content, general content and form. At some times, in trying to account for the appeal of an ideology, one may find the answer in its specific content. The idea that the Pope is the Anti-Christ may explain part of the appeal of Paisleyism in present-day Ulster in that it allows one to be anti-Catholic in general while denying that one is actually prejudiced against individual Catholics; it is the system of Catholicism that is being opposed and such a belief 'resonates' with the material and cultural interests of Protestants in Ulster. Alternatively what is important about an ideology may lie not at the level of any specific propositions but at a more general level of 'tone' of the beliefs as a whole. Thus one can see the rise of the social gospel in the last part of the nineteenth century as part of a general optimism about man's ability to develop and improve his condition. The optimistic image of man that was part of the teaching of men like Rauschenbach in America resonated perfectly with a broader optimism that characterised much of that age. But apart from content, both general and specific, ideologies also have forms and it is this feature of the ideologies of liberal and conservative Protestantism that I want to examine.

There are three important features of conservative ideology that relate to its shape or form, rather than to its content; dogmatism, stability and external authority. Conservatism is dogmatic in that it can be summarised in a set of simple beliefs which must be accepted. The IVF doctrinal basis is a good example. While more sophisticated formulations are possible, it is the fact that conservatives can reduce what they believe to such propositions that is central to my analysis. The second major feature of conservatism is its claims to stability, to being unchanging. The position of the Sovereign Grace Advent Testimony makes this clear: 'Our manifesto is as up-to-date now as when originally framed and requires no amendment. The Word of God does not change and therefore simple exposition of that Word does not need amendment' (Watching and Waiting, XXXI, 9:130). Conservative Protestant groups have a habit of talking about keeping to 'old paths'. Conservative magazines readily reprint the sermons and writings of divines long dead without any apology or justification and in so doing they constantly affirm the proposition that it is truth and falsity that matters, not modernity. Truth is not altered by time; if Spurgeon was 'useful' a hundred years ago then he is still useful now.

The third feature of conservative ideology that is important for analysis is its views of authority. Conservatism claims to possess (and to rest on) an objective and external source of authority in the Bible. To return to a point made in the introduction, it does not matter to me whether these claims are justified or not. One scholar (Barr, 1977) has recently spent a lot of time demonstrating that conservative evangelicals (whom he confusingly calls 'fundamentalists') have in fact changed their beliefs considerably. This is not particularly important for my analysis. For the sociologist explaining people's actions, what they think is the case is usually more important than what 'really' is the case. People act on the basis of their own interpretations of the situation, however misguided such interpretations might be. The very fact that conservatives insist that their beliefs have not changed (even if they have) gives them more confidence in those beliefs than they would have if they recognised that their beliefs changed.

In contrast to this model of conservative Protestantism, liberalism is not dogmatic, consciously promotes change, and involves denying that the Bible can be used as an objective, external source of revelation. As I noted in the introduction, the liberal view of revelation is a progressive one. The Bible cannot be directly apprehended; it requires interpretation and translation. The terms in which we interpret change with our culture. Hence there can be no final and complete statements. There is always 'new light'.

IDEOLOGY AND ORGANISATION

Having established the key features of the form or shape of these different types of Protestantism, I now want to look at the consequences these have for behaviour. To declare my destination before departure: I intend to show that many of the problems of liberal Protestantism stem from the form of the ideology itself. It is the form that is central to this discussion. It can also be argued that the content of liberal Protestantism ceased to have strong appeal to a certain culture. Here I want to limit myself to establishing that, whatever the connections between the content of the belief system and the interests of potential believers, the form of the ideology is such that it is extremely difficult to preserve and to promote. Naturally I want to argue the converse for conservative Protestantism; whatever the appeal of its content, general and particular, it has advantages over liberalism in terms of the suitability of its form for organisational preservation and promotion. Some of the organisational consequences that I discuss may seem obvious and hardly worthy of attention. They may be obvious (it is one of the problems of a discipline that deals with everyday life that we are tempted to justify ourselves by finding explanations for ordinary things that ordinary people would never think of; such explanations are, for obvious reasons, usually nonsense) but unless one presupposes mass ignorance, then the obvious is a good place to look for good explanation.

(a) Product profile

The first thing that follows from the dogmatic nature of conservative Protestantism is a strong 'product profile', to use the language of the salesman. Conservatives know what they believe and it is therefore not hard for conservatives to recognise each other or for outsiders to identify them. In comparison, liberalism is very poorly defined. By its very nature it cannot produce creeds and so it tends to be associated with some very general and vague perspectives and identified by being 'not conservative'. This is not to say that there are no liberal beliefs. I do, however, want to say that comprehensive statements of liberalism are so complex and obtuse as to be almost unintelligible to anyone who is not a professional theologian. For a faith that was designed to appeal to modern man, liberalism is surprisingly bad at being intelligible without being vacuous. It is easy for liberals to mock the conservatives' belief that God is an actual living 'person' 'up there' but their replacements for such naivete - Tillich's 'ground of our being', for example - tend to the meaningless. The modernisers desire to escape the primitive language of earlier Christianity; they want to replace the objective 'God out there' with some internal existential state. This naturally puts them in conflict with the traditional language of Christianity and forces them to either coin a new existential language (which cannot be understood by most people) or to speak the old language with the key terms omitted (in which case they seem to be seem to be saying nothing). Thus the move away from conservative Protestantism involves a gradual erosion of profile, of sure identity. While any individual liberal may be sure of his own beliefs, liberals as a body cease to be well-defined and well-distinguished from the secular background.

(b) Fence Building

Not only does the dogmatic nature of conservatism allow the conservative to know what he believes, it also allows him to divide the world up into those who do and those who do not believe. Boundaries can be erected and patrolled; the saved on one side and the damned on the other. Conservatives know who is on the Lord's side. Liberals do not. In a book entitled <u>Who is a Christian</u>?, John Bowden, the editor of the SCM Press, says: 'Nor do I think that there is any point in trying to draw distinctions between Christians and non-Christians for most practical purposes' (1970:12). At the conclusion of the same work, Bowden goes further than this: "Who is a Christian? It should be clear by now that there is not going to be a straight answer. It is difficult to see how there could be' (1970:111). Whether this is 'correct' is not my problem. What should be clear is that such a position endangers the continued existence of such beliefs. Unless one can draw the boundaries around what one regards as valuable, unless one can know who is in possession of the truth and who still needs it, then the truth cannot be preserved or promoted.

One solution to this problem is to cease being a 'Christian' in the sense of having special beliefs that atheists do not have and doing things (like worshipping) that atheists do not do. This then solves the boundary maintenance problem. However, it is difficult to justify such a capitulation. The most common method in recent years has been to re-name parts of the secular world as 'really Christian'. For example, one says that it is more Christian to support the oppressed than it is to own large manses and churches. Thus, as long as there are political movements in support of the oppressed that the liberal can support, he does not feel so bad about the church declining and losing its manses and churches. Again, note that I do not question the theological correctness of this reasoning, I offer it simply as the logic that modern liberals use to justify their inability to dichotomise the world into saved and damned.

(c) Missions

This point follows from the first two. If one cannot divide the faithful from the heathen, then one has serious problems with missions. One cannot evangelise until one can identify (a) the evangel and (b) those who need it. It is no accident that liberals gave up evangelising. The re-direction of effort from saving souls to improving people's welfare is a direct consequence of the form of liberal beliefs. Unless there is absolute certainty in the exclusive saving power of one's beliefs, it is difficult to justify attacking and undermining the belief system of someone else. If they might have some of the truth and you only have some of the truth, then why should you go and try and convert them from their partial knowledge to your partial knowledge?

This problem comes about by degrees. The vital question concerns who is on the same side. One can extend identificaton so far and still have a group which shares enough and still differs enough from everybody else to have something to offer the outsiders. Thus the early SCM was Protestant and trinitarian (which excluded the unitarians). It had those two things in common and so could try and sell those two things to everyone who did not have them (atheists, Catholics, the Orthodox, Unitarians and so on). But as the notion of who could be included in the movement (and in the term 'Christian') expanded, so what united the movement got less and less and what separated it from everyone else was also reduced. The extreme liberal position is one of universalism; we are all going to be saved anyway so it does not matter what you believe. There are many other stages that stop short of this but most do not seriously try to convert people. The notion of an 'ecumenical mission' is a socio-psychological absurdity.

Even when the implications of ecumenism have not yet been worked out in this fashion, one finds a gradual failure of commitment to evangelising. As early as 1926, people within the SCM were becoming conscious of a lack of drive in the movement's missionary concerns:

> While individuals feel the missionary
> challenge in a personal way very strongly

there is among the secretariat and leaders of the Movement no corporate conviction or even opinion on the responsibility of the SCM ... compare this with the strong corporate conviction about Christ and Race, Christ and Inter-nationalism, Christ and Labour, which is the dynamic behind much that is best in the Movement's work. We seem to be sure that all men need to live in a society built upon the teachings of Christ, but not at all sure that all men need Christ as the Way to God[4].

But even where liberalism is not extended to the position of actively arguing against converting members of other faiths, even if proselytisation is still socio-psychologically possible, it is still hampered by its form. There are two areas of evangelism in which the simplicity of conservative Protestant beliefs offer considerable advantages: child evangelism and the use of radio and television.

I have already made it clear that much of conservative success is due to the successful recruitment of the children of existing believers. Even when one looks at people who were recruited from outside the evangelical milieu one finds that most were converted in their youth. Naturally, children lack the intellectual development necessary to comprehend the difference between 'demythologising' and 'correcting'. In fact, when one reviews the reception that greeted the publication of The Myth of God Incarnate in 1975 it is clear that most adults take the proposition 'the idea that Jesus was God made flesh is a myth' to be synonymous with 'Jesus was not God incarnate and anyone who says he was is wrong'. Sophisticated interpretations are required to distinguish between 'myth' and 'falsehood' and children do not normally possess such faculties[5]. The simplest interpretation of Christianity is a realistic and anthropomorphic one in which angels look like people dressed as angels, God looks like Charlton Heston and Jesus looks like a kind (if sickly) hippie. The work of the Child Evangelism Fellowship is testimony to this. The workers teach the children the Bible as though it were literally true, miracles and all. The stories are told in picture comics.

There is naturally a danger that children recruited by this simple and arresting view of the world will abandon it for atheism or modify it and become liberal as they grow older and are confronted with ambiguity and confusion, but the evangelical world offers a career of active involvement which helps to maintain the commitment of the believer. Apart from church related activities, the young conservative, converted at ten, can be a member of the Crusaders, go to seaside missions and summer camps with the CSSM, and take part in his Scripture Union group at school. There are thus lots of ways in which the faith of the young evangelical can be sustained and the problems that might result from his dogmatic beliefs coming up against a complex and ambiguous world are kept at bay until the belief system has been deeply internalised.

Simplicity is also an advantage in working with the impersonal communications of the mass media. In the first place, the speaker has to arrest the listener. The dissembodied message of the radio or the television can easily be ignored; the channel can be changed or the instrument switched off. It is far more difficult to terminate a personal interview or to leave a church service or rally. Much of the concern about the power of the mass media misses the point that it gives the consumer a great deal of freedom to pay attention or not. The mass media also has the problem of possibly competing with other distractions; people talking, tasks such as the ironing being done at the same time, and so on. Furthermore, until recently, the media were hampered by poor reproduction. Thin sound on the radio and small, feeble, black and white pictures on the television serve to reduce the effectiveness of the channel. With these inherent limitations, the radio and television are clearly not going to be very useful in conveying reasoned, qualified and humble beliefs, presented without the conviction that these beliefs are absolutely and essentially necessary for salvation. Although it is difficult to prove, I suspect that television and radio are not very effective in selling soap powder. Where what is at stake is more important they are probably even less convincing but for all that, the conservatives seem to have made much better use of the new media of mass communication than have the liberals. To put it metaphorically, the problems of the impersonality and optionality of the mass media reduces its effectiveness in the way that atmospheric hiss reduces the clarity of a radio programme. The only voice that penetrates the hiss is the loud, shouting, insistent voice of the true believer. The reasonable qualified uncertainties of the person arguing that things <u>are</u> as complex as they look do not carry.

(d) Witch Hunting

Being able to dichotomise the world is essential for building and maintaining an identity. One way in which boundary maintenance assists the internal cohesion of the group is by making witch hunting possible . Durkheim long ago recognised the value that could be derived from a community identifying and punishing a criminal act (Box, 1981:26). Every time a person is punished for infringing a norm, that punishment reminds others of where the line is, it reinforces that norm. In practical terms, the hopeless sinner is a useful character in that his nature reminds the sanctified believer of the advantages that he possesses. The conservative lives in a world that is full of heretics, with all the benefits in terms of maintaining identity that such a world confers. For the liberal, 'heretic' is meaningless.

(e) Membership

Knowing what they believe, conservatives can not only periodically identify heretics and punish them, they can also regularise this mechanism into routine membership tests. People who do not have the right beliefs and attendant behaviour are simply not allowed into membership. The liberal SCM never managed to produce an agreed basis which was actually used by most member Christian Unions as a membership test. Strict membership requirements serve at least two purposes. The first is the obvious one that I have already mentioned; they keep out the unbelievers and so maintain internal cohesion. But there is a second way in which cohesion can be maintained by strict requirements and that is through the intervening factor of personal commitment. Beliefs that are sharply differentiated from those common in the secular world usually require behaviour that is similarly differentiated. In joining the member thus gives up objects, types of behaviour or aims that he or she once possessed. In this sense, joining an exclusive religious organisation usually requires an 'investment', even if that investment is only giving up dancing or something of that order. The more people invest, the less likely they will be to withdraw. Putting it another way, strict membership requirements draw out of the new member greater commitment than do lax requirements, and an organisation that can generate commitment at the time of joining is liable to be able to maintain it better than an organisation that requires little. In support of the general proposition one might note that very few social groups have ever disappeared because the membership qualifications were too rigorous.
But extreme exclusivity does hinder rapid growth and spread. A tight knit cohesive community, radically separated from the rest of the world, should be relatively immune to erosion and assimilation by the world. The faith will be maintained but growth will be limited to what the faithful can produce. The Hutterites have always been fertile and have managed to grow. The Shakers adopted a policy of celibacy and hence died out. In order to grow at a rate faster than the group can reproduce, there must be contact with the world. UCCF has developed a fine balance of the two

imperatives of exclusivity and inclusivity. The organisation has three levels of participation. The local Christian Unions organise meetings which are open to anyone and in the case of those that are designed to be evangelistic, non-believers are deliberately encouraged to attend. The second level is that of ordinary membership. This category is open to all of those who can declare 'I accept Jesus Christ as my Lord and only Saviour' or some such formula. The category of office holder and staff member requires subscription to the full detailed doctrinal basis. In this way, 'searchers' or young Christians who have the right sort of faith can be allowed into association with members of the Christian Union but prevented from holding office and exercising power until their beliefs come into conformity with the basis.

(f) Separation

Until the discussion of membership tests and commitment, I had talked of separation from the world mainly in terms of ideas, of believing things about the world that were not believed by most other people. Such beliefs are, of course, associated with different types of behaviour. The association can work both ways. Deviant behaviour both results from deviant belief and reinforces that belief. Just as the <u>beliefs</u> of the liberal represent a process of <u>accommodation</u> with the world, so the <u>behaviour</u> of the liberal is not differentiated from that of atheists of the same class and culture. Liberals do not huddle together. They do not form professional associations for liberal Protestant doctors or lawyers[6]. Instead they join the appropriate secular organisations. Conservatives constantly form groups to 'witness' to their distinctive beliefs and behaviour. Liberals listen to secular music; conservatives listen to gospel music. Liberals listen to the secular radio; conservatives listen to cassettes of sermons from their favourite preachers. Liberals go to secular film shows; conservatives watch evangelstic films and go to crusades. There is a conservative evangelical world in this country that provides alternatives to many secular institutions and activities (although this process is not as developed as it is in the United States where there are Christian universities and colleges and a far greater number of Christian radio and television shows)[7]. Christians can get discount insurance from Christian brokers if they are teetotal and do not smoke. One travelling salesman is compiling a list of Christian bed and breakfast houses for the use of other Christian travellers. Most important of all is the Christian holiday. Most evangelists have a regular holiday each summer at which they minister to those of their followers who want to combine a holiday with spiritual edification. One evangelist organises tours of the Holy Land. Stephen Olford invites his followers to join him for a week at Butlin's camp at Filey. Dick Saunders organises a week at a Pontin's camp. To quote from a brochure of the Evangelical Movement of Wales: 'a week at camp offers all the attractions of a holiday - games, swimming, enjoyable company, excursions and the rest - plus Christian warmth and hospitality, and teaching in the truths of the Bible'. For an obvious reason sacred holidays are more important in the maintenance of the evangelical world than are other elements of the parallel evangelical world; people come to associate their religious beliefs with being part of a joyful company. Piety and pleasure become associated in the believer's biography.

To a large extent conservative Protestants inhabit a world that is separated from that of either the liberal Protestants or the rest of us. However, a few important analytical points must be made about the relationship of the evangelical world to the mainstream world. I used communitarian groups like the Hutterites as my paradigm case of an introversionist response to the secular world; total separation. I argued that the conservatives are more clearly separated from the secular world than are the liberals. But there is a considerable difference between the isolationism of the Hutterites and the separatism of the evangelicals. The Hutterites are publicly and obviously separated. To use Goffman's term (1974:92-113), they would be unable to 'pass' as non-deviants even if they so desired. The evangelicals are nowhere near as radical. They do not drink, smoke or countenace sexual laxity. They tend to avoid being in debt. They dress in conservative styles. But then, for all sorts of different reasons, lots of other people share these characteristics. Thus the separation of the conservative Protestant can pass unremarked by many outsiders who simply would not notice. The degree of separation varies from group to group. The Exclusive Brethren distinguish themselves by refusing to join any organisation with unbelievers, which prevents them from going to university and joining trade unions or professional associations. They also refuse to eat with non-believers. On the other hand, the Midwest Bible Church required only that its members refrained from joining any secret societies. It is this latter degree of separation that is the norm in the world of the conservative Protestant. There is another way in which the typical conservative and the Hutterite differ and that concerns the focus of the deviant activity rather than its degree or visibility. Marty noted of fundamentalism: 'its rhetoric implies a turning from the world to Christ. In actuality, however, it integrates initiates into a new approved "o.k.

world", one that calls the members to leave behind virtually no elements of the surrounding success culture' (1979:597). Marty has an important point. The conservative Protestant does not reject any vital part of the economic world of production. His deviance is at the cognitive level of interpreting the world or confined mainly to the arena of leisure options. Catherwood's A Better Way: the Case for a Christian Social Order (1975) has nothing in it that is especially Christian and poses no threat to the ruling class in capitalist society. The issues evangelicals feel most strongly about are ones which could be accommodated within the prevailing economic order. The Hutterites are posing a challenge that is fundamental. They deviate on issues (such as the ownership of private property) that are central to the economic order of modern capitalism.

The main point of this discussion is this; while the conservative Protestants are more clearly separated from the secular world than are the liberal Protestants, this separation does not concern fundamental economic issues, and moreover, it is not essentially world-rejecting. By and large, the separation is a temporary one, based around culture rather than economy, which can, in the conservatives eyes, be resolved when they re-establish the dominance of their values.

(g) Theocracy and Democracy

The points I have been making so far derive mainly from the first two characteristics of the form of the two ideologies; dogmatism and stability. The final point derives from the third characteristic; the existence or non-existence of some objective external source of authority. In recognising that revelation cannot be directly apprehended the liberal introduces himself, as the interpreter, into the process of discovering the truth. This immediately raises problems of conflicting interpretation. Once one allows that the gospel needs to be 'demythologised', how does one know which of the many possible translations is the correct one? In the course of my research, many conservatives have made cutting remarks about the lack of consensus among liberals. 'Put three liberals in the same room and you have three different faiths' is representative of the jibes that are offered. There is, for all the malice, an important element of truth in such a judgement. If one thinks of 'becoming more liberal' as a process, it is a process of widening choices and interpretations. The biographies of the pioneers of ecumenism show clearly that it was precisely this opening up of options which was the main appeal of the new perspective. The organisational consequence of lots of people 'opening up their options' has to be diversity and a decline in homogeneity. When this is coupled to the modernist emphasis on 'relevance' as a criterion for translating the timeless truths into appropriate messages, one has the problem of conflict and diversity between generations. What is relevant for one generation may not seem so appropriate to another. This intergenerational conflict can be seen clearly in the disputes within the SCM in the nineteen sixties and seventies. Obviously evangelicals are part of the general wider culture, as well as part of the evangelical milieu and there is the possibility of differing generational interests, but the emphasis on the unchanging nature of revelation, and the constant return to the Bible as the final source, act as a brake on new generations developing new relevances. For evidence of this one need look no further than the present popularity of the Banner of Truth paperbacks, which are reprints of the works of the Puritan divines.

I have spent so much time on this analysis of the consequences of the form of liberal and conservative ideologies for the simple reason that it is an area which is easy to overlook. Even committed and articulate spokesmen for these alternative perspectives tend to overlook the limits that ideology puts upon human behaviour. Conservatives, for example, tend to view the lack of consensus among liberals and their failure to set forth creeds that state their core beliefs as being attributable to moral or intellectual failure. They fail to appreciate that these things follow logically and socio-psychologically from the form of liberalism. Likewise, the liberals' view that conservatives are narrow-minded and bigoted misses the point that such characteristics are not characteristics of the individuals who become conservative evangelicals; they are logical and socio-psychological consequences of the belief system. This point also needs to be made against sociologists such as Kanter (1968) who, by concentrating on mechanisms developed by organisations to produce commitment from their members, imply that these mechanisms are available for any organisation that has the appropriate will. This is not the case. One can only be bigoted about beliefs that can be framed dogmatically. One can only build separatism around beliefs that are sufficiently different to those shared by the rest of the world. The organisation is secondary to the ideology.

THE GENERAL PROBLEMS OF A DIFFUSE BELIEF SYSTEM

Finally, I want to summarise the points I have made so far and draw the themes together around the two problems faced by any voluntary association; those of maintaining consensus within the organisation and generating action. The advantages of consensus can be seen in a comparison of schools work in IVF/UCCF and SCM. Both organisations were interested in building some sort of school 'youth arm' which would prepare potential university students. IVF/UCCF does rather well in this respect. School teachers who lead Scripture Union groups cooperate to promote the university Christian Unions by either passing on to the Christian Unions the names of any of their children going to university, or by giving the prospective student the name of a Christian Union member to contact. Thus the evangelical child is steered by the Scripture Union into the IVF/UCCF Christian Unions. Those evangelical students who become teachers then help run Scripture Union groups. The important thing to note is that this mutually supporting system is not kept in operation by any formal organisational connections. The Scripture Union has no formal ties with IVF/UCCF. They continue to cooperate to maintain evangelical beliefs because they share a common, narrow and well-defined body of doctrine. The various attempts of the SCM to build a similar environment for itself regularly failed because there was not the same degree of consensus or homogeneity among liberal Protestants. Not only is it in the nature of any form of liberalism to produce divergence, but liberal theology contains one special feature – the commitment to the idea of making the faith relevant – that guarantees conflict between generations of liberals. What was 'relevant' to the students of the nineteen sixties was not the same as that which was relevant to the previous generations. Liberals not only share less with other liberals of the same generation; they have less in common with liberals of other generations. One can see this very clearly in the easy way in which the young undergraduates in the evangelical Christian Unions invite their seniors to address them. There is a continuity in conservative Protestantism which is patently missing among liberals.

Consensus is the basis for action. Unless a group of people are agreed on what they stand for and what it is they wish to achieve they cannot act together. Although there may be local reasons for the recent demise of the Irish Humanist Association (Wallis, 1980) humanism in the wider context has declined because of its inability to produce sufficient consensus among humanists about what they stand for (other than opposition to religious beliefs) and what they ought to do (Budd, 1967; Wallis, 1980). In such circumstances, humanist associations are always open to competition from other groups organised around narrower and more specific issues, which are better able to mobilise people. An important part of the appeal of any organisation or movement is its perceived ability to attain results, to get things done, and humanism, like liberal Protestantims, is such a diffuse belief-system that its adherents never share enough in common to be able to generate any action. What makes the problem for liberal Protestantism even more crippling is again the commitment to relevance. One of the themes that run through all the policy discussions of the post-War SCM is 'building bridges'. If the students were not interested in Christianity but were into Marxism then the SCM had to build a bridge to the Marxists by showing what a lot they really had in common. If Freudianism was this year's flavour, then the SCM had a conference on Christ and Freud. When many young people became attracted by the idea of communal living, lo and behold, the SCM discovered that there was really a strong communal streak in Christianity too and built their own commune.

This was done for two reasons. It was ideologically sound. These compromises with the interests of the secular world were exactly 'what Christians ought to be doing'; taking religion out of the cloisters and putting it back where people were. But it was also justified as a means of recruitment, both to the SCM and to Christianity. Conferences on Christ and Freud were intended both to educate Christians about psychoanalysis and to recruit students who were into Freud for the SCM and for Christ. Whether this was ideologically sound is not my concern, but it can now be seen to have been organisational suicide. The bridges that were built to the secular world did not serve to bring new blood into SCM or the Christian Church. Instead, these bridges served as paths of defection for SCM members. Rather than Marxists becoming Christian, the Christians became Marxists. One year the whole Edinburgh branch left the SCM to become a cell of a Trotskyite party. One leading staff member left the SCM during its commune period to join a 'real' commune. In competition with other groups and organisations built around a more specific set of beliefs, an organisation built upon a diffuse and general belief system must lose.

The Camel's Hump

The analysis in this discussion has mainly been at the level of features of belief systems, independent of the actual content of those beliefs. In comparing conservative and liberal Protestantism, I have been interested in the notion of organisational strength coming from a tight and specific belief system, and in the precariousness of a diffuse belief system. At the more concrete level of actual beliefs, conservatives have one major advantage over liberals; they can make sense of being a small minority. The conservative can reason that Christ was ridiculed and persecuted; I am ridiculed and persecuted; therefore I am Christ-like. It may not be good formal logic but it makes a lot of psychological sense and provides a way of re-interpreting failure and unpopularity as signs of grace. The conservative can also, of course, see success and the confusion of his enemies as alternative signs of grace. Either way, the conservatives can find satisfaction and confirmation. Being able to accept and rejoice in minority status has enabled conservatives to retain their morale for long periods in the ecclesiastical wilderness. Some sects actually seem to find their minority status so satisfying that they make little effort to proselytise at all[8]. The main plank of the liberal platform is relevance: translating the faith into terms appropriate to modern Western man in a rational and secular world. To have modern secular man display utter indifference to one's efforts undermines the certainty that one has got it right. Whereas either popularity or unpopularity can be seen as confirmation for the conservative, only popularity can do that for the liberal. The conservative is like the camel; ideologically equipped for extended periods of draught and able to sustain himself on his 'old paths in perilous times' until he comes across the next oasis of revival.

Notes

1. This chapter draws heavily on my doctoral research (Bruce 1980) and I would like to acknowledge the helpful remarks of Professor David Martin of the London School of Economics who examined the thesis.

2. Accounts of the split are given by Tatlow (1933), Pollock (1953), and the CICCU (1913;1933).

3. To put it very simply, the 'sitz im leben' school of Biblical criticism argues that the Gospels cannot be seen just as accounts of what happened; they had <u>uses</u> and took their forms from the context in which they were used (perhaps for teaching a moral). Hence their meaning had to be interpreted in the light of what is known about the life of the early Christians. This is simply one aspect of a general tendency to rationalise the supernatural out of the Bible.

4. This quotation comes from an internal SCM memo written by Laura Jackson, the missionary secretary, in 1926. All the SCM records and office-files are in an archive in the Central Library, Selly Oak Colleges, Birmingham, and I am grateful to the Librarian, Miss Francis Williams, for her permission to work with this material.

5. Against the conservatives, who accuse them of believing nothing, the radical theologians insist that they are still 'Christians' and normally go further to say that they are the 'real' Christians. It is interesting then to note that one of the authors of the <u>Myth of God Incarnate</u>, Michael Goulder, has since resigned his holy orders, stopped going to church and declared himself an agnostic (Guardian, 7th December 1981).

6. For example, one might contrast the Christian Medical Fellowship (CMF) mentioned in Chapter 3 with the nearest liberal Protestant equivalent, the London Medical Group (LMG). The CMF was an offshoot of IVF which attained financial independence but which remains a professional body for evangelical Protestants. The LMG was originally part of the SCM. Its general secretary sat ex officio on the SCM General Committee and it was supported by SCM from 1966 to 1972. It then cut its links with SCM and developed a general 'mission' to provide a forum for discussing medical ethics independent of any particular religious faith.

7. One can now update this observation by noting that some English evangelicals are trying to catch up with the Americans in these respects. A number of schools have been founded using a system of programmed learning called ACE (for 'accelerated Christian education') and a group of evangelicals have formed a television production company called LELLA to promote wholesome family entertainment. LELLA has recently collaborated with the BBC to produce a Christian news magazine programme called Day One.

8. Revelling in elite 'cognoscenti' status is not unique to conservative Protestants. O'Toole (1975) notes a similar phenomenon in a small left-wing political party.

5 Crusades and conversions

The purpose of this chapter is to look at modern evangelical crusades and to consider the problem of explaining conversion at these events. There remains a great deal of public ignorance about crusades and those people who think of them as involving much prostration, hysteria and 'enthusiasm' would be surprised (and probably disappointed) by the 'serious' tone of most tent meetings. Given the popularity of evangelical Protestantism in Ulster and the province's history of revivalism it is not surprising that tent meetings are still common and popular events. In the summer of 1979 (and there is no reason to suppose there was anything unusual about that year) there were two major missions, at least ten smaller tent missions and a visit from the cross-towing American evangelist Arthur Blessit.

BARRY MOORE

The first large crusade of that summer was held in Belfast's Ormeau Park, situated on the edges of the largely Protestant areas of East and South Belfast. The tent held some 4,000 people and the first impression on entering was of the circus; the same smells of tarred rope, canvas and damp trodden grass. At one end there was a large stage with, banked up behind it, the seats for the choir. On either side of the platform there were large speaker units designed to carry the evangelist's voice through the tent hall. To one side there was a smaller tent; the counselling area where those who went forward at the altar call would be taken for prayer, counselling and processing. Ushers were on hand to pass out the booklet of specially chosen hymns and choruses, to welcome the newcomer with a handshake and, as the tent filled up, to show people to their seats. The choir were dressed in black and white.

The meeting begins with the arrival on stage of the team: Barry Moore, his soloist who acts as master of ceremonies, a pianist, a vocal trio and a number of local clergymen from the sponsoring committee. Introductions are made. One speaker makes a point of telling the audience that the costs of the crusade have already been covered and that a collection will not be taken although there are boxes at the doors for those who wish to make donations. There then follows a sequence of prayers, hymns sung by the choir, the trio, the soloist and by everyone. In this part of the meeting there is a distinct restlessness, an expectancy as the audience waits for Moore's address. The prayers and hymns are attended to with seriousness and even some enthusiasm, but the address is the main part of the meeting. Many members of the audience are regular attenders at revivals, and just as regular concert goers will discuss in detail the performances they witness, so those who frequent revivals become connoisseurs of sermons. This is especially true of those from Presbyterian churches where members may be actively involved in choosing their ministers by audition. We wait to see how Barry Moore compares with other preachers we have heard.

The main aim of the crusade sermon is not the careful teaching of correct doctrine. Rather it is the forceful presentation of the need for a personal commitment to Christ, and the urgency of the matter of salvation. This aim, allied with the sheer size of the audience being addressed (and hence their physical distance from the speaker), makes drama more important than exposition. Since the pattern for the revival meeting was established by Charles Finney and developed by Dwight Moody and others, there has been little change except that developments in electronics, especially the use of very sensitive 'tie-pin' microphones, have given the evangelist the opportunity to use a much greater variation in volume and tone of speech while still remaining audible and mobile. The evangelist's message - that Christ died for our sins, and that the acceptance of that truth is the only way to salvation - is a simple one and one that is ideally suited to presentation in a short address. The skill of the evangelist lies in his making this message live for the listener. In a two week run the evangelist will use each evening's address to approach the same theme from a different angle, lacing his sermon with humorous anecdotes and

96

references to scripture, strung around a coherent underlying structure that builds towards the climax of the altar call.

Moore talks rapidly, striding backwards and forwards across the wide stage. After each anecdote, his voice rises in volume and pitch on the first part of the moral and then he turns to the audience, pauses, and dropping his voice, delivers the punch. Hectoring alternates with beseeching, kneeling posture with strident pacing and arm-waving. His assistant in this presentation is an imaginary stooge, someone who 'knows' the truth, but who vacillates about accepting it, who offers rather pathetic excuses, who says 'Barry, you are right but I don't want to do it right now, give me some more time'. Using this stooge as a surrogate for the audience, Moore presents these trivial objections in a weak voice, standing side on, and then whips round to confront the listeners and booms: 'Well, there may not be any more time!'.

The key to success for the preacher is his ability to use anecdotes from everyday life which the varied audiences to which he preaches can identify with and understand. This is the reason that stories about families and children are so common. To illustrate the immediacy of the need for conversion Moore tells the story of a father who was too busy to give his little child one kiss for every year of his age. He tells the child to come back later when he has more time. The child goes off to play and drowns. The father naturally regrets that he turned the child away. Evangelists are fond of anecdotes about family life. Billy Graham tells the following story

> Someone had loaned us a boat - a little motor boat and my son said 'Daddy, can I drive the boat?' So I turned the controls over to him and, well, within about one minute he was headed right towards the rocks and I said 'No, Ned, give the controls back to Dad' and he said 'No, No, No, No, and I said 'Yes, Sir!' (pause while audience laughs). But you see, when we want to run our own lives we run them into the rocks. We make a mess of it and then we want to take that mess to the Lord.

The selection of family anecdotes allows the evangelist to avoid the sorts of faux pas that result from trying to be relevant to a strange audience without being well prepared. The night before he impressed the audience with his boat story, Graham made the mistake of trying to illustrate the problems of modern life in high rise urban housing by saying; 'And you have a television programme called FAWLTY TOWERS', which being a reference to a popular comedy series about a badly run seaside hotel, only impressed the listeners with Graham's lack of preparation[1].

The climax of the presentation is the altar call. Finney invented 'the anxious seat'; a bench at the front for those who came under conviction of sin during the address. Modern evangelists ask those in the audience who have 'got saved' to signal this declaration, or intention, by walking to the front of the tent where they are met by trained counsellors, before being taken aside for further assistance. As Barry Moore asks people to come forward the choir softly sing 'Just as I am' and then 'He is Lord'. When the hymns are finished, Moore asks for an encore to give more time for those who are still considering to make up their minds. Eventually, with some 20 people now standing at the front, the meeting is closed with a short prayer and we file out, leaving those who have gone forward to be counselled and to have their names and addresses taken so that they can be 'followed up'.

DICK SAUNDERS

While the Canadian, Moore, was working in Belfast, Dick Saunders, a well-known English evangelist, was holding a tent crusade on an industrial estate just outside the town of Bangor, County Down. The different locations produced a slight difference in the composition of audience. Moore's, like most church congregations, was older than the general population and had a very high proportion of women. Saunders' audience, drawn from the surrounding countryside, as well as the seaside town, was older still. The format of the meeting was similar. There was a large, locally recruited choir, a soloist singing moving ballads, and a sequence of prayers and hymns before the main address. There were, however, some interesting differences in style and emphasis. Barry Moore's show was expensive and sophisticated. The soloist performed the introductions, and Moore himself was distanced from the event, as if he was the 'guest star' of someone else's show. Saunders worked on a smaller stage with a less efficient PA system which restricted his delivery. He also performed his own introductions and announcements, advertising "special offers" on records and cassettes of the soloist Midred Rainey. Where Moore was almost aloof, Saunders was the jocular 'warm up man', reminiscent of a Butlin's Redcoat.

Although the message of salvation was the same, the two evangelists choose to emphasise rather different consequences of 'getting right with the Lord'. A regular theme in conservative evangelical thinking is that most (and for some, all) of our problems can be solved through salvation. There are, of course, good grounds for this where the problems are ones of individual behaviour, such as the poverty and marital difficulties that can result from serious drinking problems. Asceticism is still a very effective way of raising one's standard of living. Barry Moore intorduced one of his patrons, Robert McLintock, to give his testimony. McLintock had been born in Ulster and raised as a Presbyterian before emigrating to Canada. He began his career as a labourer with serious drinking difficulties. Through the intervention of his young daughter, he sought spiritual advice, and was saved. Since then he has risen to be the head of one of Canada's largest construction companies. The moral is simple; the transition from sinner to saved is matched by the move from drunken labourer to successful entrepreneur. Some other evangelists, such as the American Oral Roberts and Ulster's Leslie Hale, have developed this into a totally mechanical model; you put so much money in and God gives X times as much back[2].

Using the statement of Jesus about casting your bread upon the waters and having it return ten-fold, Roberts and Hale preach salvation as miraculous investment: 'If you want God to supply your financial needs, then give SEED-MONEY for HIM to reproduce and multiply' (Roberts, 1970:21). The translation of miracles into business success offends many evangelicals and fundamentalists, who regard it as a trivialisation of the gospels. Nonetheless, worldly success is still a strong theme with evangelists and there is evidence for the attraction of such a message. A large proportion of the converts of one of Graham's New York crusades joined the church of Norman Vincent Peale, the author of the best-selling Power of Positive Thinking and one of the major modern proponents of Christianity as a means to material success and this-worldly competence.

While the message of worldly success would not have been rejected by Saunders, he chose to emphasise the benefits of salvation for relationships between people; especially in restoring families. McLintock's testimony would have been appreciated by Saunders' audience as a sign of the Lord's power, but, given that most of them were female, and near or over the age of retirement, the prospect of entrepreneurial success would not have been a personally alluring one.

BOBBY BRYSON AND HARRY ANDREWS

The Moore and Saunders crusades represent the top end of the United Kingdom market. Both were large, well-organised, popular and supported by all the local evangelical clergy (with the exception of the Revd. Ian Paisley who was not invited to take part in sponsoring Moore's crusade even though it was held only two minutes walk from his church). I now want briefly to look at two small events.

One small crusade was organised by the Churches of Christ. Clearly they did not expect a small crusade as they had booked the massive Ulster Hall and advertised in the Belfast Telegraph but their average attendance was barely about 100 and most of those people were members of Church of Christ congregations. At these meetings there were more young people than had been at the larger crusades and the ministers of the congregations made a point of mixing with the audience and introducing themselves to newcomers. The evening was also much less formal; as we waited for an electrician to repair the PA, a family led us in unaccompanied singing. Bobby Bryson, a Church of Christ minister from Huntsville, Alabama, preached in a fashion very similar to that of Barry Moore. Given the much smaller audience it is not surprising that his altar call drew on one evening only one person, and on another evening no one at all. The one person who came forward was a young girl, a member of one of the congregations, who had been saved some time ago but who felt that since making her decision she had been slipping. Bryson talked to her for a few moments and then introduced her to the audience (many of whom seemed to know her already) and asked us to pray for her.

In the summer of 1980, a group of independent Gospel Halls arranged a tent mission on the Stranmillis embankment in Belfast and invited Harry Andrews, a part-time evangelist, to conduct the meetings. The small tent, holding about 100 people, was filled most evenings with members of the Gospel Halls. Andrews clearly recognised many of the people there and peppered his address with a number of jokes and asides about the piety of 'the Ormeau Road lot'. Although the message was one of salvation, no altar call was given at the end. This is characteristic of some independent churches, and of the Brethren who believe that one presents the message and leaves it up to the Holy Spirit to do the rest. They see calling people forward as pre-empting the work of the Spirit.

THE NATURE OF CRUSADES

I have spent some time on detailed descriptions of different types of crusades in order to give a feeling of these events and to clear up some misconceptions. From my own research and from the work of others, the following points can be made.

(a) The crusade itself as become a highly routinised affair. Charles Finney laid the foundations of what were then called 'the new measures' in the 1820's when he captured the spirit of enthusiasm of the great frontier revivals and toned it down for the sophisticated urban audiences of the east coast. Later revivalists such as Dwight Moody in the 1870's, and Billy Sunday and Billy Graham in this century refined the procedures, especially in regard to recording details of the convert's residence, church affiliation and so on to facilitate 'follow-up', but already by the 1850's the revival had become a formalised, and in many cases annual, event. One no longer waited on the Spirit, but instead arranged regular events at which it was hoped the Spirit would move.

(b) There is little or no 'enthusiasm' at the crusades. The frontier revivals in America in the 1780's did exhibit a great deal of emotionalism. During meetings that lasted day and night for a week or more, people fainted, went into trances and cases of catalepsy were reported. As Weisberger (1958) argues in his history of American revivalism, these were hard people who lived a rugged life in constant combat with natural and human forces. There was no place in their normal lives for displays of emotion, and when they got religion, they got it like they did everything else; hard! By the time revivals had become accepted and common in the urban centres of the east, prostration and catalepsy were no longer a part of normal audience reaction. By the turn of the nineteenth century, the audience was almost totally passive while the evangelist, on stage, produced what enthusiasm there was[3]. If the changes in American revivalism are well documented, the case is not clear for Ulster. There were reports of prostration and extravagant behaviour in the revival of 1859, but there are reasons to be cautious of these. Both believers and critics have good reason to exaggerate the ecstasy of these events: believers to show the power of the Spirit and critics to point to the dangers and excesses of unregulated religion. What is well known is that enthusiasm is related to social status. The wealthy and prestigious prefer their religion regulated with themselves as observers or as participants in a well-ordered ritual while the poor prefer fire and vigour, taking active part in much more losely organised events. It may well be then that the increasing 'sophistication' of crusades represents, not only the introduction of business methods (one author called his book on Billy Graham <u>Evangelism Inc</u>. (Target, 1968)), but also the failure of the churches to retain any stronghold on the poorer sections of the community.

(c) Cooperation between different denominations provides a reason for regulating the event. In an interesting study of the Faith Mission, an interdenominational organisation that sends pairs of itinerant evangelists around the country areas

of Scotland and Ulster, Warburton (1969) argues that the
Mission's desire to court the active support of the clergy of
the main denominations was the main reason for the
formalisation of the organisation and the tightening of the
leadership's control over its evangelists. In order to be
genuinely 'interdenominational' one has to be very careful of
treading on denominational corns. Many controversial points
of doctrine and practice have to be avoided if one is not to
give offence. The less opportunity there is for lay
participation, the less chance there is of members (and
especially clergy) of some denomination taking affront at
something untoward. Large crusades which are sponsored by a
committee of ministers of various denominations tend to be
more highly formalised. Small events with audiences from one
denomination or with an 'undenominational' approach have less
need for control.

(d) Crusades are not for the conversion of the heathen.
'Revival' is a suitable term. The majority at such events
are regular churchgoers. I do not want to enter into an
argument as to whether these people are 'real' Christians or
not. Suffice it to say that most people who go to crusades
are already well versed in the teachings and life of the
Churches. The people who go forward are almost all the sons
and daughters of believers. What they signify with such a
move is not that they have just found a new and previously
alien belief-system convincing but rather that they have come
to make a positive commitment to a set of beliefs with which
they are already familiar. This is an important point for
understanding conversion and I want to offer some evidence
for this proposition.

The conservative nature of the dress of crusade audience
(the wearing of hats by women, for example) suggests that
these people are already churchgoers. Most members of the
audience bring their own Bibles with them and show great
skill in rapidly turning to the portions of scripture being
read. Likewise, the competence in singing revival choruses
suggests that the typical audience is already acquainted with
the Christian culture in a way that the general public is
not. This 'already-churched' nature of the audience is
constantly recognised by the evangelists themselves, who
direct their sermons, not at the heathen, but rather at the
regular church attender who has not 'really' been saved. To
make this point with a recent observation; one service in the
Luis Palau Glasgow 1981 Crusade began with the master of
ceremonies welcoming all the various church bus parties and
asking them to wave their programmes in the air as their
church was named. To the observer this quickly revealed that
almost every member of the audience (between four and six
thousand) had been bussed in with a church party. In one of

his addresses Palau said 'All of you here love this land and most of you know the Lord Jesus already ... what must happen if we are to expect a revival in Scotland?' (my emphasis).

If one prefers statistics, the technique of recording the details of the convert and passing them on to ministers to 'follow-up' allows us the opportunity of finding out more of the religious history of those who go forward. Crusade, a pro-Graham evangelical journal, evaluated the results of the 1961 Manchester campaign five years later and found that of 325 enquirers referred to the churches, only 137 were still regular attenders and 121 of these had previously been regular churchgoers. It is possible that those who were 'saved' and then dropped out were all previously unchurched. But even in that extreme case, it is still true that more than one third of those who went forward were regular churchgoers. It is actually likely that at least some of the 188 who had dropped out also had some previous church connections. The London Evening News followed up some of the converts of Graham's 1954 Harringay Crusade and found that of a sample 336, 226 said they had been regular attenders at a church before their conversion (Target, 1968:264-5). Graham's 1956 Glasgow crusade was one of the most efficiently integrated mass evangelism operations in this country. Land lines were used to relay the Kelvin Hall meetings to a number of other centres and months of work, both before and after the crusade, were given by Church of Scotland ministers to try to combine the public attraction of an American evangelist with the preparation and follow-up of a national chruch-based campaign. Allen (1956:108) shows that at least 62% of those going forward were regular church attenders. It is true that there were more church-goers in Britain in 1956 than there are now but it is also true that mass evangelism was then novel and popular and more likely to draw in the unchurched then than now. In a sense, though, it is the nineteen fifties that I am concerned with because it is from that period that Sargant's explanation of conversion, to which I will turn shortly, comes.

A recent survey of a large Billy Graham crusade in the Seattle/Tacoma area in May 1976 (called by Decision magazine the 'most exciting and successful US Billy Graham crusade in years') found that only 16% of those who responded to a questionnaire three years after they 'came forward' had not been regular church attenders at the time of their decision (Firebaugh, 1981). Other studies could be cited (for example; Whitman, 1968, and Altheide and Johnson, 1977) to the same effect. If mass evangelism is not actually preaching to the converted, it is certainly talking almost exclusively to those who are well acquainted with its central themes.

(e) Crusades do a great deal for the morale of some of the Christians involved in organising them. The staging of a large mission requires the active participation of hundreds of people. There are roles for fund-raisers, singers, music arrangers, publicists, stewards, counsellors and sponsoring clergy. It can be argued that although the returns from mass evangelism are small in the first place, there is a secondary effect in that actually helping in something that is clearly the Lord's work raises the morale of local Christians, making them more confident and reminding them of their obligation to spread the Word. Local Christians then witness to their children and to people they meet. Mass evangelism may thus be more effective indirectly than directly. Set against this, naturally, is the despondency that can set in after a crusade if it is thought to have been a failure.

(f) Crusades provide some badly needed Christian entertainment. There is the pleasure of being part of a choir of three or four thousand singing a ringing chorus of 'He is Lord'; the novelty of a new preacher with a new sermon; and the warm emotion of a good soloist putting feeling into a pious ballad. There is very little for the upholder of conservative moral values in the products of the mass leisure industry. The traditionalists can band together to prohibit the showing of some particularly offensive film but they cannot force major film companies to make films they would like to see. Increased affluence and technological development have increased the opportunities for pious home entertainment of a professional standard; many evangelists produce cassette recordings of their services and a number of small record companies produce and market a lot of sacred music. But just as television did not kill the attraction of 'going out' for the secular world, cassettes and records have not diminished the entertainment value of the live crusade.

EXPLAINING CONVERSION

Accounting for conversion is a difficult business. There is a voluminous literature in sociology and psychology concerned with the circumstances and conditions under which people change their beliefs in a dramatic fashion. Here I want to examine the notion that the evangelist manipulates the environment and certain symbols (such as 'hell') in order to persuade, or coerce, or 'trick' the listener into making decisions that under other conditions he would not make. This 'brainwashing' theme is part of a general approach to conversion which sees it as something that is done to the convert; it is the product of forces acting upon the individual rather than an action which the individual engages

104

in himself. The public form of this line of thought derives from the work of psychologists such as William Sargant, and I want to look in some detail at his book Battle for the Mind.

Sargant offers a brief summary of Pavlov's work on conditioned reflexes in dogs, paying special attention to the flooding incident when the fear of drowning disrupted the dogs' conditioning. From this he argues that fear in some way destroys the normal working of the brain and central nervous system. To make the case that observation from dogs is generalisable to humans, Sargant reviews the 'shell-shock' literature of psychologists working with sufferers of battle fatigue. He eventually concludes that 'various types of belief can be implanted in many people, after brain function has been sufficiently disturbed by accidentally or deliberately induced fear, anger or excitement' (1957:132). In his chapter on religious conversion, Sargant refers to the diaries of John Wesley and Jonathan Edwards' A new narrative of the revival of religion in New England with thoughts on that revival to argue that conversion results from the effect of fear on the brain. Wesley's talk of hell, for example: 'affected the nervous system of his hearers very much as the fear of death by drowning did Pavlov's dogs in the Leningrad flood' (1957:78).

Battle for the Mind is subtitled 'the physiology of conversion' and the term 'physiology' is the key to Sargant's perspecive. In essence he is saying that circumstances act on the nervous system of people to make them more gullible. Conversion is no longer about people abandoning one belief system in favour of another because they believe (a cognitive matter) that their new worldview is a superior guide through troubled times, or seems more sensible than what they believed before, or even that it feels better. Sargant is no longer interested in the reasons that people may have for changing beliefs, because he regards the cognitive element as irrelevent in an account of conversion; that is, he believes that conversion is not reasoned behaviour.

This line of thought has not lost credence since Sargant wrote and if anything, seems to be reviving with public interest in new religious movements. A textbook popular enough to go into a third edition (Thouless, 1971) makes no explicit mention of Pavlov, but follows a similar argument. Thouless begins by asserting that 'it is not principally through reasoned demonstration that the beliefs of an individual' (1971:20) are changed. It is through suggestion. Suggestion is interestingly defined as: 'a process of communication resulting in the acceptance and realisation of a communicated idea in the absence of adequate rational grounds for its acceptance' (1971:21). Suggestibility on the part of the audience is increased when they are in a hyponoidal state; something like being half awake. This condition is thought to result from such things as the preacher droning in a monotonous voice, soft singing, rhythmic dancing and chanting. In considering the traditional appeal for souls at the end of a revival meeting, Thouless says: 'the closed eyes, the monotonous singing, and the repetition of the word "come" tend to produce in the audience an approach to the hyponoidal state' (1971:26).

My criticism of the Sargant/Thouless approach is based on two separate issues. There is the question of how well it fits with the crusades I have witnessed, and then there is the issue of the general adequacy of this type of explanation. The first point is easily dealt with. As suggested in my introductory account of the typical modern crusade, there is little or no enthusiasm. Nor is there any evidence of tension. There is little about the modern crusade audience that fits with the literature on crowd psychology. What one has is a large number of people engaged in highly routinised and predictable behaviour which, like most such behaviour, is perfomed with some degree of 'role distance'; that is, there is often an evident self-conscious awareness of playing a role. Far from there being a uniform commitment on the part of all the members of the audience to become totally involved (which is what is implied in talk about enthusiasm or tension), there are various degrees of involvement. Girlfriends chat about attractive boys and vice-versa. People criticise the singing. There is often much impatience with the poor sound equipment that produces muffled and distorted versions of the sermon. One vignette perhaps captures this mood. At the call to come forward the evangelist usually tries to introduce some solemnity by having the audience bow their heads in prayer. This also means that no one should be watching as those who decide for Christ go forward. However, as one might expect, many people do look up to see how many people are going forward (is it a success?), and who is going forward (is it anyone I know?). Observations are then made about what is seen. Far from being held in the thrall of tension and emotional pressure, most members of the audience unwittingly contribute to undermining the theatre of the climax by their desire to 'see what is going on'. The same restless curiosity also undermines the possibility of any 'hyponoidal state'.

It may well be the case that crusades have changed since Sargant wrote The Battle for the Mind. I have occasionally seen elements of the sort of enthusiasm that is produced by people immersing themselves in their performances at very small Pentecostal missions, but it is utterly absent in the reality of the typical conservative Protestant crusade. This may be a product of changes in religious and social behaviour over the last 25 years but I cannot think how such a case could be argued. Suffice it to say at this stage that

Sargant's accounts of behaviour and responses at crusades has little in common with my observations of similar events in the period between 1978 and 1981.

Although this book is not centrally concerned with Pentecostalism, the question of enthusiasm might as well be pursued. At the Dales Bible Week some 7,000 people, most of them committed Pentecostalists associated with the Harvestime Fellowship churches, gather and the main evening worship does have elements which superficially conform to the stereotype of an atmosphere heavy with hysteria and edgy with emotion. The same simple gospel chorus is sung over and over again, sometimes for ten minutes and more. People raise their arms to heaven and dance in the aisles. Even the platform guests and speakers hop and skip to the music, twirling each other round while praising the Lord. But what emotion there is, is not the result of preaching on the subject of hell; far from it, it is produced by the combined satisfaction of 7,000 people who all believe that they have some treasured prize that the rest of us lack. That is, the emotion is the result of a certain set of beliefs, and not the cause of them (although obviously such services, if constantly enjoyed by the participant, will act to confirm the beliefs that inform them). To further confound the Sargant argument, one might point out that all this hopping and skipping occurs at the start of the service and is not preceded by any preaching. The sermon comes after the singing, and the atmosphere during this is invariably quiet, with the audience relaxed but attentive.

How satisfactory Sargant's work is as an account of crusade conversion in his own and earlier times is another matter. His use of the revivals of Wesley and Edwards as examples of how high emotional tension could be created, is suspect. He gives little thought to the reliability of the reports of the work of these men, and rather too readily attributes motives to them when there is considerable disagreement about their motivation. Wesley is accused of having deliberately created tension in his audience by preaching on hell and damnation. This is a gross exaggeration; Welsey did not preach a great deal on hell. Edwards was short-sighted and he read his sermons in something approaching a monotone, pausing whenever a member of his audience interjected. It is by no means sure that Sargant has chosen well in his examples. As I have already said, there is good reason to be cautious of taking at face value accounts of enthusiasm and prostration in early revivals.

Furthermore, not all great revivals of religion have been accompanied by reports (let along the reality) of prostration. Moody's main campaigns were always described as well-ordered. It could be argued here that 'high emotional tension' might not always be visible, or the focus could be shifted from extravagant behaviour to presumably passive 'hyponoidal' states. Target, for example, argues that the sombre serious tone of modern crusades actually creates <u>more</u> tension than the old-fashioned mayhem of the Frontier meetings (1968:200-5). But this re-writing of the argument only preserves it at the cost of stripping it of any value. If everything can be interpreted as signs of 'high emotional tension', the explanation ceases to explain.

Returning to the general question of evidence, Sargant does nothing to demonstrate the truth of his assertion that preaching on hell affected the central nervous system of the listeners. Even if we suppose that the accounts of Wesley's Newgate prisoners falling to the ground and moaning are reliable, changes in the central nervous system are not the only causes that could be found for such behaviour. There is a readily available cognitive explanation which would argue that people who become convinced of their sinfulness may well want (note the implied rationality here) to demonstrate to their Lord their regret at having sinned by prostrating themselves. This seems as plausible an explanation of prostration as that offered by Sargant, and has the advantage that it does not commit us to assuming that other people's behaviour is not rational. Sargant gives us no evidence for his physiological account; he presents no proof of changes in the central nervous system of crusade audiences.

It is no great sin to build theory ahead of evidence, but the Sargant account actually ignores two rich sources of material. He does not talk to converts. We cannot ask Pavlov's dogs why they acted as they did, but we can ask converts. As far as I know, there are no accounts by believers which attribute their going forward to physiological causes. Given the nature of the explanation, this is not surprising. Most converts talk about the combination of two things; their own will and reason, and the presence of the Lord. Clearly any explanation in the realm of social science will not use the presence of the Lord as an independent variable but that is not a good reason to ignore the first part of the account and move straight to some unconscious cause.

Where one might find limited support for the Sargant view is in the accounts of 'lapsed' converts. Those who regret what they did often do offer an account that mentions environmental pressure and manipulation but we need to be very cautious here. Most lapsed converts are in the business of justifying a temporary departure from conventional behaviour and belief[4]. We are rightly suspicious of self-justificatory stories in other circumstances (such as the 'it was the drink that made me do it' defence for deviant acts). The general methodological principle is that we should always be aware that actors' accounts are often designed for some moral or political purpose in addition to their nature as reports of what was done (see Wallis and Bruce, 1981). The point remains that Sargant bypasses such accounts, not because of methodological problems of interpretation but because of an a priori theoretical assumption that the explanation of conversion must involve causes that are unknown to the actor. If actors' accounts are the first source of information disregarded by Sargant, the second type of datum to receive the same treatment is the analyst's own observations. There is no indication that Sargant actually went to crusades and immersed himself in that milieu. His own observations and experiences would have given him an insight into the processes he infers from a superficial acquaintance with journalistic accounts and possibly unreliable historical accounts.

A second point emerges with consideration of the factors mentioned by Sargant as relevant to an account of conversion: fatigue, uncertainty, tension, seriousness, and the use of brutal language all figure. Of these, only the first is unambigiously physiological. All the others involve a large and essential cognitive factor. The same things do not produce tension in all people. Whether something produces tension depends on what that thing signifies to the audience or to the individual. Whether any symbol or story is tension-producing depends on a complex pattern of prior experiences and significances with that symbol. A moment's thought on what counts as, for example, attractiveness in different social groups should make it obvious that 'ability to produce tension' is not a property of any object or symbol but is a property of the reaction of the group to that object or symbol, and such reactions can vary enormously.

I can sit through any amount of preaching on hell and damnation without feeling any fear or tension because I do not have a predisposing set of values and beliefs which make 'hell' a potent symbol. Sargant is making an enormous error of analogy in transferring the Leningrad flood to crusades. Pavlov's dogs had their susceptibility raised by the tension induced by the reality, the direct stimulus, of impending death. Edwards' audiences had no such material stimulus. The stimulus that Sargant wants to substitute for 'death by drowning' is a symbol which only acts as a stimulus to people who already hold the beliefs necessary for that sound, 'hell', to have the symbolic quality of pain and dread. It should be clear that Sargant's sequence: 'hell' produces tension which produces conversion, can only work if we introduce various pre-existing beliefs. Thus it would read 'hell', acting upon an existing disposition to believe in hell, produces tension which produces conversion. But once it has been expanded to that stage there is no longer any pressing need to have 'tension' in the sequence at all. If one believes in hell, one probably also to some degree, believes the other parts of the conservative Protestant package. If there really is a hell, then conversion is perfectly rational. A public gesture, a slight change in behaviour, these things are not a high price to avoid what, if it exists, is a dreadful place. Thus, if we recognise that 'hell' is a tension-producing symbol only for those who already hold certain beliefs, the irrationalist view that it is the tension that causes the conversion can be replaced by the explanation that proceeds at the cognitive level.

The core of this problem is Sargant's transference of a mechanical stimulus response explanation of behaviour from lower animals to man; what Koestler called the 'ratomorphic' view of man (1981). How adequate such an explanation is for animals is itself a problem. On the general question of the validity of generalising to humans, it cannot go unremarked that Pavlov himself did not believe that such a generalisation could be made. Pavlov, in his later work, recognised that the faculty of language, by giving humans symbolic communication, freed us from the necessity of responding mechanically to stimuli. Pavlov, and his students Luria and Vygotsky, recognised the limitations of the stimulus response model, and developed a social psychology in which the symbolic nature of human thought and communiation was emphasised (see Lindesmith et al, 1977:40). It is ironic that the pioneer of conditioned response psychology should realise its limitations while his western interpreters should fail to do so.

The next general criticism of the mechanical approach to conversion also touches on a fundamental issue; in this case, the rationality of the beliefs to which people convert in crusades and the rationality of the grounds for such a conversion. What seems clear is that Sargant and Thouless, and others who follow this type of argument are either atheists (hence 'belief in hell' is not rational and requires a different sort of explanation to 'belief in Wales'), or they are believers who think that conviction should come gradually and not dramatically. Thouless refers to a story told of Brownlow North, a prominent Victorian evangelist who came to fame in the 1850's. North was asked by a young man how God could have permitted sin and North replied that God could do what He liked, and that if the young man continued to cavil at God's power and wisdom than what God would like to do would be to cast the man into hellfire! Thouless sees the fact that this story had the desired effect of leading the man to the Lord as evidence of the 'suggestibility' of the young man. It is 'suggestion' because the assertion that God is all-powerful and should not be challenged does not, for Thouless, provide 'adequate rational grounds' for belief change.

This is difficult to support. The argument here hinges on what is meant by 'adequate rational grounds'. If we mean that anything which is not demonstrated in logical steps, supported at the appropriate places by experimental evidence, is 'suggestion', then there is little that we believe which is not the result of 'suggestion'. Most of us rely for most of what we know on the statements of those we regard as authoritative. I have no knowledge of atomic physics or advanced mechanics yet I live in a world which I believe (clearly as a result of 'suggestion') to run along the lines of the models offered by advanced science. It may well be that this is a road Thouless would be happy to go down. He may well hold that most of what we believe and do _is_ a result of 'suggestion' and thus he may want to explain most human behaviour in a mechanical way. My own view of human behaviour is quite different and it is based on the proposition that human activity is 'meaningful'. People do things in order to try to attain certain ends. While they may not be doing a very good job of constructing their action, construct it they must. This is not to say that all human action is rational in the strict sense that Thouless endeavours to reserve for that term. As I have suggested, little would be rational in Thouless's sense. I do believe, however, that most human action is understandable in the sense of being 'reasoned', even if it may not appear to be 'reasonable' to us. The Sargant/Thouless model is based on a dichotomy of normal and abnormal belief[5]. It seems to me improper procedure to employ different types of explanation (I learnt what I know; you were brainwashed) for why people hold certain beliefs, without first providing good evidence for the initial dichotomy. Are there any grounds for saying that people who commit themselves to Christ at crusades are changing beliefs in a manner different in form to that followed by others in more 'normal' circumstances? To return to the story of Brownlow North and the young man, the young man is convinced by North's assertion of the power of the Lord. This is conviction by authority and seems no different to the myriad instances in our 'normal' lives in which calling forth of suitable authority is sufficient to establish propositions and resolve conflicts. 'Because he says so' may not satisfy the philosopher as rationally adequate grounds, but it is precisely the principle that most of us use most of the time.

The critics of revivals and the proponents of mechanical models of conversion usually share a common error; they assume that the whole of the change that has to be explained has happened in _one_ meeting. It is the rapidity of the change which separates it in their minds from a process such as 'learning'. They have fallen for the myth of the Pauline conversion. An essential element of the style (if not the theology) of Victorian evangelicalism is the identifiable moment of conversion. Willie Nicholson, the Ulster evangelist who was popular from around 1920 to 1940, often began his addresses by introducing himself with his 'date of birth': the day when he was saved. This sort of rhetoric should not blind us to what is obvious from a reading of the biographies of evangelists. John Wesley was not a heathen before his conversion; he was a pious clergyman perfectly well acquainted with the faith. Torrey Johnson, a successful American evangelist who started the Youth for Christ crusades that brought Billy Graham to prominence, had the following biography:

> he has been raised in a Christian home, two doors from one of the country's greatest churches, under the ministry of one of the great pastors of the day, possessing a perfect Sunday School attendance record of 10 years, going to church every Sunday without fail, sitting in on revival meeting after revival meeting - but yet not a Christian! (Larson, 1945:16).

Although Johnson is something of a virtuoso, his story is a model for the biographies of must crusade converts.

To summarise this section, I have argued that the mechanical model of conversion that Sargant presents is unacceptable because it assumes that what goes on in crusades is radically different from what is called 'learning'. Without offering any evidence for so doing, he ignores the accounts of converts themselves, and substitutes an implausible physiological explanation, for which again there is no evidence. My own view is that crusades offer an important 'rite de passage' for young evangelicals which has a social role identical to that of confirmation and first communion in other religious traditions (for an account of a Graham crusade in such terms see Clelland et al, 1974). Crusades do not cause conversions; they provide opportunities for people to claim a conversion experience, to commit themselves to a set of beliefs and practises that they think and feel might be better than the lot they have at the moment. For many the experience involves little or no movement in terms of worldview. They are simply making a public commitment to a view of the world and our place in it which they have grown up with or acquired gradually through their social interactions with other Christians.

112

Mechanistic explanations of belief change are not confined to the realm of psychology. One finds similar models in sociology, the main difference being that the forces that are thought to produce the change are now located outside, rather than inside, the convert. It is no longer faults within the central nervous system that cause people to be unusually gullible, rather it is social facts, faults within the social structure, that produce this willingness to believe things they would not normally believe. Aberle's account of the rise of the Peyote cult among the Navaho Indian is a case in point (1966). His explanation of Peyotism views the cult as a compensation for the loss of status and autonomy that affected the Navaho with the destruction of their economy and traditional culture. In many sociological accounts, as in most psychological stories, conversion is something that happens to people either as a direct result of some prior event or through some event reducing people's normal standards of reasoning. In either case, the convert is an essentially passive creature. In recent years there has been a growth in a literature of conversion that does not begin from such a view but which instead views the convert as an actor, as someone who is doing something. The most vigorous statement of this position is by Roger Straus (1976:1979) who has popularised the notion of the convert as 'seeker'. This type of person, common in the America of the post-nineteen sixties, is active in searching after various forms of enlightenment. Straus makes the often forgotten point that many converts are quite consciously in the business of sampling different worldviews and types of behaviour in the hope of finding some 'trip' that suits them. A similarly active image of the convert is offered by Shupe and Bromley (1979) when they suggest that one might be mistaken in assuming that people change beliefs and then behave differently. They argue that some conversions proceed by people trying out the new types of behaviour, acting 'as if' they did hold all the new beliefs; and then as they find the behaviour acceptable and continue to play the role, so they gradually come to accept the beliefs that support and make sense of the new role. In both of these views, conversion is an accomplishment. It is something that the convert does in association with other people.

This very different view of changes in beliefs and behaviour can be given analytical substance by putting it into the context of a general sociology derived from Berger and Luckmann's The Social Construction of Reality (1973). The starting point of their position is the realisation that humans do not simply react to objective stimuli from the world around us. We deal with the symbolic representations of that world; we act not with 'things' but with what those things _mean_ to us. The meanings in question are social creations. Our dealings with the world are compiled into what phenomenologists call our 'stock of knowledge'; our everyday solutions to the problems and experiences that confront us. This 'stock of knowledge' is not our novel creation. By and large we continue to work with the stock passed on to us by those people who bring us into the world and first interpret it for us. By and large we accept the stock that is presented to us as authoritative and when the presentors are not our parents and close acquaintances in childhood, they are powerful institutions. One can think of a 'perspective' as being the general background to a stock of knowledge and these perspectives are supported by social groups that continue to affirm them. To give an example, a man cuts his finger. If he is one of those who work with the dominant stock of knowledge for such cases he will wash the cut and then bathe it in antiseptic. His views of what to do here are obviously informed by the medical profession's germ theories of infection. If he is a pentecostalist, he may work with a very different stock of knowledge that involves not germs and antiseptic, but the Devil and healing faith. He will then pray and possibly call other believers around him to pray. Thus different stocks of knowledge produce very different solutions to the same objective problem.

A vital feature of the sociology of knowledge approach concerns its approach to 'truth'. It is not our concern whether the germ theory or the evil theory is more correct. One does not need to look far afield to realise that to say that something is true does not explain why people believe it. Whether something is true or false, and whether or not people will believe it, are, for the sociologist, two different questions, and we are mainly concerned with the second one. What matters for the persistence of a perspective is its social support. More than anything else, what makes a set of beliefs or practices plausible is the number of people who share them. Thus a Muslim in Britain has problems maintaining his view of the world in the midst of a culture that gives his view very scant support. In Iran, he has no such problems. At every turning, every conversation, every glance around him, he finds people who believe what he believes, who act on his beliefs and who accept his world as the 'normal' everyday world. A Western atheist finds that sort of constant confirmation in the West, but would find himself a part of a very small deviant minority with curious views if he went to Iran.

One can be more specific about this. In practice we do not live in 'Britain' or 'our society'; we live in small social groups and we have relationships with a small number of people who are of great significance. The rest of the world is dealt with in a very transitory role-based fashion: I buy a ticket from this busman; I buy my meat from that butcher; I exchange pleasantries briefly with an attractive stranger in the park. In constructing our views of the world and in maintaining those views it is our relationships with the small number of people who are significant, to whom we 'refer' (Shibutani, 1955), which are vital.

This analysis can be turned into a number of specific propositions about changing beliefs.

1)   If an individual accepts a new group of people who have a different perspective to his own, as his 'reference group', then he is likely to convert to that perspective. This simple observation is recognised by many evangelistic organisations which deliberately train their evangelists in making friends and winning the trust of potential converts. In his study of recruitment to the Oxford Movement (Moral Re-Armament), Eister (1950:11) notes the importance of the close bonds that the 'soul surgeon' develops with the potential recruit. John Lofland's study of conversion into one of the first Unification Church groups in America (1966) shows that an important link in becoming a 'Moonie' was the development of close friendship ties with existing members. Some organisations combine this process of building links between the potential convert and people who are already movement members with a deliberate policy of cutting the ties between the potential convert and his old reference group which supported his old view of the world. One of the key steps in the evangelical work of the Moonies is to persuade the potential convert to come to one of their camps where they are befriended by experienced members, and kept isolated from their old world, in the hope that new bonds will form with existing members. In addition the Moonies also discourage potential recruits from interacting with each other in case they begin to construct their own view of the significance of the event in opposition to the official one. In this proposition I am thinking of the 'seeker' moving into contact with a new reference group. There is also the situation where the individual remains static, in the same social relationships, but the perspective of his reference group changes around him. One can think of this as the case where the new beliefs 'travel' through stable social relationships.

2)   If the individual remains with the same reference group but other members of that group change their perspectives, then the individual is likely also to convert. There is plenty of evidence for this proposition in the many studies of how beliefs spread. One tradition expects that social movements, episodes of less than rational collective

behaviour, will be most common in mass societies; in those formations in which local communities and voluntary associations break down to leave a mass of isolated individuals (Kornhauser, 1959). While one can see the logic of such a theory, it has not been borne out by the research which, on the contrary, shows that isolated individuals are precisely those people most difficult to mobilise into any form of collective behaviour. Beliefs can only spread through contacts and connections. Gerlach and Hine's study of the diffusion of pentecostalism and black power ideology shows that these new perspectives spread from friend to friend, and relative to relative (1968:1970). Bibby and Brinkerhoff's work shows that one important way of being recruited to conservative Protestant churches was through one member of a family 'accommodating' himself to the views of another member who was already part of such a church (1973). Bainbridge (1978) makes the same point about recruitment to an occult movement.

There are a number of reasons why this should be the case. In the first place (and this is so obvious that it is often missed) we can only convert to something we know about. We have to have some contact with the new belief system. We need to be informed of the existence of alternative worldviews, and the source of the information affects how we receive it. Information that is transmitted to us by someone we know, love or trust is clearly more legitimate and plausible than information that comes to us from some impersonal source. A personal recommendation is more convincing than an invitation from a wall poster. Our buying a new religion is similar to our purchase of any major item; we ask our friends what brand of, say, washing machine they recommend. The principle that applies to the purchase of some consumer durable applies a fortiori to investment in new beliefs and patterns of behaviour. It is awareness of this that makes those who are engaged in evangelism keen on 'witnessing' the success of the new product in their own lives. A demonstration of the validity of the new world is much more convincing than an account of it. This is the significance of the personal testimony that is part of the evangelistic repertoire of many religions. The testimony normally consists of two parts. In the 'before' part, the movement member tells us that he too was once like us. He was a hopeless sinner, or confused, or whatever it is that the movement aims to alter. In this part he identifies with us as we are. In the second part of the testimony, we are presented with the 'after' story; an account of who the member now is, with emphasis on the improvements between the two states. In this part of the story we can see what we might and can become. The lives of people who have already made the transition are thus presented to us as demonstrations that show us why we ought to convert, and at the same time show us that such a change is possible. Consideration of this suggests a further proposition about conversion and person relationships. The more extreme the new beliefs and the more change that is required in the transition, the more important it is that such beliefs be legitimated by close friends and kin. Even in cases where the new perspective appears to have been acquired from some part of the mass media such as television or radio, one often finds that the convert was listening to the broadcast in the company of believers who reinforced and made plausible the message by their own presence and agreement (Gerlach and Hine, 1970:88).

Loss of Plausibility

Critics of evangelistic movements often make much of the fact that such movements attract the miserable and the incompetent. Movements like the Unification Church are accused of preying on the weak and the inadequate. This is based on an observation that is superficially valid but never pursued to its conclusion. I am not likely to become a 'born again' Christian, despite the years spent reading the literature of convinced Christians and attending innumerable crusades, because my view of the world is, for the present, satisfying. I am at home in the cognitive world I inhabit and to date my atheist rationalist stock of knowledge has served me well. This is, of course, no guarantee that it will continue to do so. People who are competent and adequate are hardly likely to be in the market for a new view of the world. <u>Conversion is for people who wish to change</u> and these are typically the people who are least happy and content with their lives as they are (which does not preclude the possibility that a movement may convince people that they are, in fact, missing something and thus create a need for change, rather than simply servicing an existing and recognised need, but this does not materially change my argument).

The sociologist can now pursue the lines of Berger and Luckmann's thesis and consider the sorts of structural changes that might put people in a position where their views of the world lose some of their plausibility. The first case can be considered under the heading of <u>mobility</u>. This is part of my proposition (1) above. People's views of the world can become precarious when they are separated from the reference group (or in wider terms) the culture which supported that perspective. The mobility can be geographical. One of the things that erodes traditional religious belief is large-scale population shifts such as occurred in Britain with the move from the land into the new industrial centres during the industrial revolution. The mobility can also be _social_, as in the case of individuals or groups improving their class and occupational position and then accommodating their religious beliefs and practices to suit those of the new reference group. The second case of perspectives becoming precarious can be termed _marginality_. Isolation from one's culture, even if not part of a process of becoming integrated into a new reference group, can result in a lose of plausibility for one's view of the world. The faculty of memory allows us to sustain our worldviews for considerable periods of such isolation because it allows us to interact with the recollection of our reference group even though it is not present in body. The caricature of such behaviour is the Englishman in the heart of Africa, still dressing for dinner even though there is no one present for whom such action has any significance. But memory is a poor substitute for a genuine reference group and hence one has to suppose that marginality presents problems for the maintenance of a worldview.

The third main source of precariousness is _novelty_. Talk of the social construction of reality should not mislead us into supposing that there is no obdurate reality, that there are only as many mirages as people wish to create (although there are enough groups of people with sufficiently strange views of the world to offer more than a little support to such a position). The stock of knowledge is after all a way of dealing with the world and people can be confronted with new problems and circumstances for which they have no ready solution within their present perspective. In such situations, people are liable to be in the market for new solutions and new perspectives. Thus one can expect that novelty can cause problems for the individual and that, at a social level, rapid social or economic change could put whole groups in the position of being receptive to new views of the world. This is not the same as saying that social change _causes_ changes in perspectives, rather that social change offers an opportunity for people to change perspectives, and presents them with a challenge to do so. There is no need for them to accept such a challenge, and certainly no inevitability about the process that warrants describing the occasion for reconsidering one's worldviews as 'the cause' of whatever is the outcome of such a reconsideration.

Predispositions

My point about people being in the market for a new picture of the world when their old one seems to fail them, might suggest that the potential convert is a clean slate upon which any movement could write its message if it happened along at the right time. This would be a mistake. People have biographies and a consciousness that is cumulative. We have predispositions. But this must also be qualified. I do not wish to argue, as many psychologists would, that people's behaviour can be explained as simply the 'working out' of pre-existing attitudes. A man may begin to climb a hillside with a plan of the line he intends to follow only to find that the lie of the land causes him to move first one way and then another to reach his goal. He may even change his mind en route about where he wants to end up. Most human action is similar. We may begin with a scheme, informed by pre-existing attitudes, but once we begin to interact with other people, and with our assessments of the circumstances in which we are acting, schemes change. Thus predispositions cannot be used as causes of behaviour. They are nonetheless important. I have already argued that conversion to evangelical Protestantism is greatly assisted by the presence of an existing belief that 'the Bible is important'. Without such a belief being held, a crusade evangelist carries no conviction; every time the evangelist says 'The Bible says ...' the listener mentally replies 'so what?'. Predispositions in this sense not only make it easier to accept some beliefs; they effectively block others. Schein, in a study of the attempts made by the Chinese to convert American prisoners to communism, says: 'the witnessing of a single act of brutality could almost inoculate the prisoner ... against being coercively persuaded because no amount of subsequent experience could make the Communists a credible source of information for him' (1961:167). Greil (1977) notes that many of the recruits to the Cryonics movement (people who believed that bodies could be preserved in freezing solutions until cures had been found for whatever had killed them) were science fiction literature enthusiasts. These points about predispositions concern particular and general beliefs. There is another level of predisposition that is important, and that is 'cognitive style'. In addition to actual beliefs, people have general patterns of thought, and one may find people attracted to a new ideology which seems superificially hostile to that they already believe but which shares similar principles of cognitive style. I will return to this in Chapter 8 when I consider the curious affinity between conservative Protestantism and natural science, and the nature of conspiracy thinking.

Conclusion

My main aim in this chapter has been to describe and explain what goes on at evangelistic crusades. I have spent a lot of time criticising the 'brainwashing' thesis of William Sargant because it is still the common view of such events. Having

119

detailed the problems with mechanical explanations of conversion, I introduced a very different view of conversion, a view in which conversion is seen as something that the actor accomplishes rather than as something that is done to him.

Notes

1. This story was told by Graham in Oxford on the 1st February 1980. I am grateful to the ATV <u>Jaywalking</u> programme for the invitation to attend Graham's Oxford meetings and to take part in their documentary on Graham.

2. Hale says 'God has plenty of money. He can supply you with an abundance' (n.d.:47). Sadly for Hale, one of his best advertisements for the success of his supernatural investment plan was found to have achieved his prosperity by the short cut of swindling the government out of the various agricultural grants and subsidies.

3. Billy Sunday is a good case in point. His audiences remained largely impassive while he performed his sermons in the style we now associate with the term 'holy roller' (Rodeheaver, 1936).

4. The manipulation story has at least two distinct values for the lapsed member of a deviant religious movement. In the first place, it allows him to admit that he did these deviant things while retaining a self-conception that is 'normal'. The 'blame' for the aberration is shifted from the ex-member to the organisation that recruited him. The second value is rehabilitation. The media and various anti-cult organisations such as the Deo Gloria Trust offer a career as a 'denouncer' to people who are prepared to tell manipulation stories about their involvement in new religious movements. In the eyes of both the general public and the ex-member's family, the manipulation story is a much more satisfying account of the deviation than the story that these things were done because at the time it seemed the best course. This latter account is dangerous because it leaves open the possibility that new religious movements may actually have something worthwhile to offer.

5. One might note that this sort of dichotomising is common to much social science. To take an example from the field of social movements and collective behaviour, there is a tendency of some authors (Lipset and Raab, 1971, for example) to work with an implied distinction between normal political activity (voting for the major parties) and abnormal activity (such as joining the John Birch Society). The first type of activity is thought to need no explanation while the latter is explained by identifying some cause of anxiety for which people then compensate, such as status inconsistency. This system

of division tells us more about the prejudices of the authors than it does about the episodes of collective behaviour apparently being explained.

6 Creationalism, Christian rock and counselling

To appreciate the present strength of conservative Protestantism it is not enough to show, as I have done, that it has survived and in some places grown in a period when liberal Protestantism has been in decline. One needs to be aware also of the rise in confidence, in assertiveness, and in the strength of morale in the conservative world. Conservatives seem to be more willing to fight the secular world on issues, such as the origins of the world, which have been almost undefended for 25 years. Evolutionary explanations of the origins of species have long been accepted by the secular world. They have also been accepted by liberal Protestants. More than that, Darwin's work played an important part in the development of liberal theology. Certainly a belief in evolutionary progress has the value that it resolves what would otherwise be an embarrassing problem for liberals: their claim to an insight superior to that of earlier divines. Evolutionism justifies the idea of 'new light' in two ways. It can be used to suggest that humans become more acute and aware as they evolve and hence our generation is more able to see what God intended than was the generation of Knox. It can also be used in some suggestion that the Lord gradually reveals more of himself over time. Either method provides subtle psychological support for the implied claim of the liberal to a better theology than that of churchmen at any previous period. Even if the claim is not presented in this form, evolutionary thinking is important to the liberal because it establishes the premise that man _changes_ and hence theology must also change to be appropriate and relevant to man in his new circumstances.

Someone who believes that the Bible, taken at something close to face value, reveals the Word of God naturally cannot accept evolutionism. Nonetheless the period from the First World War to the late nineteen sixties is remarkable for the timidness of conservative Protestants when faced with evolutionary arguments. It is as if they continued to believe Genesis but recognised that they could hardly expect anyone else to follow them. That they have begun to fight back over the teaching of Darwinism in schools and to challenge evolutionary science on grounds other than that it is wrong because God says so, suggests a new assertiveness.

A similar spirit can be seen in the willingness of conservative Protestants to assimilate various cultural forms of the secular world. The adoption of rock music and psychotherapeutic techniques are two cases of such assimilation. Like most new movements in conservative Protestantism, these changes appeared first in America and are gradually being adopted by British conservatives. Before discussing creationism, Christian rock music and Christian counselling, I will briefly offer some indication of a similar spirit of expansionism among British evangelicals. My own research on the conservative student organisation, the Inter-Varsity Fellowship (or Universities and Colleges Christian Fellowship, as it now is), discovered a gradual broadening of interests among evangelicals. The publication lists of the Inter-Varsity Press make this clear. When the enterprise was first launched it confined itself to countering the productions of the Student Christian Movement Press. Its main interest was in making available to students doctrinal and devotional literature of impeccable orthodoxy. This would provide an antidote to the liberal Protestant and atheistic teaching students would be confronted with in college. Christian Unions would supply their members with lists of readings which gave them stock responses to dangerous ideas. In some places this is still done but by and large the present generation of evangelicals is no longer on the defensive and is far more willing to consider the implications of their faith for a variety of issues and problems that before were ignored. Although they retain the same commitment to a well-specified set of doctrines, they are not solely concerned with an introspective cultivation and preservation of those doctrines. Now that the Student Christian Movement has ceased to be an effective force the evangelicals do not feel obliged to avoid social, economic or philosophical problems in the way they did when such topics were identified as 'SCM business'. The decline of liberal Protestantism has allowed the conservatives the luxury of being expansionist in their interests and has given them the confidence to believe that they can co-opt problems and cultural forms from the secular world without having their identity eroded. I now want to look at three examples of expessions of conservative confidence.

CREATION SCIENCE

For most liberals and atheists, creationism was buried in either 1860 or 1925 depending on whether one is British or American. 1860 was the year of the Oxford meeting of the British Association at which Bishop Samuel Wilberforce (known as 'Soapy Sam' for his unctuous manner) attempted to ridicule Darwin's work and was humiliated by Huxley's eloquent defence of his absent friend. 1925 was the year of the trial in Dayton, Tenessee, of John Scopes, a school teacher who had taught evolution in his biology classes. Scopes was defended by a team of lawyers headed by Clarence Darrow, a man who had spent more than 30 years defending radical and minority cases. He was prosecuted by William Jennings Bryan, the Populist politician and preacher who had built a career on speaking for the 'small people' of traditional rural and small town America (Russell, 1976). Confronted with a judge who was a Methodist lay preacher, a jury of whom six were Baptists and four were Methodists, of whom nine were farmers, and of whom three testified that they read nothing but the Bible, the conclusion was foregone. Scopes was found guilty but this verdict rather got lost in the publicity that followed the death of Bryan shortly after the trial finished. The verdict was later quashed by the Supreme Court of Tennessee on a technicality and the charge was dropped, thus effectively preventing Darrow having the whole argument pursued again to what he hoped would be a more satisfactory conclusion. The Scopes trial and the death of Bryan marked the end of the creationists. Although total faith in the Genesis story remained common in such pockets of fundamentalism as the Appalachian mountains, the rest of America grew up taking Darwin for granted.

Those who opposed Darwinism did so on the same grounds as Bryan. They maintained that if science came into conflict with revealed religion then science was wrong. While this reasoning might go down well within the community of the Saints, it did not provide a viable basis for arguing in the public arena of a pluralistic society, especially one which owed so much of its improved standard of living to the products of technology. Creationism ceased to have any major public voice, and evolutionism gradually asserted itself in the public consciousness as the accepted, taken-for-granted, explanation of the origins of the species. However, in 1969, the California State Board of Education ruled that 'scientific evidence concerning the origin of life implies at least a dualism or the necessity to use several theories' (Peter, 1970:1067). This and other similar decisions mark a clear change of direction in the debate between creationists and evolutionists. The California decision was the product of intensive lobbying by the Creation Research Society which argues, not that religion trumps science but that Darwinism is not good science. Creationists have accepted the terms of the secularists. They have recognised the amount of authority that scientists possess and decided to equip themselves with the same devices of legitimation. Membership of the Creation Research Society is restricted to those people who have a second degree in some science (although it is noticeable that few of them are biologists), and publications concentrate on either challenging evolutionist positions with results of scientific research, or on compiling research that seems to support a creationist view.

The campaign has been very successful. A number of local school boards have decided to require 'equal time' for evolution and creation in their classrooms. While electioneering in Texas, Ronald Reagan was asked his views on the issue and he replied that evolution is 'a scientific theory only, and it is not believed in the scientific community to be as infallible as it once was believed'. He went on to add 'if it is going to be taught in the schools, then I think the biblical story of creation should also be taught' (Time, 16th March 1981:50). This is a position that is becoming popular. In the first quarter of 1981 and the year preceding, legislators in 14 states introduced bills requiring creationist views in science classes. All failed to be passed but the fact that such bills could be introduced at all seems to have frightened many teachers and biology book publishers into evasive action, passing over the whole question of the origin of life[1]. Between 1974 and 1977, the section on Darwin's life in a major biology text was reduced from 1,373 words to 45. Text on the theory of evolution shrank from 2,750 to 296 words. If book publishers are going to respond so easily to pressure from creationists then legislative victory will not be necessary. Whether Creation science is or is not good science is a matter which I am not qualified to judge. However, even if it is, it is not the fact of being right that explains the recent successes of creationism. It is rather the changing self-image of natural science that is important.

It was once hoped by some scientists, Haldane and J.S. Huxley for example, that natural science would replace religion. Scientific rationalism and materialism would take the place of primitive superstition. Such a hope was undermined by those scientists and philosophers who argued for a much more humble and restricted view of science. A good example of this diminished conception of science can be found in Karl Popper's philosophy of science (1979;1978). Popper claims to have solved the problem of induction, which, as Hume pointed out, is that because every case so far observed verifies our theory does not allow us to suppose that there might not be a disconfirming case tomorrow. Thus complete verification is never possible. Popper's contribution to the solution of this conundrum was to point out that verification and falsification were not symmetrical. While the former is impossible, the latter is very easy. One single instance that does not fit is enough to falsify a proposition. A science based on falsification does not proceed by establishing immutable laws and accumulating these into a recognised body of truth. Instead it proceeds by falsifying present theories and formulating better ones that last longer, until they in turn are falsified. Thus science gets better not by accumulating 'truth', but by moving gradually further from error. Whether or not one accepts this particular philosophy of science, it does seem to be a good representative of the more limited claims that recent scientists have been prepared to make. Furthermore, one might note that the majority of those philosophers of science who disagree with Popper want to go further in undermining science's claims to producing valid, objective knowledge[2]. Certainly even the Popperian view of science, as 'the best we know for this week', is a long way from the new religion of Haldane and Huxley.

The rise in the popularity of the social sciences made people more conscious of the social construction of reality and knowledge. The idea that all knowledge was really only ideology became popular. And enter the irony. The purpose of the qualifiers and the relativisers was to destroy absolutisms. Claims to absolute truth were to be criticised by showing the social roots of ideas and by showing how social forces affected whether or not ideas were accepted or rejected. Yet the main consequence of the new humility and relativism was to allow the old absolutisms to re-establish themselves. Absolutists 'relativised the relativisers'. In the first part of his A Christian Social Perspective (1976), Storkey argues that modern sociology cannot be scientific because it cannot escape the confines of its own values and culture. Sociology is a social construction of a certain period and a certain place and as such cannot produce timeless truth. Thus the sociologist's work is turned against him and he is left in the technically absurd position of someone who wants to make the truthful statement that he always lies. Once the relativiser has been silenced, the Christian then asserts that the only way out of the trap is to accept the truth which is found in revealed religion.

A similar line of argument is used by creationists. Reymond (1977) first notes that natural scientists claim to be neutral and objective in their work. He then argues that such neutrality is not possible. All human thought must involve some starting propositions which cannot be scientifically established and these propositions destroy the 'objective' nature of such work. Thus even natural science can only produce knowledge that is relative to some culture and some values: 'for all the talk of scientism regarding the facts and laws it possesses, it in reality possesses none for sure' (Reymond, 1977:19). Reymond then proposes the same solution as Storkey; if we have to have values, then they should be the 'correct' ones. The only rational basis for 'true' science is a commitment to fundamentalist religious beliefs. Thus the relativism of those who wanted to destroy the old absolutisms based on supposedly objective knowledge is used to undermine that relativism, and to reassert an absolutist position.

Another creationist method is to use the humbler and more restricted claim that scientists now make as a lever to widen the gap of the 'possible'. Anyone with a cautious Popperian view of science has to allow that most things are 'possible', provided one takes 'possible' in the widest sense. The slightest hesitancy on the part of evolutionists, the merest expression of doubt that every single piece of evidence supports the evolutionist position, is snapped up by the creationists and used to demonstrate that 'there is not one single piece of proof for evolution'. One recent convert to fundamentalism has offered 25,000 dollars to anyone who can produce any proof for evolution. His prize is as yet unclaimed, presumably because he is using the word 'proof' in a very narrow way, in the pre-Popper sense of evidence that would verify beyond all doubt an explanation. But, of course, there are no reputable scientists who hold such a view of science. Thus the creationists put their case by using 'possible' in the broadest sense, which makes their story 'possible', and then use 'proof', when applied to evolution, in the narrowest sense, so that they can establish creation as being as scientifically legitimate as evolutionism. In fact, creationists have become so adept at toning down the Bible references and presenting Genesis as legitimate science that some conservative Protestants are now concerned that the creationists are implicitly accepting the superiority of natural science over God's word (Cameron, 1980:3).

The Genesis account of the origins of the world is important to the conservative Protestant because the Bible says God made the world in that fashion, and the Bible is the revealed Word of God. It is also important because it is the basis for one of the most common arguments for the existence of God; the argument from design. Things that have order must have been made. Where there is a watch, there must also be a watchmaker. Where there is a garden, there must also be a gardener. Where there is a magnificently complex world, there must have been a creator. A cogent evolutionary account destroys a lot of the appeal of the argument from design, although not all; one still has the problem of how the process began in the first place. There is, however, a third good reason for the conservatives' commitment to special creation and that concerns the supposed ethical consequences of evolutionism. Creationists want to blame Darwin for most of the evils of the modern world. They do this by arguing that evolution erodes the differences between humans and lower animals and hence justifies inhuman behaviour. Thus abortion, homosexuality, racial integration and all other evils are thought to have resulted from the denial of the uniqueness of human beings. While this reasoning is not often used in public apologetics, it does form a major part of the internal appeal of creationism to conservative Protestants.

To summarise this section, the changed conceptions about the nature and status of science, and, in particular, the increased awareness of the problems of values and the relativity of knowledge, opened a line of attack for creationists. They reduced their reliance on scripture and increased their attacks on the scientific status of evolutionary theory. They also collected as much material as they could which either made creation plausible or showed conflicts within the evolutionist camp. In these ways they managed to exert pressure on many school boards, text book publishers and biology teachers either to accept creation as an alternative hypothesis, or to avoid Charles Darwin.

CONTEMPORARY CHRISTIAN MUSIC

The rise of creation science is an example of conservative Protestantism's new confidence displaying itself in attack. The development of Christian rock music is a case of such confidence appearing in an ability to take over a cultural form previously thought to be too dangerous for contact. As in many of my earlier discussions, the story must be told with a degree of generalisation that will mean the neglect of the views of this or that minority. Such generalisation is, however, necessary if one is to go beyond the particular to the description and explanation of trends.

As late as the start of the last century many Protestants still rejected the use of music. Even today the Reformed Presbyterians and Scottish Free Churches sing, without mechanical accompaniment, only metrical versions of the Psalms of David. Any other form of music is rejected from worship because it is regarded as human (rather than divine) in origin. During the crusade of 1872, Moody's soloist, Ira D. Sankey, was much abused for using an organ (described by an irate Calvinist as a 'kist o'whistles'). But the Scots outside the Highlands and the Reformed Presbyterian Church soon developed a taste for accompaniment. English dissenters developed a strong musical tradition; North of England chapels spawned choral societies and brass bands. Welsh chapels produced a tradition of choral singing that is still unrivalled. For all this the Protestant suspicion of music remained. In part this is rooted in a distrust of anything 'elaborate'. Elaboration holds suggestions of priestcraft. Just as elaborate decor and dress are associated with Catholicism, so elaborate and sophisticated music is thought to be connected with liturgies and other 'high' forms of worship.

Complexity is not the only aspect of music that causes problems for the Protestant. The music at the other end of the market - the riotous, stomping, hand-clapping, enthusiastic singing of the Black churches - is equally suspect because it is thought to replace intellectual belief by an emotional commitment. Giving free rein to the emotions opens the door to the Devil. For most conservative Protestants music in worship means poorly sung, and weakly accompanied, versions of hymns for the last century. Outside of the church there was only secular music which the conservative Protestant would largely have ignored because it was not 'serious'. I have always been struck by how little music there is in the houses of evangelicals who are in their forties or older; where there is a record player there are usually very few albums.

Modern Christian popular music takes a number of forms. In Scotland and Ulster one finds a strong Country and Western culture which can be made distinctly religious simply by amplifying the elements of Protestant piety that are already present in the normal lyrics of Country and Western songs. A well-known performer in this idiom is William McCrea MP, a minister in Ian Paisley's Free Presbyterian Church, who has recorded in Nashville. In England the most common form of popular Christian music was always the acoustic guitar/vocals sound of folk music. As one practitioner noted, this was more acceptable than electric music because 'you could hear the words' (Allan, 1980:6). In youth fellowships and church socials, young people strummed their guitars and tortured 'Sinner man', 'A cowboy carol' and innumerable negro spirituals. Rock music was treated with suspicion:

> You read it in the evening papers,
> you hear it on the radio.
> Crime is sweeping the nation,
> this world is going to go.
> We need a nationwide revival
> to put the love of God in our souls.
> We need a whole lot more Jesus
> and a lot less rock 'n' roll!
> (Wayne Rayney, quoted in Allan, 1980).

There are two main reasons for a dislike of rock music. Firstly there is opposition to the hedonistic culture associated with rock music (the culture celebrated in the title of Ian Dury's song 'Sex 'n' drugs 'n' rock 'n' roll'). There is also the notion that the rhythms and volume of rock music 'brainwash' the listeners. As one writer put it in a recent Hour of Revival Association prayer letter:

> While many parents dislike rock music, most
> are unaware of its dangers – as I was a decade
> ago. The vast majority of young people too
> are totally ignorant of its effects ... Rock
> music is harmful, not only the beat of the
> music, but also the lyrics which often promote
> drugs, promiscuous sex and revolution (quoted
> by Hutchings, October/November 1981:14).

The writer goes on to say that rock causes hysteria and, in the long term, schizophrenia. Eric Hutchings added: 'Pray that Christians may realise that demonic powers can enter under the pulverising effect of this "drug" (noise)'. The more liberal Evangelical Alliance seems also to have subscribed to the brainwashing thesis. One of their publications includes a discussion of gospel music that asks 'and if some pop music is deliberately intended to be used for psychological manipulation, can these methods be used for the Gospel?' (Chapman, 1968:11). It may not be surprising that conservatives should believe that loud rock music brainwashes people but it is ironic that this thesis should come from the same tradition of psychology, criticised in the previous chapter, that asserts that conversion at evangelistic crusades (which Eric Hutchings promoted) is itself produced by psychological manipulation!.

For some conservative Protestants the manipulation has the result of a weakening of the listener's resistance to the Devil and his forces. Such a view is given some foundation in the use by a lot of 'heavy metal' bands of vaguely Satanist rhetoric and symbolism. Chick Comics publicise the claims of an American preacher called John Todd to have been a record producer, a druid High priest and a member of the Illuminati. He asserts that the melodies for rock songs come from old Druid manuscripts and that the lyrics are spells. Reverends Dan and Steve Peters believe the Top Ten to be 'one of the largest Satanic forces in the world' (Daily Express, 21st September, 1981). Reverend Alton Garrison of Texas holds record burning events as does the Zion Christian Life Centre in Minneapolis. Traditionally the Beatles have been the focus for much of this attention. They were (and still are) immensely popular; they flirted with Indian mysticism and drugs; and John Lennon stated at a press conference that the Beatles were more popular than Christ. One should not suppose, however, that all conservative Protestants share such views. The prestigious American evangelical magazine Christianity Today criticised the 'rock music as Satanism' position of John Todd. The situation can be most accurately depicted by thinking of an axis of conservatism. The more conservative the theology of any group, the more likely it is to hold to the Todd view.

The most important influence in changing the relationship between conservatism and opposition to rock music was the 'Jesus movement'. The background to the conversion of a large number of flower children and 'freaks' to evangelical religion is neatly sketched by Ellwood:

> In 1966-67 it was the Flower children. By 1968 many of them had taken off for the rural communes, and many of those left in the cities had become radically political. The political surge culminated with the McCarthy campaign. The disappointment of its failure produced, viscerally expressed in the formation of the 'Yippies' and the Chicago riots of 1968, a more traumatic shock than most outsiders realised. Yet that wing of the 'movement' suffered another equally battering blow in the upheaval following the Cambodia invasion and the Kent State shootings in 1970. After these events the new community felt futile, depressed, and oppressed ... by then it was apparent that its utopian communal dreams had ended in squalor, bitterness and economic failure augmented by violent opposition from without. The 'drug scene' and the 'crashing' districts of runaways were riddled with disease, psychological wreckage, crass exploitation by racketeers, perverse kinds of occultism, and despair. The new heaven had become a hell (Ellwood, 1973:16).

The conversion of members of the counterculture to conservative Protestantism produced a new cultural synthesis, with the dress style and mannerisms of the hippies being yoked to a new ideology and a new set of moral precepts. The movement was not itself long lasting. Some elements of it gradually returned to mainstream society and culture, moving into the evangelical churches of their parents while others (the Children of God, for example) developed their own beliefs and practices away from evangelical Protestantism and into new cults and sects. What the movement did produce that endured was the conversion of a number of rock musicians to 'born again' Christianity. Larry Norman is a good example. Were one to ignore the lyrics of his songs and listen only to the music one would find it hard to separate Norman from any other hard-driving rock act. A product of the same era, Randy Stonehill, could also pass as a competent act in secular rock festival.

In Britain the focus for Christian rock is the Greenbelt festival, first held in 1974. Beginning rather awkwardly with an uneasy mixture of evangelistic addresses, Bible studies, rock music, and an audience of 2,000 the festival has grown to rival secular festivals and, in 1981, it received coverage by BBC Radio One and drew 19,000 attenders. While isolated figures such as Cliff Richard have been professing their faith for over a decade, it has been the example of Norman, Stonehill and other Americans which provided the impetus for Christians actively to engage in rock music, and to seek a professional standard as high as that expected in the secular rock business. The organisational structure of this movement also has American elements[3]. The first major Gospel management company, Musical Gospel Outreach, grew out of Buzz magazine but folded, and the British arm of the American-based Youth for Christ organisation saw the potential of rock acts as an attraction for evangelistic crusades and offered regular employment to a number of rising British acts.

Bob Dylan

While not wishing to understate the significance of Norman, Stonehill, Pantry and others, the impact of Christian rock owes a great deal to the 'second generation' of converts and especially to the conversion of Bob Dylan. Since his arrival on the New York folk scene in 1962/63, Dylan has been regarded by his vast army of followers as something close to the conscience of a generation. His was the voice of the Civil Rights protestors and the anti-Vietnam war demonstrators. When his songs were direct attacks on corruption, hypocrisy, racial bigotry and authority, they were sung and resung at every rally and meeting. 'The times they are a-changin' and 'Blowin in the wind' were the anthems of the youth culture of the late nineteen sixties. When he moved in completely surreal imagery, his lyrics were probed for direction and meaning. For all that he counselled 'Don't follow leaders' in a 1965 song, (Dylan, 1973:268), millions followed him through every change of musical and lyrical style. In 1979, rumours appeared in the music press that Dylan had foresaken his Jewish heritage (which he had flirted with at various times in his career) and had been 'saved'. The album Slow Train Coming left no one in any doubt. The obscure imagery had gone, to be replaced by a direct and unambiguous fundamentalism. The song 'Gotta serve somebody' made it clear that this was not the vague pantheism that is commonly invoked by rock musicians looking for bombastic images. If that was not clear enough then 'I have been saved (by the Blood of the Lamb)' and 'When they came for Him in the Garden' should have made the point. As Dylan said at a concert in San Francisco's Warfield Theatre on 1st November 1979: 'all old things are passed away'.

In retrospect, Dylan's conversion was not totally unsignalled. Although his early repertoire included the hilarious send-up of redneck anti-communism, 'Talkin John Birch Paranoia Blues', Dylan also performed traditional American folk songs and blues that made use of the symbols of a deeply embedded Protestant piety. He could happily sing 'Meet me, Jesus meet me/ Meet me in the middle of the air/ If these wings should fail me, Lord/ Meet me with another pair'. Those critics who remind Dylan that he once condemned people who made 'flesh coloured Christs that glow in the dark', forget that the verse ends 'it's easy to see without looking too far that not much is really sacred'; it is shallow commercialism rather than the core of revealed religion that is being attacked. Noel Paul Stookey, the 'Paul' of Peter, Paul and Mary, claims that Dylan was influential in his own conversion as early as 1967. Stookey was going through the classic nineteen sixties 'seeker' syndrome of trying to discover the 'meaning of life'. His quest finally took him to Dylan's house in Woodstock where Dylan is supposed to have advised him to return to his home town and to read the Bible (Stookey, 1979:38). Whatever the reliability of this story, it is certainly true that Dylan's next released album, John Wesley Hardin, was full of religious imagery and language. Shortly after Hardin, Dylan went to Nashville again to record Nashville Skyline, which is signficant in featuring a duet with Johnny Cash, himself a classic model of the conversion of a popular, hard-drinking musician to 'born again' Protestantism. One of Dylan's songs from 1970 requires no devious interpretation to produce religious referents; 'Father of Night' is pure theism:

Father of grain, Father of wheat,
Father of cold, and Father of heat,
Father of air and Father of trees,
Who dwells in our hearts and our memories,
Father of minutes, Father of days,
Father of whom we most solemnly praise.

But for all these signs, Dylan's conversion came as a shock to most fans (myself included). It naturally delighted young evangelicals who found a musician of stature added to their camp. They could now open the secular music papers and find a reputable performer saying:

> You can come to know yourself but you need help in doing it ... The only one who can overcome all that is the Great Creator Himself. If you can get His help you can overcome it. To do that you must know something about the nature of the Creator. What Jesus does for an ignorant man like myself is to make the qualities and characteristics of God more believable to me, 'cos I can't beat the Devil. Only God can. He already has ... Satan's working everywhere ... If you can't see him he's inside you making you feel a certain way, he's feeding you envy and jealousy, he's feeding you oppression, hatred (New Musical Express, 15th August, 1981:31).

In itself there is nothing noteworthy in Dylan and a handful of other well-known musicians walking the glory road. Famous musicians have converted to many faiths and probability alone would lead us to expect a trickle in the 'born again' direction. Nor should one exaggerate the public impact of these conversions. One Scottish Highland minister, who had been at university in the late sixties, had never heard of Bob Dylan (although once I had told him the story he expressed himself pleased at the man's conversion!). It is not especially important that some conservative Protestants have adopted a new cultural form, but it is significant in this context; it shows the confidence of current evangelicalism that it can assimilate and turn to its own ends an art form that was once seen by many as a satanic threat.

In this section, I want to consider the nature of counselling and psychotherapy in the secular world, and the conservative Protestant versions of these enterprises. First, I will try to explain the rise of counselling and psychotherapy. The private world has not always been with us. It is very much a modern creation. It comes into being as a result of the increased autonomy of the world of production. The industrial economy has its own internal logic (of which a major part is the concern with ever greater efficiency), and it tends to be separated from other areas of social activity, especially the family[4]. Modern man, man in the age of technology (Gehlen, 1980), moves in at least two worlds; the public and the private. This opens the possibility of two identities. We are confronted with two 'selves'; the public self and the private self. Some people invest entirely in their public self. Celebrities, politicians, people with absorbing and time-consuming jobs, may well identify almost entirely with their public persona. For most people this is simply not possible; their jobs are so mundane and trivial that there is no room for creative expression and absorption. In the modern world, jobs are not only rendered almost meaningless by the division of labour but also made short-lived. It is no longer uncommon for someone to lose more than one trade in a lifetime because that job has ceased to exist. In such circumstances most people tend to <u>play</u> their public self, either hammed up or tongue-in-cheek. It is the private world that has become the primary one for modern man. To anglicise Berger's expression (1965:36), it is as if the individual was saying: 'Don't judge me by what I do here – in the City I just play a role – but come home with me to Ruislip and I'll show you who I <u>really</u> am.'

The second main point about the modern world concerns the difference between human beings and other animals. Most animals have their behaviour determined for them by patterns of instinct and their environment. They possess instincts that are detailed and specific. In contrast, humans have little or no instinct. We talk loosely of 'sex drives', the 'will to survive' and so on. But a comparison of the many and varied forms in which sexuality can be expressed suggests that the instincts we do have are not good guides to actual behaviour in any particular situation. Nor are we constrained by our environment. A species that can build heated swimming pools in Alaskan oil fields is clearly not determined by the ecology of its world. Humans are thus in a curious position of 'openness'. We could do and be almost anything. All is potential and possibility. Gehlen argues that this potential and lack of predictability is intolerable. We simply do not have the mental capacity or the energy to live in a world in which any thing could be any way, and where everything has to be decided anew. We could not function in a world where the behaviour of others was not largely predictable. Our solution is to create an artificial order of institutions that imposes a framework of regularity on our activities. We agree to drive on one side of the road. We agree to have only one wife at a time (or ten; it does not matter what the agreed pattern is so long as there is one). Stable patterns become part of the 'taken for granted' part of our world and cease to be a matter for conscious examination; it is 'just like that'. We create institutions to regulate large parts of the social world and thus free ourselves to be active and creative within a small stage that is left free for examination and decision.

The problem of modernity is that it undermines and erodes institutions. The economy is characterised by constant innovation. Productive practices are scrutinised for ways of improving their efficiency and changed accordingly when such methods are found. The spirit of critical examination cannot be confined to the productive world. The attitudes that characterise economic activity cannot be kept entirely separate from other spheres of life (although many people try hard to maintain separate watertight compartments for their different worlds). One can imagine a stable society of yam-growing cousin-marriers. The institutional pattern of cousin marriage may continue until eternity, provided there are no problems with the supply of cousins. But then they discover that a new system of crop rotation improves their yam growing. If an experimental attitude develops in the field of yam growing, it will not be long before someone questions cousin marriage: 'I don't like any of my cousins. I like this other girl. We've changed the old ways of yam growing, so why can't we change our marriage patterns?' Of course, institutions do not crumble overnight. When Gehlen talks about the impact of technology on human institutional patterns he is talking about changes that took place over a period of a hundred years.

The new stress on the private world and the erosion of institutional patterns forces modern man back on his own performance. It raises doubts and fears about our 'selves'. It forces us to put effort into being our 'selves'. After all, if the person I am at home is going to be the real 'me', then I ought to be concerned about whether that 'me' is as good as he could be. The combination of these two things produce that novel phenomenon; the rise of the psychotherapies. There is a recent paperback which lists more than 250 varieties of psychotherapy that range from Creative Agression therapy to Vita-Erg therapy, and runs through some other curious techniques on the way (Herink, 1980). While this obsession with improving the self is still a predominantly American concern, it has clearly had an impact in all Western cultures. In traditional societies, it is only the very, very strange who are thought to be subjects in need of having their selves changed. In the modern world, the coming ethos is that we could all do with some remedial work in order to liberate our true potential/find our real selves/really relate to other people, and so on.

There is a perverse irony in these changes. Max Weber (1976) argued that the spirit of capitalism, the constant critical examination of methods of working, was an indirect consequence of the Puritan's obsessive concern with their moral lives. Many of the Puritans kept detailed diaries which served as ledgers for their spiritual state. Signs of grace and signs of sin were recorded as if they were the credit and debit sides of an account book. Attitudes that had their roots in religious and spiritual concerns then spread into the economic sphere. What we are seeing in the modern world is a further turn of the screw. Some people now apply the same restless critical improvement ethos to their private leisure worlds. Instead of becoming more efficient producers of ball-bearings, we are now concerned to be more efficient human beings. Thus while the world of work has been replaced by the private world as the main focus of interest for modern man, the nature of that interest seems to owe much to the ethos of the world of work.

Another feature of the technological world that is relevant to this discussion of the rise of personal counselling and psychotherapy is the popularity of manuals. This is part of the technological fantasy; things are amenable to manipulation, and the recipies for manipulation can be recorded and passed on. Manuals are immensely popular. Some publishers depend almost entirely on the sale of magazines that explain 'how to' (do almost everything from crochet to sexual intercourse), and build into an extended manual. All problems are solvable with the right tips. No matter what your problem - sexual frigidity to faulty electrical wiring - there is a book that shows how to deal with it. There is nothing new in the manual itself but what has changed is the part of the social world for which advice is given. There seems to have been a clear shift from Benjamin Franklin's Advice to a Young Tradesman, which is a tract, written in 1748, on honorable and legal ways of becoming rich, to the 1970's best seller Zen and the Art of Motorcycle Maintenance, which has very little to say about motorcycles and a lot more to say about 'the self', human potential and 'oneness'.

These brief remarks identify certain features of the modern technological world and the sort of consciousness it produces. They also allow us to understand the rise of counselling and the idea that psychotherapies are products which can be consumed by all of us, and not just the extremely odd. The concentration on the private leisure world and the private 'self', combined with the erosion of previously institutionalised patterns of thought and behaviour, has produced a market for guidance and direction for this new <u>private</u> individual. Modern man is in need of what Dylan called 'road maps for the soul' and I want to look at various secular 'maps'.

Rogerian Client-centred Therapy

Carl Rogers is the man who, more than anyone else, has been responsible for altering psychotherapy's basic image of human nature. Freud's human is possessed of a nasty, carnal nature. Rogers promoted the view that the essence of human being was benign. The central premise of Rogers' work is the idea that 'the individual has a sufficient capacity to deal constructively with all those aspects of his life which can potentially come into conscious awareness' (1973:24). For Rogers, humans are driven not by sin or greed but by a desire to 'actualise' their potentials. Quite what these potentials are, or what someone who has successfully actualised them would look like, is not clear. Rogers seems to assume that the end products of 'actualising' would be flexible rather than rigid in their thinking, open to others rather than defensive, and independent rather than dependent on others (Nye, 1975:90-100). Rogers is not prepared to offer detailed guidelines on how people should behave. His view of why some people are unhappy is a relativistic one. There are no rules that would suit everyone. People are unhappy because they are not actualising <u>their own</u> potential, which may, of course, be different for different individuals. Problems are relative to the individual's own interests and not to some objective set of rules or ethics. The good client-centred therapist does not give moral direction to his client; rather he aids him to be himself. Moral relativism does have one major problem and that concerns treating vicious and vindictive people. To take an extreme example, does the client-centred therapist assist someone who wants to actualise his potential to kill people with a chain-saw? This sort of case actually exposes the weakness of non-directive types of therapy. The notion that moral judgements are not involved is a thin rhetoric which disguises a profound morality. What the Rogerian does is to argue that the desire to kill people with a chain-saw is not part of someone's 'true' potential; it is a piece of social wreckage that has floated into the individual's personality and there sunk, so that it <u>appears</u> to be an essential characteristic of the person. Thus the therapist can protect his initial claim that people are 'really' good (which is essential to the morality of not directing them but only helping them to be themselves) from falsification, simply by attributing negative attitudes and desires to society, and positive attitudes and desires to the 'raw' person.

There are very good reasons for counsellors advocating a non-directive position. We live in a pluralistic society made up of a number of different cultures. Different people have different beliefs, attitudes and aspirations. A counsellor who followed the traditional sense of the occupation and gave <u>advice</u> would find his clientele limited to the culture for which he can speak. In order to appeal to the widest possible market, the counsellor has to remove his practice from a particular culture by disguising its moral content. If what one offers is not advice, but an apparently neutral technique which can assist anyone from an Eskimo to a New York Jew to actualise their potentials, then everyone becomes a potential client. The emphasis on technique rather than advice has the value for counsellors that it mystifies the business. The basis for a lucrative profession is the claim that one possesses some rare and valuable skill that is not available to everybody. Anyone's grandmother can give advice, but only a trained Rogerian can give client-centred therapy.

Clinical Theology

Until recently, Christian counselling, if it meant anything, meant the work of the Lake brothers and their attempts to combine clinical psychology with theology. The introduction of theology is also the introduction of moral direction: 'the goal of pastoral care, and the goal of psychiatry in so far as it sets out to help Christians who are theologically aware, is not the goal of self-realization, or of psychic completeness, but of Christ-realization' (Lake, 1966:xvi). The psychiatric element in the system is heavily Freudian. 'The passivity of infancy' and other problems of childhood cause innumerable problems which Lake likens to the agony of Christ in his crucifixion. Christ and the Holy Spirit play an important part in the cure of psychic ailments and the Church attempts to make bearable what cannot be removed. The important question is to what degree does Clinical Theology differ from secular psychiatries? There is much talk of Christ and the Holy Spirit, but it seems that the traditional Christian doctrines have been psychologised and secularised. For example, the 'schizoid' condition (a common problem, in Lake's view) seems to be the result of alienation from Christ, oneself and others. But Christ himself seems to have been 'existentialised' from being God incarnate to being some sort of psychological superman. The Fall seems to have been altered from being a historic event that was the real cause of our sinfulness to being a metaphor, a symbolic representation of a process of alienation that happens to every human being in early infancy. One has the feeling that Lake is engaged in the modernist Protestant habit of translating the Bible from being a story about what actually happened to real people then, into a metaphor that helps us to understand what happens routinely to us now.

Clinical Theology accepts the validity of secular psychology and psychoanalytical theory, and then adds a Christian element to the insights derived from these perspectives. As in many other Christian social services (residential homes, for example) only the original motivation for wanting to help is especially Christian; the theory and practice of what is actually done largely adopts whatever is current in the corresponding secular form of care and service. It is also the case that most clergymen pass on to other people many of the problems that are brought to them for counselling. A survey of American clergy of most denominations found that cases of 'vague mental disorders', 'alcoholism', 'sexual problems in marriage', 'psychoses, paranoia and schizophrenia', 'divorce and separation' and 'psychopaths and mental defectives' were typically passed on to other groups of helpers (Cumming and Harrington, 1963). Thus even in a period when it was supposed that the clergy were interested in developing new roles to replace that of purveyor of religious truth, the clergy were recognising the superior claims of other professional groups, such as psychiatrists and child psychologists, to deal with the problems that were brought to them.

The work of the Presbyterian Calvinist Jay E. Adams stands in complete contrast to this surrender to the secular world and I now want to turn to this assertively Christian approach to personal problems.

Adams' Nouthetic Counselling

> Since other disciplines (engineering, business, medicine and even non-clinical and non-counselling psychology) seem to be able to arrive at some measure of order and cohesion - enough at least to produce concrete results, must not something be radically wrong with counselling? The answer to that question is 'yes'. Something is radically wrong with counselling, and this is it: almost to a man, counsellors have rejected the only true standard of human values, beliefs, attitudes and behaviour. Yet those matters comprise the stuff of which counselling is made. They have

> looked everywhere else, tried everything else,
> but have totally ignored the one Book that can
> bring order out of chaos. Only a word from
> God himself can properly tell us how to
> change. In the Bible alone can be found the
> true description of man, his plight and God's
> solution in Christ. Only the scriptures can
> tell us what kind of person we must become ...
> counsellors are in their present state of
> confusion, swayed by every new fad, precisely
> because they have rejected the one and only
> perfect and lasting textbook on counselling
> (Adams, 1977:6-7).

Nouthetic Counselling has become very popular in the United States in the last decade and is now beginning to be used by clergymen in the United Kingdom. It offers a considerable contrast to Lake's work in that is starts from a critique of psychiatry. Adams' follows Thomas Szasz (1974, 1976) in arguing that most psychiatry is stepping over its bounds in peddling moral direction in the guise of medicine. Like Szasz, he accepts that there are some problems that result from diseases and wishes to confine psychiatrists and psychologists to such diseases and the working of the central nervous system. Matters of belief and behaviour, however, are moral matters and as such are in the province of religion, not medicine. In contrast to the optimism of Rogers, Adams' view of basic human nature is that man is utterly sinful. Far from having a natural tendency to decency, man (since the Fall) has a natural tendency to evil which is further exacerbated by the day to day activities of the Devil. What people need is not less external control but more external control (if one calls God external). Adams' attacks Carl Rogers on the grounds that Rogers is doing theology, but doing it wrong. To make any statement about human nature is, for Adams, theological, and believing that one can solve problems without the aid of God is itself a theological position.

The Adams' system begins with conversion: 'the Christian counsellor must recognize that it is fruitless to offer anything other than minimal help before evangelizing; apart from the resources of the Word and the Spirit all counselling is superficial' (Adams, 1977:67). Thereafter it is concerned with confronting the counsellee with his behaviour and Biblical principles in the hope of changing the counsellee. Far from being 'non-directive', this form of Christian counselling is nothing but directive in that it has borrowed the language of counselling and some of the technique of secular counselling and harnessed these in the service of a set of dogmatic beliefs.

Adam's system is one variant of an explicitly Christian counselling that is acquiring adherents. One can readily see its appeal. It offers a jusification and technique for adding a new dimension to the traditional preaching and teaching roles of the conservative Protestant minister. It offers a new professional status ('counsellor') and the satisfaction of becoming competent to assist people in their difficulties and it does so while avoiding the problems of trying to be 'non-directive'. The difficulties of trying to help others without imposing one's judgements and values do not arise. The intellectual angst of liberal Rogerians experiencing tension between their values and the values of the client is not a problem for the heavily directive Christian counsellor.

Nouthetic counselling is only beginning to establish itself in Britian. Five or six ministers, usually from theologically conservative churches, are now offering such counselling. One focus of the Christian counselling movement is the Crusade for World Revival (CWR); an evangelistic organisation with charismatic and pentecostal tendencies which holds crusades and ministry training sessions and publishes a glossy magazine, various booklets and cassettes. The founder, Selwyn Hughes, has always emphasised personal counselling in evangelism and CWR recently began a quarterly called The Christian Counsellor's Journal. This does not support one particular brand of Christian counselling but rather has an eclectic flavour, publishing articles on a number of different varieties of Christian therapies. Some give more credence to secular psychology and psychoanalysis than does Adams but not a great deal more. Perhaps the simplest way to think of these is to consider an axis which has the Bible at one end and secular therapies and theories at the other end. On such an axis, Adams' nouthetic counselling lies at the religious end, most of the contributions to the CWR's journal lie between that pole and the middle, and the liberal Protestants who do engage in this sort of thing are found at, or near, the thoroughly secular end. In 1975, for example, the Student Christian Movement offered courses in what they called GOAT; the initials stood for 'Gestalt Orientation and Alinsky Training'. Apparently the course was going to be called 'Personal Relationships and Organisational Development' but this produces the acronym 'PROD' which has significance in Ulster! Gestalt Psychology is a secular therapy created by Fritz Perls which offers the usual 'actualising one's potentials' or as one student put it: 'the basic underlying belief is that all these fragments are part of my whole self and the job of life is to integrate and own them in order to grow into my living wholeness' (Zipfel, 1974:1). The Alinsky training component came from the teaching of Saul Alinsky on community politics and organisation. The interesting feature of the SCM's rationale for putting on this course is the total absence of any specific reference to Christianity. The word 'Christ' does not appear and the only overt mention of religion comes in a curious passage that seems to owe more to the Manichean heresy than to traditional Christianity.

The recent rise of explicitly Christian counselling is important for an understanding of conservative Protestantism for two reasons. In the first place, it is a symptom of the increased confidence and strength of conservative Protestantism. As is the case with Christian rock music, ideas and techniques from the secular world are being borrowed, stripped of their sinful associations, and turned to the Lord's work. But it is more than that. Christian counselling has a significance that goes beyond that of Christian rock music in that it shows the influence of the modern world on conservative Protestantism. I have sought to show that the rise of counselling perspectives is part of a much wider set of transformations that result from modernisation. Modernisation produces the private world. It stresses the individual rather than the community. It fragments identity between the public and private self. The extensive division of labour reduces the ability of the world of work to provide us with meaning, and we react by developing an instrumental orientation to our work. Work, the public world, is valued only to the extent that it provides us with resources to develop our private worlds. Conservative Protestants, as evidenced by the rise of perspectives like that of Jay Adams' Nouthetic conselling, shows a similar movement of attention from the public to the private. In the second chapter, I made the point that there was a brief period in the last century when revivalist religion was associated with social reform; when it had something to say about social action and matters of economics and politics. When one appreciates the individualistic emphasis of conversionism - the idea that every individual must undergo a personal change of heart - this period must appear as a temporary aberration. For conservative Protestantism is the paramount religion of the individual, isolated 'self'.

This is not to say that conservative Protestants have nothing to say about economy and society. In the next chapter I will be examining various political interventions of conservative Protestants. My point is that lack of success in these enterprises poses no problems for conservative Protestantism. Liberal Protestants who favour social interpretations of the Christian tradition are threatened by the failure of their social witness. Faiths of communities such as Catholicism and Judaism are undermined by the modernising trend to emphasise the private world over against the public world. While conservative Protestants may be troubled by the failure of the economy and the polity to respond to their moral and ethical teaching, the nature of their faith allows a parallel shift of attention from dogmatic preaching to dogmatic counselling; from advertising the public benefits of their product to offering improvements to the personality, family life and close inter-personal relationships. If it cannot save the world, it can improve family life.

Notes

1. This section was written before the Arkansas state
    legislature passed one such bill. According to reports,
    this legislation was passed with minimal discussion and
    with few of the state senators being aware of its
    importance. The American Civil Liberties Union has
    challenged the legality of the bill on the grounds that
    it involves the introduction of religious beliefs into
    the classroom and hence violates the constitutional
    guarantees of the separation of state and church. Thus
    in December 1981, the creation arguement was once again
    raised in a courtroom, this time in Little Rock,
    Arkansas. Given the interest in the issue it is
    unlikely that the case will stop with the judgement of
    that court which went against the creationists and one
    can expect a long trial through the legislature to the
    Supreme Court.

2. See, for example, the arguments in Lakatos and Musgrave
    (1970).

3. One of the 'centres' of this movement is the glossy
    quarterly New Christian Music.

4. Much of the thinking behind this section (and much of
    the book) has been greatly influenced by the writings of
    Peter L. Berger, especially Berger (1965), Berger and
    Luckmann (1973), and Berger, Berger and Kellner (1973).

7 Conservative Protestant politics

Most people take the term 'conservative Protestant' to indicate someone who is a Protestant and has conservative politics. In most of this book I have used the term in the religious sense, to indicate someone who holds certain theological positions. The common-sense interpretation is, however, not all that far from the mark. Traditionally those with conservative theologies have also held conservative political positions. There have been honourable exceptions. The piety of Wilberforce and the Saints led them to support and initiate a number of progressive reforms. The anti-slavery movement was a product of evangelicalism as was Shaftesbury's factory legislation. Early American revivalism was reformist; Finney was opposed to slavery (although one of his assistants was a noted anti-semite!) In both Nazi Germany and the Soviet Union the strongest opposition to the state has come from the conservative rather than the liberal end of the theological spectrum.

Furthermore, by far and away the dominant political posture of conservative Protestants is quietism. The desire to maintain purity, combined in many cases with the belief that the Day of Judgement will be coming in the reasonably near future, does not encourage active involvement in the affairs of the world. In some Protestant sects this position is specified in the ideology and behaviour of the group (the Exclusive Brethren, for example); in other groups it is simply taken for granted. Usually conservative Protestants display no more involvement in politics than is typical in

their society and the nature of their politics is usually
determined by the class background of the believer rather
than by his religion. Thus the typical English conservative
Protestant will either not vote or vote for the Conservative
party. The politics of the evangelical will be similar to
those of the atheist in the same class position and this will
be Toryism because most evangelicals are middle-class. Only
in those cases where the evangelical is working-class does
religious belief have a marked effect; it will be
considerably easier to be a Christian socialist if one has a
liberal theology than it will be if one is an evangelical.

Having said that, I now want to consider those cases
where conservative Protestantism and extremist right-wing
politics have combined.

AMERICA: THE OLD NATIVISM AND THE NEW RIGHT

American right-wing movements have mostly been 'nativist' and
have thrived in those periods when the white Protestant
settlers have felt themselves to be under threat from some
newer arrival. If one defines 'nativism' as a body of
social, political, economic and religious traditions common
to the first wave of white settlers and their descendants
(Moffat, 1963:127), then the modern period has seen many
nativist movements. 'Know-nothingism', so-called because its
supporters were instructed to answer 'I know nothing' to any
enquiries, reached its peak in 1855 when the first wave of
immigration also peaked. Another peak in immigration
coincided with the formation and spread of the America
Protective Association. Both of these movements were
anti-Catholic. While maintaining that they were not
attacking the civil rights of individual Catholics, the
followers of these movements asserted that Catholics were
untrustworthy as citizens because they owed a superior
allegiance to Rome than to America. As will become clear
from the nature of the other targets of right-wing extremism,
the idea of real or potential disloyalty is a central theme
in the right's identification and stigmatisation of target
populations.

One of the best known nativist organisations is the Ku
Klux Klan. It was founded in the Southern states shortly
after the Civil War as a vigilante movement that could
establish law and order in an area characterised by
banditry. The Klan's early targets were apparantly 'aliens,
idlers and slackers, immoral women' (Moffat, 1963:6). At its
most popular around 1875, the Klan faded when many members
concluded that stability had returned to the South. The
organisation was revived in 1915 as a commercial venture by a
W.J. Simmons, the son of a preacher who had been a salesman,

a founder of fraternal societies and a 'Professor of Southern History'. By the middle of the nineteen twenties the Klan was at its peak, with about 100,000 members. Its centre was, surprisingly enough, not the old South but rather the area west of the Mississippi (North and East Texas, Arkansas, Oklahoma and North Louisana) and it was successful in California and then Oregon. Writing in 1924, Moffat guessed that there were more Klan members in Ohio and Indiana than in all the states east of the Mississippi. This fits with Moffat's other observation; that the Klan in this period was not primarily racist. It was anti-Catholic. A canvas of the main motives for Klan membership produced 'anti-Catholicism' as the most common with 'one hundred percent Americanism', support for law and order, anti-semitism, 'the purity of womanhood' and racism as the most popular subsidiary concerns. The fact that maintaining white supremacy was not at that time the primary interest of the Klan does not mean that those Klan members were any more friendly towards blacks than were Klan members of the nineteen fifties; it simply means that blacks were not, at that time, seen as a serious threat.

In the nineteen thirties the focus of much Christian right-wing politics again shifted. The rise of fascism in Europe and the growth in the influence of the Soviet Union made anti-semitism and anti-communism the main props of right-wing belief systems. These are not, of course, exclusive and some novel combinations were produced. Gerald B. Winrod, for example, hated both Catholics and Jews; a combination he justified by arguing that Roman Catholicism was Judaism mixed with paganism. Winrod also thought that Eisenhower was a front for Jewish communists (Roy, 1953:12-19). Robert Welch, the founder of the John Birch Society, agreed that Eisenhower was a communist but he dropped the 'jewish'. The Klan was legally dissolved in 1946 for failure to meet its tax bills but in the small local groups that remained, anti-Catholicism was largely replaced by a 'bitterness towards Jews and broadminded Protestants' (Roy, 1953:127) and Catholics who shared that bitterness joined the Klan. The presence of Catholics was even more marked in the John Birch Society. Named after a young Baptist missionary reputedly killed by Chinese communists, this organisation was founded by Robert Welch in 1958 with the aim of alerting Americans to the threat of communism without and within. Surprisingly, Welch was not himself a Biblical fundamentalist. He spoke of having broken out of the shackles of narrow Southern fundamentalism and he attended a Unitarian church. However, an overwhelming proportion of the JBS membership was fundamentalist. Other anti-communist organisations of this period included Billy James Hargis' Christian Crusade, Bundy's Church League of

America and Fred Schwarz's Christian Anti-Communism Crusade (Pierard, 1970). Bundy gathered and circulated (usually inaccurate) information about 'leftists'. Hargis, a John Bircher himself, used radio evangelism to spread an anti-communist message and he used a number of leading conservative Protestants, including Robert Welch, Bob Jones, Snr and Jnr, and Ian Paisley, as guest preachers. The use of the latter brought out the theme of changing targets for right-wing extremism. Hargis is reputed to have warned Paisley to lay off anti-Catholicism and to stick with anti-communism (Bestic, 1971:66).

THE MILIEU AND SECTARIANISM

The idea of a 'milieu' is used for a certain type of loose social organisation where a large number of individuals and organisations share certain common values, beliefs and patterns of behaviour without actually being part of one formal organisation (Bruce, 1980). The sharing of common interests is the basis for individuals to move from one organisation to another within the milieu; for individuals to engage in a number of different activities within the milieu; and for individuals to maintain contacts and alliances with other like-minded people. In this sense there is a distinct fundamentalist world and there is a distinct right-wing world and these two milieux have tended to overlap. The same names appear in both worlds. Hargis, for example, was ably assisted by L.E. White, a shrewd public relations man who had worked as a 'booster' for the faith-healing evangelist Oral Roberts. Within the milieu there is usually cooperation based on an awareness of sharing an identity that is distinct from everyone outside the boundaries. However, from time to time, one finds the cooperative tendency being over-ruled by sectarianism. Someone like Billy James Hargis already believes that most of the world is peopled by communists, or the dupes of communists. Only himself and his small band of close followers are the possessors of the truth. Such a style of thought is seductive and one finds that the number of others who are allowed to possess some of the truth is gradually reduced. Bob Dylan's <u>Talkin' John Birch Paranoia Blues</u> (1973:30-1) is the story of just such a progression.

> Well, I was feelin' sad and feelin' blue,
> I didn't know what in the world I was gonna do.
> Them Communists they wus comin' around,
> They wus in the air/They wus on the ground.
> They wouldn't give me no peace.

So I run down must hurriedly
And joined the John Birch Society.
I got me a secret membership card
And started off a-walkin' down the road.
Yee-hoo, I'm a real John Bircher now!
Look out you Commies!

Well, I investigated all the books in the
    library,
Ninety percent of 'em gotta be burned away.
I investigated all of the people I knowed,
Ninety-eight percent of them gotta go
The other two percent are fellow Birchers ...
    just like me ...

Well, I finally started thinkin' straight
When I run outa things to investigate.
Couldn't imagine doin' anything else,
So now I'm sittin' home investigatin' myself!
Hope I don't find out nothin' ... hmm ... Great
    God!

There is a clear connection between the dogmatism of the
beliefs and a tendency to schism and factionalism which can
be seen in the biography of Carl McIntire, a leading
fundamentalist preacher and political extremist. McIntire's
personal involvement in schisms began when he was a student
at Princeton theological seminary. He was there at the time
when J. Gresham Machen was involved in a number of
controversies with others in the Presbyterian Church about
the apparent drift towards liberalism. When Machen left
Princeton, McIntire went with him to his new college,
Westminster (named after the Westminster Confession of
Faith). For a time he was a minister in Machen's new
Presbyterian Church of America but he split from that body
over two issues. He wanted to make pre-millennialism part of
the stated doctrine; Machen refused. Generally McIntire
wanted to increase the amount of specified doctrine and
reduce the number of beliefs that were left as matters of
conscience.

In 1938, the Presbyterian Church of America divided into
Machen's Orthodox Presbyterians and McIntire's small Bible
Presbyterians. Eighteen years later, the Bible Presbyterians
dumped McIntire and withdrew from the two ecumenical
organisations that he led: the American Council of Christian
Churches and the International Council of Christian
Churches. Once again McIntire began to rebuild his
organisations. He was successful in establishing a large
theological college but in 1971, the president of the
college, more than half of the students and all but two of

the staff, left in protest at McIntire's leadership and his public rallies for total victory in Indo-China. This second point unites him with fundamentalist leaders of this period who were unanimous in arguing that the Vietnam War could be won with the right will. Bob Jones was fond of suggesting using nuclear weapons on Hanoi to finish off the North Vietnamese. McIntire's ability to alienate fellow conservatives can be seen in the fortunes of his American Council of Churches. In 1941, it had 15 member denominations with a total of around 200,000 members. By 1974, this had only grown to 250,000 in a period when the membership of conservative denominations had grown by about 50%.

Like Hargis, McIntire derived his financial support from responses to his radio show, the 'Twentieth Century Reformation Hour'. Audience figures for these shows are notoriously inaccurate but in 1975 the show was being broadcast on some 600 small stations and could well have had an audience of 10 million listeners. Unlike Hargis, McIntire was reluctant to work with the secular right and it was not until the Presidential election of 1964, when McIntire supported Goldwater against Lyndon Johnson, that he became seriously active in promoting another part of the right-wing milieu (Clabaugh, 1974:92). Ironically McIntire's first cooperative action for years produced another split. His own American Council of Christian Churches threw him out for getting involved with people who were not 'born again'!

One could hardly review the extreme right in this period without mentioning Senator Joseph McCarthy and the House Committee on Un-American activities. McCarthy, like Father Coughlin in the thirties, drew a large Catholic following and thus created a problem for the fundamentalists. He was not saved and his supporters were not predominantly Protestant but for most fundamentalists, McCarthyism was just too good an opportunity to be anti-communist to pass up. McIntire gave the committee the names of clergy whom he suspected of leftist views. Billy Graham introduced Fred Schwarz (leader of the Christian Anti-Communism Crusade) to various senators as an 'expert on communist threats'.

In the climate of the nineteen sixties and the early seventies, the stock of the right fell drastically. John Birchers became figures of fun and ridicule in the youth culture. Those who campaigned against the Vietnam war triumphed. Alger Hiss was made a hero of the 'new left', and Richard Nixon, who had played a part in Hiss's conviction for treason, was forced to resign the Presidency. The McCarthy era was mocked in The Front: a film starring Woody Allen and Zero Mostel, directed by Martin Ritt. Allen plays a very small-time bookie who is asked to serve as a 'front' for three of his friends, playwrights who have been blacklisted by the studios for suspicion of leftist sympathies. The film itself is a funny and vicious attack on McCarthyism and the motives of those who 'testified' against others, but the rub comes at the very end when the names of the actors and production team are screened. Under each name (except that of Woody Allen, who was too young) there is 'Blacklisted' and the year of blacklisting. More than any other single item, The Front demonstrated the decline in the status and power of the right-wing. Artists who had been unable to work 18 years before because of their political views (or in the case of many, their ethical views; many people were blacklisted simply for refusing to inform on others) could now wreak their revenge on Joseph McCarthy.

The position of the extreme right is perfectly captured by Norman Mailer:

> a huge indigestible boulder in the voluminous ruminating government gut of every cow-like Democratic administration, an insane Republican minority with vast powers of negation and control, a minority who ran the economy, and half the finances of the world, and all too much of the internal affairs of four or five continents, and the Pentagon ... and nearly every policeman in every small town, and yet finally they did not run the land, they did not comprehend it, the country was loose from them, ahead of them, the life style of the country kept denying their effort (1968:61).

Still possessing vast economic power, but divorced from the dominant culture and from the centre of political power, the conservative Protestants did not die but rather withdrew to develop their own private world. While the centre of the American stage may have been occupied by Johnson's Great Society and the hippies, the conservative Protestants founded or continued to develop alternative institutions. If the public schools were going to teach Darwin's theory of evolution, then the conservative Protestants would found their own schools to teach the creation account. Colleges and universities were established by leading fundamentalists. One of the largest, Bob Jones University, has about 3,500 students (of whom only one or two are black). Oral Roberts has his own university worth some $100 million. Herbert W. Armstrong, the founder of the Worldwide Church of God, has his own college. The creation of a distinctly Christian education system allowed the conservatives to raise their children apart from the permissiveness and promiscuity of the secular world.

Fundamentalist films, books, cassettes, radio and television and live entertainment in the form of crusades and church, all provided an alternative culture. It was in this alternative culture that the germs of the new right were incubated.

In an earlier chapter, I made the point that the nature of the conservative variety of Protestantism made it well suited for presentation through a narrow and superficial medium like radio and television. While the liberal papers and magazines sneered at the florid style of the 'holy roller' television evangelists, the audiences for such a product grew until leading evangelists such as Robert Schuller, Billy Graham, Rex Humbard and Oral Roberts found themselves fronting billion dollar enterprises. In Schuller's case, his success was made public in stunning style with the erection of a massive glass structure which cost $16 million. It is both cathedral, television studio and open air crusade. The walls at one end open up so that those who park in the car park can watch the service from their cars while listening on speakers and headphones; a 'drive-in' church. Humbard, in slightly more modest style has built himself a 'Cathedral of Tomorrow' in Akron, Ohio, at the cost of a mere $3.5 million. Roberts, Graham, Schuller and Humbard all share one thing in common and that is that they have ceased to be 'holy rollers'. They no longer sweat. Roberts has joined the Methodists; Schuller wears clerical garb; Graham preaches to Roman Catholics and has been described by a serious fundamentalist, Bob Jones, as 'doing more harm to the cause of Jesus Christ than any other living man' (Frady, 1979:248); and Humbard preaches an anodyne gospel that seems to be little more than 'Jesus loves you' dressed up in the language of prophecy and the coming end of the world.

There is, however, a new generation of media evangelist and it is this new generation that is involved in the new religious right[1]. Jerry Falwell began his own Baptist church in an old factory in Lynchburg, Virginia, in 1956. He now has a very large congregation, a university with 2,000 students and a television show that is syndicated on 304 stations. Jim Bakker's PTL Club (PTL stands for Praise the Lord) has amassed some $50 million in the first seven years of its existence. Pat Robertson founded the Christian Broadcasting Network (CBN) in 1960 and it now has an annual budget of $65 million. Its flagship programme – the 700 Club – with its chat show format of celebrity guests, born-again politicians and prayer phone-ins, is one of the most popular American religious shows. This new generation of evangelists formed part of the 'new right'. Another element was provided by Anita Bryant. Bryant, a successful singer on the churches, state fairs and conventions circuit, became involved in a campaign to prevent homosexuals establishing themselves as a minority who deserved guaranteed and protected equal employment opportunities. Bryant's 'Save Our Children' campaign, built on the thesis that any legislative protection for homosexuals would undermine the nuclear family, soon achieved its immediate goal (repeal of a particular Dade County statute) and a lot of public notoriety. Anita Bryant was invited to appear on Falwell's Old Time Gospel Hour show on Mothers' Day. She was also sponsored by the Florida Conservative Union whose guest speaker was Ronald Reagan. Her reputation brought with it the inevitable public pressures to adopt stands on other issues and Bryant became associated with opposition to the Equal Rights Amendment (ERA).

The ERA was passed by the Senate in 1972 and would have become part of the Constitution had it been ratified by 38 of the state legislatures. An interesting analysis of the women who campaigned against ratification shows them to be people who believe in a domestic communist conspiracy, who believe that 'big government' is a threat, and for whom the moral state of the nation poses serious problems. For most of them, it is their conservative protestantism that is the main source of their politics. What is important is that, contrary to the expectations of some scholars, the women who campaigned against the ERA were not isolated, disillusioned, ill-educated, poor rednecks. They were well-educated, middle to upper middle class, political conservatives (Brady and Tedin, 1976:574).

The problem with the movement until 1979 was the lack of an organisational centre. This was provided with the formation of the Moral Majority. Howard Phillips, a former Nixon aide and organiser of the Conservative Caucus; Paul Weyrich, a leader of the Committee for the Survival of a Free Congress; the Reverend Robert Bilings, an Indiana Republican; and Ed McAteer, a former Colgate Palmolive marketing man, all joined to persuade Falwell to front a new national movement. The Moral Majority soon grew to claim 72,000 ministers and four million lay members. Groups were established in every state and some $5 million were raised. While these things were important, perhaps the most important success of the Moral Majority was breaking the quietist tradition of conservative Protestantism. The Moral Majority claim that they persuaded four million people to register to vote for the first time. The Reagan organisation estimated some two million new conservative voters but even this total may have been significant in an election decided more by absention than by anything else (Time, 13 October, 1980:42).

The major problem for the new right was to provide some unified focus for the aggression of the WASPs. This was done through the 'targeting' policy. In common with the Religious

Roundtable and the west coast Christian Voice, the Moral Majority developed a score card for members of the Senate and Congress. The card rated their voting on a number of issues dear to the conservative heart; abortion, the ERA, the Panama Canal treaty, trade union legislation, the bussing of schoolchildren, the SALT talks, and so on. In explaining the system and giving instances of how it worked, a conservative said:

> Adlai Stevenson of Illinois is zero family ... meaning if they voted against the interests of the family, if they voted for the homosexual amendment then that would be a black ... If they voted for federal funding of school bussing then that would be against the private rights of the family. Schweicker is 90% family. Birch Bayh in Indiana is zero family. Senator Kennedy is zero family, zero business, zero farm ...

By taking the way a legislator voted on a number of pieces of legislation, an overall score was developed which claimed to identify those who were 'pro-family' and those who were 'anti-family'. On the basis of these scores, 32 leading liberals were selected for 'stopping'.

The targeting system at first sight seems to have been highly productive. Twenty-six of those singled out for the attention of the right were defeated and that number included some leading liberal politicians, among them Goerge McGovern, Frank Church and Birch Bayh. It appears that the right was not too concerned about accuracy in compiling the ratings. Church, for example, has always been opposed to abortion except in very limited cases of medical problems. This did not stop his opponents distributing leaflets accusing him of being a child murderer. Goerge McGovern pointed out the more general weakness of the system; that it divorces how someone votes at a certain time from their more general qualifications as a public servant. It thus produces the incongruity of Florida Congressman Richard Kelly who was given a 100% rating by the religious right, and was then caught on the undercover films of the FBI's 'Abscam' corruption investigation stuffing wads of used dollars into his jacket. A further embarrassment was Congressman Robert Bauman, another hero of the right, with a 100% score and a history of active campaigning against homosexual rights, who was arrested on a homosexual morals charge. Such inconsistencies do not seem to have troubled Falwell and other new Christian right leaders.

In understanding the success of the Moral Majority and the other new right movements it is not enough to appreciate how the ideology they have developed appeals to deep seated values, aspirations and fears of certain parts of the population. Having an appropriate ideology is important in any political victory but one also has to mobilise this ideology. People's discontent has to be converted into political pressure and this brings me to the question of organisation. The backbone of the new right's recent successes was formed by the work of two direct mail specialists, Richard J. Viguerie and Bruce W. Eberle. Direct mailing is a form of communication that avoids the wastage of public advertising. Mass advertising is charged on the basis of the total number of people likely to be reached and this is clearly wasteful if one is sure that only one tenth of those reached will be at all sympathetic to one's message. The method of direct mailing is to acquire the names and addresses of people who are known to be sympathetic to one's cause, perhaps by collecting letters written to congressmen on right-wing issues. With advanced (and expensive) computer technology, lists of people who are pro-guns, anti-bussing, anti-ERA and so on, can be assembled. The machine writes letters to these people and addresses the envelopes. Direct mailing can be used to solicit funds (and the lists can be amended to show only those who responded) or they can be used to prompt public opinion. The method here is to send to some supposed right-winger a standard letter addressed to his or her representative stating a position on some contentious issue. The recipient of this package signs the enclosed letter and posts it on to the congressman who then receives thousands of letters, all supporting one position. Providing the standard letter or a tear-off card is an effective way of orchestrating a protest because it requires far less of the protestor than does a request that they themselves write to their representative. What direct mailing does is to give millions of isolated individuals some political power and influence.

Like the barrow loads of petitions that the anti-slavery campaigners used to pour onto the floor of the House of Commons, the direct mail gives symbolic weight to the claims of its users that they represent a very large number of 'small' people. Whether these 'small' people are being 'represented' by this system or being manipulated is contentious. Although they are clearly influenced by the material that is mailed to them these people are not dupes. Nothing forces them to post the tear-off card. One can only suppose that they feel their own interests to be served by the spokesmen for the Moral Majority.

The 'electronic church' also links very large nubers of small people into a potential movement and a coherent source

of public opinion. The television evangelists do not rely on
the patronage of a small number of wealthy men (as did early
evangelists such as Dwight Moody) but rather solicit small
sums from the millions who watch their shows. They take the
widow's mite seriously and encourage the widows to send it
in. While there are disputes about the size of the audience
for religious television and radio, there can be no doubting
that it is massive. In the build-up to both the Senate
elections and the presidential elections Falwell, Bakker,
Robertson and Robison made no bones about their political
preference. Although they would have lost their charitable
status had they openly supported any particular candidate,
the evangelists got round this problem by supporting a set of
positions and attacking politicians who did not vote the
right way on key issues.

Explaining the Rise of the Right

No change as radical as the rise of the right from its
defeats in 1960 and 1964 to its major electoral victories in
1980, can have causes that are less than complex. For
simplicity's sake I will consider the question under the
separate themes of organisation and appeal. A great part of
the success of the right was due to its superior organisation
and technology. The left had simply not come to terms with
the new media, especially direct mailing. This in turn is
partly explained by differences in wealth. The right had
both its traditional wealthy patrons and its income from the
millions of people contacted through the electronic church
and direct mailing. The left had neither wealthy patrons (or
to be more accurate, had far fewer patrons), nor means of
encouraging their mass following to make donations. In
addition, changes in the electoral funding laws, drafted by
the liberals to prevent the corruption of Nixon's
fund-raising, actually worked against the left. Under the
new laws, corporations could not make contributions to
campaign funds; but then nor could unions. Individual
members or corporation hierarchies could make donations and
being considerably wealthier than the typical union official
were likely to give far more to the right than the left
received from its traditional allies. Thus while the changes
in the law restricted the income of the right, they cut the
left's funds dramatically.

But good organisation is not enough. One has to explain
why so many people felt that the message of the Moral
Majority about the spiritual decline of the country should
have had so much appeal. The answer to that question can be
found in comparison with the rise of McCarthyism.
McCarthyism coincided with a period of threat to American
power and pride. The Russians had nuclear weapons. The

response to that threat had three components; it promoted a nativist longing for some earlier period of better fortunes (which involved invoking the symbols of that period such as 'God'); it brought a directly religious response from some believers ('this is God's judgement for America's sins'); and it promoted a search for a traitor. This third element is important because it is the saviour of the logic of populism under threat. The populist claims that he speaks for the common people, the masses rather than the elite. His is the view of the silent majority. Yet he usually wishes to argue that his beliefs and values are being threatened and undermined. His is thus the voice of the majority which is also a beleagured minority, and the simplest way of reconciling this contradiction is to postulate an internal traitor. For the McCarthy era this traitor was internal communism; 'pinkoes' within America who had betrayed the majority of Americans. For the Moral Majority the threat has come from inflation, the raising of the price of oil, Soviet expansionism, the loss of the Vietnam war, and Iran's taking of American hostages. The traitor is no longer the communist but the permissive modern cosmopolitan. It is a small unrepresentative group of liberal intellectuals who have ruined America for decent Christian family life and capitalist free enterprise. The Moral Majority's analysis of the state of America and the causes of that condition was clearly acceptable to many conservative Americans.

This is not the place to engage in sweeping analysis of the politics of the modern world but it is worth noting that the rise of the new right in America has coincided with discernible shifts to the right in many other European countries; the notable exceptions being France and Greece which were already exceptions in not having been liberal and social democratic administrations during the late sixties and early seventies. It does seem that the obduracy of problems like poverty and racial prejudice, and the fact that progressive income tax and other measures of social reform have not produced the 'great society', either in the United States or Europe, have lessened public faith in the liberal agenda.

The Right in Power

It is easy to exaggerate the influence of the fundamentalist right-wing. For many commentators, the active involvement of 'born again' Christians in politics, and the possibility that they might win, caused an over-reaction and a lack of critical judgement about the importance of this movement. In the first place, the presidential election was lost by Carter, not won by Reagan. It was the abstention of those who had previously voted for Carter that cost him his second term in office. Only a quarter of those who did not vote for Carter the second time transferred to Reagan. In the second place, it is clear that that the fundamentalists do not have the influence of more traditional class-based Republican groupings. Reagan's nomination of George Bush as vice-presidential running mate was known to be unpopular with the Moral Majority, who thought Bush too liberal, but it stood. While the arch-conservative Baptist lay-preacher Jesse Helms has increased his power in the Senate he is still defeatable. His favoured candidate for the post of Head of State Department Office of Human Rights and Humanitarian Affairs, Ernest Lefever, was rejected by Democrats and liberal Republicans because of Lefever's known support for some of the less pleasant Latin American dictatorships and his opposition to majority rule in Rhodesia. In September of 1981, the Senate voted by a narrow majority against Helms on the question of military aid to El Salvador. The House was considering a motion that suspended all military aid to the military dictatorship until that regime guaranteed elementary human rights. Helms tried to add an amendment changing the stated conditions into 'goals' which El Salvador should claim to be working towards, but this move was blocked by the Sanate.

Another blow to the right wing came from their President. One of Reagan's first major public appointments was that of Sandra Day O'Connor to the Supreme Court. O'Connor was immediately opposed by Falwell and the Moral Majority as being 'soft' on abortion and being for the Equal Rights Amendment. This in turn produced disagreement within the right. Senator Barry Goldwater, a man sufficiently right-wing to have been supported by Bob Jones and Carl McIntire, is reputed to have rejected the Moral Majority position with the statement: 'I thing every good Christian ought to kick Falwell in the ass! (Sunday Times, 12th July, 1981). The Senate endorsed the appointment by a record 99 votes in favour and none against.

SCOTLAND AND ULSTER; THE WEARING OF THE ORANGE

The political situation of religion in Ulster and Scotland is clearly quite different from that obtaining in America. The extreme right in the United States has traditionally had a number of target populations; Catholics, Blacks, leftists and Jews. The fact that Roman Catholics were only one possible target and that they themselves were involved in attacks on the other targets loosened the tie between conservative Protestantism and the extreme right. In Scotland and Ulster the division between Catholic and Protestant has so dominated politics that Protestant political activity has been concerned almost exclusively with anti-Catholicism. As has already been mentioned in the second chapter, there was a period when the Presbyterians in Ireland were persecuted by the Episcopalian ruling class, and when it seemed possible that the Presbyterians could join Roman Catholics in a nationalist republican movement but the view that prevailed among the Presbyterians was that their interests were best served by Loyalism. Under the leadership of Henry Cooke, the theologically conservative Protestants aligned themselves with the Episcopalians (practically, by joining the Orange Lodges; Roberts, 1974) and they even defended the Church of Ireland during the debate about the 'established' status of that Church. The argument of Cooke and others was that it was better for the state to support a Protestant church (even though it was the wrong one) than to support none at all. From about 1880 onwards then, ministers of the Presbyterian Church were to be found either actively promoting Loyalism and Protestant political and economic domination or simply taking it for granted.

Again, one has to be wary of overstating the connection. Although there were obvious connections between religious belief and political position, especially over the central question of partition and the Ulster state, it does not seem to be the case that the theologically conservative Protestants are dramatically more involved in such politics than are liberal Protestants and those one might call nominal or ethnic Protestants. Rather the Protestant church as a whole gave mostly passive support to the dominant Protestant politics, with only a small number of individuals such as the Reverend Martin Smyth, the Grandmaster of the Orange Lodge, and the late Reverend Robert Bradford M.P., being actively and publicly involved. The two small Presbyterian Churches that are notably conservative in their religious belief reject the political involvement of clergymen. The Reformed Presbyterian Church still maintains a position of non-involvement in the political process of the state. Its members do not stand for office, even at the level of local government, and they do not vote. The Evangelical Presbyterian Church, formed this century by members of the Irish Presbyterian Church, who felt that it was becoming too liberal, has no specific doctrine that requires such quietism but its members by and large, take no part in politics and those who do vote normally vote for the Official Unionist party rather than for the party of the Reverend Ian Paisley.

Ian Paisley and the Use of Tradition

Where theologically conservative Protestantism is actively coupled to right-wing politics is in the biography and party of Ian Paisley[2]. Since he founded his own church, but especially since the beginning of the current period of 'troubles', Ian Paisley has built himself and his party into a major spokesman for Protestant opinion in Ulster. Standing on a populist platform, Paisley has gradually undermined the hegemony of the old official Unionist party and the Orange Order. This success is often explained by reference to Paisley's 'charisma'. This is totally misleading. When Max Weber popularised the concept of 'charisma' in his types of leadership and authority, he had in mind the type of leader who overthrows previous traditions (1970:245-248). He had in mind the Christ figure who asserts 'It was written ... but I say to you ...'. 'Charisma' was used to describe the relationship between a revolutionary leader who claimed no authority other than that of his own person and his own revelations, and his followers.

Moses David, the leader of the Children of God, is a charismatic leader. He claims divine revelations as the source of his pronouncements and is bound by no tradition, not even that established by his own previous revelations (Wallis, 1981). He is quite prepared to deliver a new judgement that contradicts those he gave earlier. Far from being charismatic, Paisley is traditional. His claim is that he is the best spokesman for a tradition. He offers no new revelation but insists that his positions are the old ones.

What gives Paisley the edge over other poeple who claim to speak for Unionism and Loyalism is that his rhetoric, his actions and his whole demeanour reinforce his political positon. In his sermons he makes constant reference to Knox, Calvin, the Westminster Confession, Charles Spurgeon, William Nicholson and Hugh Hanna. In his political speeches he uses references to Carson in order to locate himself as the defender of the faith, religious and political. A good example of his presentational style was exhibited at the opening of the first directly elected European parliament in Strasbourg on July 17th 1979. The news that evening reported that Paisley had publicly (and apparently offensively) protested that the Union Jack was being flown upside down (which is a distress signal). As a result of his behaviour, he was asked to leave the auditorium. To many on the mainland of Britain and to many of the Ulster middle classes, this display was seen as further confirmation of the boorish and ill-mannered nature of the man. But to many working class and lower middle class people in Northern Ireland this was seen as further confirmation that 'Big Ian' would always stand up for what he believed in. It is this style, the hearty loud Ulsterman who speaks his mind, that gives 'added value' to Paisley's Unionism. It is not so much that his politics are pronouncedly more conservative than those of the Official Unionists, but rather that while his style amplifies his symbols, the rhetoric and manner of the Official

Unionists tends to diminish their presentation of similar messages. One of the leaders of the Official Unionist Party, Enoch Powell, is English. Most of them have an air of statesmanship, of being concerned more with Westminster politics than with Ulster politics, of being just a bit too refined. This allows Paisley constantly to paint them as potential traitors, and leaves him with the appearance of being the reliable Unionist, the one man who will not compromise.

It is in the mastery and deployment of the symbols of Unionism that Paisley's religion is important. Even for those who take no active part in worship, religious symbols have a powerful attraction. Certain hymns remind us of our childhood; mothers sitting by the fireside and so on. Even in the secularised culture of mainland Britain, such symbols can produce nostalgia for a previous age (which is part of the attraction of television programmes like Songs of Praise for those who have not set foot in a church throughout their adult lives). In the Ulster context such traditional attachments are still stronger for two reasons. In the first place the culture is not as secularised as that of the mainland. More people still go to church and those who do not are still close to a specifically religious culture. Secondly, there is a more realistic connection, for Protestants, between the ties of their youth and their parents' time, prosperity and the strength of religion. People on the mainland may connect the smell of churches, the sound of sermons and the tunes of the Wesleys with their childhood and with an earlier time when the world was more simple and prosperous. Protestants in Ulster can make the same connections with the added element that they were actually more propserous and more secure in the days of the old times. Thus even for those people in Ulster who are not members of Ian Paisley's Church, who do not share his theology, Paisley's religious beliefs and activities do add to his appeal in that they represent an earlier period when the shipyards were working and when the Protestants ran Ulster from their own parliament at Stormont.

Ideology and Compromise

One of the main differences between the politics of the American fundamentalists and the conservative Protestants in Ulster has already been mentioned. While the right-wing in America has attacked a number of targets, the Ulster conservatives have been concerned almost exclusively with Catholics. It is worth remembering that Protestantism of any form is, in essence, an anti-Catholic movement. The Reformation was against the Catholic Church and its teachings. This is worth recalling if only to be clear about the relationships between Protestant religious beliefs, anti-Catholicism and 'bigotry'. Liberals tend to associate anti-Catholicism with 'bigotry', as if attacking the Roman Catholic Church was some sort of aberration produced by a diseased mind. Such an implication requires a profound ignorance of the nature and origins of Protestantism. After all, the identification of the Pope with the anti-Christ is not a novel invention of Ian Paisley; it is contained in the Westminster Confession of Faith of 1647 which is still recognised by most Presbyterian Churches as being their doctrinal standard. Given that Protestantism recognises the existence of heaven and hell, and asserts that the teaching and practics of the Catholic Church are a hindrance to attaining salvation, it is hardly surprising that Protestants are opposed to Catholicism. The assumption that it is the open anti-Catholicism of Paisley and not the ecumenical stance of liberal churchmen that needs to be explained, can only be made by someone who knows little, and understands less, of Protestantism.

My point is the simple one that opposition to the Catholic Church (and all other faiths that are not conservative Protestant) follows quite simply from a commitment to Protestantism as it has been conceived until this century. Now this opposition may be further promoted by a personal hatred for Catholics. Protestant organisations and spokesmen are usually at pains to point out that they oppose the system of Catholicism out of compassion for individual Catholics (who will, unless they get 'saved', burn in eternal damnation). They state that they do not condone prejudice or discrimination against individual Catholics. In practice, this distinction is sometimes hard to identify. The Orange Order, for example, asserts that it is not antipathetic to individual Roman Catholics, but the lyrics of the songs sung by Orangemen display a less than charitable attitude toward 'taigs' (see Roberts 1974:57). Thus bigotry may be involved in the reasons why any particular conservative Protestant is anti-Catholic but it is certainly not the case that Protestantism was somehow ecumenical and tolerant towards Catholics until it was distorted and led astray by a small group of bigots. Anti-Catholicism is the heart of Protestantism. It was Catholicism that the reformers were trying to reform!

That the border and state question has remained the centre of Ulster politics has kept anti-Catholicism to the fore in the concerns of the extreme right. This does save people like Paisley from having to make difficult decisions on alliances with right-wing Catholics. The American fundamentalists had this problem once they turned from Catholics to what appeared the more pressing evils of blacks, Jews and communists. Although there are some exceptions, the

dominant response of the fundamentalists has been pragmatic.
They have normally worked by taking their religion as the
source of certain political attitudes. Those attitudes in
turn generate positions on specific issues and the
fundamentalists have then been prepared to support any
politician who shares those positions, <u>irrespective of his or
her reasons for so doing</u>. They have thus been willing and
able to work with people who are not 'born again' provided
that they are saying the right things about the issues.
Anita Bryant, in her Save Our Children anti-homosexuality
campaigns, enlisted the support of conservative Catholic
priests and Jewish Rabbis[2]. The leadership of the new
Christian right contains fundamentalists, Catholics, Jews and
Mormons. The most obvious example of pragmatism was in the
fundamentalists' choice of their 1980 Presidential
candidates. Jimmy Carter and John Anderson both have been on
the record as being 'born again' for a long time and both are
active in theologically conservative churches. Ronald
Reagan's claim to be a 'born again' Christian is a recent one
that comes suspiciously close to coinciding with the rise of
the fundamentalist right as a potent political force. He is
an ordinary member of the Presbyterian Church of America, a
broad liberal denomination that is affiliated to the World
Council of Churches. For all their suspicions about his
spiritual state, the fundamentalists supported Reagan because
he had the right positions on the issues. It is interesting
to note in passing that the one fundamentalist leader who is
on record as dissenting from the general support for Reagan
is Bob Jones Jnr who, in an address to Paisley's congregation
shortly before the election, attacked Reagan for remaining in
an apostate denomination, and suggested that perhaps God's
will for America was another term of Carter 'to bring the
country to its sense' (Jones, 1980).

In contrast to this pragmatic approach, Paisley
maintains more of an ideological purity. He can afford to,
given that all of the issues on which he might well cooperate
with right-wing Catholics (such as abortion and
homosexuality) are so much secondary to anti-Catholicism and
Unionism. That he is more pragmatic, however, than Pastor
Jack Glass, a man who in many senses is his Scottish
counterpart[3].

Jack Glass was born in Dalmarnock, Glasgow, and
converted at the age of 11 in a Salvation Army Sunday
School. During his period of national service, he was
influenced by two young Calvinists who had 'sat under' Dr
Martyn Lloyd-Jones (the pastor of Westminster Chapel and a
major influence on the Inter-Varsity Fellowship and those
churches and organisations now connected in the British
Evangelical Council). When he returned to Glasgow Glass
could find no church that combined the two features that he

now felt were essential; the doctrines of Grace (as Calvinism is sometimes called) and adult, rather than infant, baptism. Glass considered the Baptist ministry and studied at Glasgow University for what was intended to be the first year of his theology course. After a year he split from the Baptists over their continued membership of the British Council of Churches and he persuaded the Free Church of Scotland to let him study at their college as a private student. There at least he found the doctrines of Grace, if not the adult baptism. After three years of theology training, Glass began his own ministry in Glasgow. In 1968, three years after his launch, he had a congregation of about 40 people meeting in a hall rented from the corporation. He was an early supporter of Ian Paisley, whom he invited over to speak, long before his reputation was known outside Ulster and evangelical circles. Like Paisley, Glass was prepared from the first to demonstrate against liberal Protestantism, ecumenism and the Roman Catholic Church. In 1966, Glass went with Paisley, a Strict Baptist minister from London called Brian Green, and three others to Rome to protest at the meeting between Archbishop Ramsey and the Pope.

Shortly before this, Glass, Paisley and Green had united in an organisation they called the Return to the Reformed Faith Council of Great Britain and Ireland. The doctrinal statement that the three signed was a classically Calvinist document that committed the signatories to 'the doctrines of Grace' and belief in 'the total depravity of man ... sovereignty of God in election ... definite atonement ... effectual calling' and 'the final preservation of the saints'.

In 1969, in reaction to the 'troubles' in Ulster, Glass formed the Twentieth Century Reformation Movement as the political arm of his church. In a press report he likened this to Paisley's Ulster Constitution Defense Committee, the organisation that preceded the Democratic Unionist Party, and called it 'a political organisation influenced by religion' (Glasgow Herald, 10th January, 1969). From that point onwards, Glass was involved in protests and marches to support the Loyalist position in Ulster. In 1973, he attacked the government White Paper plans for a power-sharing executive in Ulster. When the Ulster Workers Council brought down the Executive, Glass arranged a celebratory rally with the Vanguard party and spoke on the same platform as Glen Barr of the New Ulster Political Research Group (the 'think tank' of the Protestant paramilitary Ulster Defence Association). By this time, however, Glass and Paisley were no longer united in their defence of Protestantism.

Paisley and Glass parted company over the doctrines of Grace. Paisley's father had been a Calvinistic Baptist; he had been educated at a Welsh Bible college and at the time he signed the basis of the Return to the Reformed Faith Council, he was clearly willing to identify himself with an overtly Calvinist document. Paisley's visits to the United States had, however, brought him into contact with leading fundamentalists, the Bob Jones family in particular, and he became increasingly influenced by fundamentalism. Paisley was given his doctorate by Bob Jones University and his eldest daughter is an undergraduate there. Although Paisley still uses the language of Calvinism and makes the same reference to men like Spurgeon, he also accepts practices such as the 'altar call', which is rejected by Calvinists because it suggests that men have free will to choose their own salvation, when the Calvinists believe that God predestines people to be saved or damned. The actual break between Glass and Paisley was prompted by the actions of Bob Jones University in sanctioning some students for Calvinist teachings; Glass now regards Jones as 'probably America's leading anti-Calvinist'. Glass believed that Paisley had abandoned his Calvinism in order to be acceptable to the large and lucrative 'holy roller' circuit in America and severed all links with him. Since then, Glass' Scottish Protestant View has often contained attacks on Paisley, once describing him as 'Mr Facing Both Ways'. The realignment can be seen in affiliation with international organisations. Paisley was initially associated with Carl McIntire's International Council of Christian Churches, which could be described as generally Calvinist. He is now part of the World Congress of Fundamentalists, which is a mostly Arminian grouping. In an interesting piece of usurpation, Paisley recently revived the British Council of Protestant Churches, which was the title of the organisation that linked Paisley and Green to McIntire's ICCC.

Throughout his career Paisley has been more willing to engage in pragmatic compromise than has Glass. Although he makes constant reference to separation from apostasy and claims to be a separatist, he is more willing to cooperate with unbelievers. He resolves the problem to his own satisfaction by drawing a dividing line between religion and politics. In the religious sphere, he asserts the Pauline principle: 'Be ye not yoked together with unbelievers. Come out from among them and be ye separate' (2 Cor. 6:14-18). The political sphere is different; here one can work with anyone who is on your side. Paisley has been willing to work with some very dubious people. To what degree he has been involved with those who have been willing to undertake acts of terrorism and violence is not clear. What is known is that people convicted of terrorist offences have sometimes blamed Paisley for their involvement. One man, charged in 1966 with the murder of a Catholic is reported to have said 'I am sorry that I ever heard of that man Paisley or decided to follow him'[4]. In the same year, the director of Paisley's Puritan Printing company, who had been the secretary of the Ulster Constitution Defence Committee, was jailed for conspiracy to provide explosives. In 1969, Paisley and his then associate Major Ronald Bunting were instrumental in organising opposition to the People's Democracy march, and when their supporters brutally attacked the marchers at Burntollet Bridge, both men were jailed for incitement. While he is on record often enough as condemning individual acts of violence and aggression, he has always been willing to use the threat of armed Protestant resistance in order to dissuade the British government from dealing with the Republic. Thus Paisley is clearly willing to work with 'unsaved' Protestants on the 'dark side' of his political career; he is also willing to work with unbelievers in his Democratic Unionist Party and his legitimate political life involves him in constant association with 'sinners'. As a member of the European Parliament, Paisley has worked with John Talyor and John Hume (a Catholic!) on matters of interest to Ulster. In 1973, he joined with the Vanguard Party, the UDA and the Orange Order in the Loyalist Action Group to oppose the power-sharing Assembly.

The difficulty with the division of politics and religion is in placing organisations like the Orange Order and the Apprentice Boys. To someone hoping to speak for Ulster Protestants (the same is true for Scotland) it is these organisations that are important because they provide the focus for 'Protestant' identity and symbolism for those who are not active church members. Paisley resigned from the Orange Order in 1961, when an Orange Mayor of Belfast

168

attended a Roman Catholic funeral. He revived the Independent Orange Order, an organisation formed in the last century by working class Protestants who resented the gentry's domination of the Order. He is also a member of the Apprentice Boys, a fraternal organisation that celebrates the actions of the Londonderry Apprentices who closed the gates of the city to the Catholic Army of James and thus created another potent symbol of Protestant resistance to the forces of Rome. Although both Orange Orders and the Apprentice Boys claim to be religious bodies with definite salvationist principles, in practice most of the members are not theologically conservative Protestants and most are not religiously active.

Glass rejects the Orange Order because it purports to be religious and yet fails to uphold the standards of the 'true religion'. His father left the Orange Order because it allowed alcohol consumption. Although he was in the youth wing until his father left, Glass was never a full member of the Order and he now campaigns against its failure to translate its rhetoric into practice by the use of strict membership criteria. In more recent years, Glass has refused a place on the Scottish Constitution Defence Committee, a pan-Protestant Loyalist organisation including Orangemen. The comparison between Glass and Paisley is interesting. Both are conservative Protestant clergymen who have founded their own churches. Both have been eloquent in the defence of the Ulster state and in their oppositon to anything that seemed to undermine the Protestant nature of the British state. Yet while Paisley has built himself a denomination with some 10,000 members, Glass leads only three small congregations in Scotland. (He is a popular preacher in Ulster and has turned down an invitation to pastor an Ulster congregation). The party that Paisley founded now has three members of the Westminster Parliament and about half of the total Unionist vote in Ulster. Paisley himself came first in the election for three members for the European Parliament. Glass stood for election in the Bridgeton ward of Glasgow in 1970 and polled an honourable number of votes. The Labour candidate was elected with 11,000 votes; the Tory polled a mere 3,000; the Nationalist candidate received 1,500 votes; and Jack Glass was supported by just over 1,000 voters. But since then he has played little part in politics and by 1975 was unwilling to cancel his Sunday evening service to picket the Roman Catholic Bishop Daly preaching in St. Giles Cathedral. Although we only have his word for it, it does seem that Glass has deliberately turned down invitations from rank-and-file Orangemen to play a role in Scottish Loyalism similar to that of Ian Paisley in Ulster. His own account is that his religion comes first and that involvement of the sort that Paisley practices would necessarily involve him in compromises, and in being seen to be associated with people who do not support the doctrines of Grace. While he would condemn such people, Paisley is not averse to being supported by drunken hooligans whose Protestantism seems entirely encompassed by the fortunes of Glasgow Rangers football team. Glass does seem to be averse to this support and certainly his rejection of Protestant fraternal organisations such as the Orange Lodges for promoting Sunday drinking clubs has effectively prevented his emergence as the leader of the West of Scotland's working class Protestants. Clearly there are massive differences in the environments in which the two men work, and the issues that confront them and their potential supporters. Working class Protestants in Glasgow have issues other than ethnicity and religion which concern them, as the massive vote for Labour in Bridgeton shows. The politics of class, and even the politics of Scottish nationalism, come before the politics of Loyalism and Orangeism. For that reason Glass is located in a far less promising environment. In terms of rhetoric, he is also hampered in that there is far less of an accepted tradition of clergymen in politics in Scotland than there is in Ulster. But one has the feeling that there is still sufficient there for Glass to work on, had he the desire to compromise his Calvinism. Were he a fundamentalist or any variety of conservative except Scottish Calvinist, he would be less committed to maintaining separation from nominal Protestants who invoke the language of salvationist religion, but who do little to provide the substance of a religious Protestantism. In the end, maintaining a consistent 'witness for the faith' transcends other considerations. Jack Glass's conservative Protestantism, which produced his Loyalism and Orange political posture, prevents active involvement in fruitful alliances with the mass of Loyalist Orangemen.

To return to the general theme of pragmatism, one can see the influence of two principles in the way in which these different types of preachers related their religion to their politics. In the first place, there is the degree of conservatism in their religion. The most conservative preachers tend to be the most separatist and the ones least willing to make the sorts of alliances and compromises that political activity requires. Hence among the fundamentalists, Bob Jones, one of the more conservative, was least involved in the politics of the new right because he would not have been prepared to work with conservative Catholics and Jews. It was also the case that the more Calvinistic, the less likely to be pragmatic. Of the leading 'holy rollers', one who was noticeably absent from the Reagan campaign was Carl McIntire. No doubt this was due in part to his abrasive personality and unwillingness to be involved in anything he cannot dominate, but it also results from a

theology that is more conservative than that of Falwell and
Robison. The second principle concerns the centrality of
anti-Catholicism. Pragmatism is <u>necessary</u> for American
preachers who wish to have political impact because the
issues that concern the right-wing are issues that transcend
religious boundaries. On the issues of bussing, abortion,
the Equal Rights Amendment, and homosexuality, conservative
Catholics and Jews share the same stances as conservative
Protestants and, given that Catholics have long been
superseded by blacks and communists as the enemy within, the
obvious interests of all are served by cooperation (if only
at the minimalist level of not attacking each other's
favoured candidates). Pragmatism is much less important for
Paisley. He only has to be able to cooperate with 'unsaved'
Protestants; the question of working with Catholics simply
does not arise. The degree of compromise that is required
here is small and is legitimated by futher appeals to the
long tradition of ministers who have been active in politics,
but it is a type of compromise greater than Glass can allow.

ENGLAND AND SOUTH AFRICA

Although such a pairing might seem unusual, there is one good
reason to consider South Africa and England together: the
question of the South African regime is one of the things
that concerns the right-wing English evangelical.
    The question of the relationships between politics and
religion in South Africa is simplified by two things.
Firstly, as is the case with Ulster, there is only one
political question. In Ulster that question concerns the
participation of Catholics in the Ulster state. In South
Africa, the question concerns apartheid and there is a fairly
straightforward division among its churches. Put at its
simplest, the Afrikaner Dutch Reformed Churches are
pro-apartheid and the English-speaking churches are opposed
to it. There are three Dutch Reformed Churches. The largest
is the Nederduitse Gereformeede Kirk (NGK) with about 1.5
million adherents; almost 40% of the total white population.
The Nederduitsch Hervormde Kirk (NHK) has some 250,000
adherents and the Gereformeede Kirk (GK) has about 113,000
white followers (Buis, 1979). The Dutch churches also have
the largest black membership, with black congregations
organised into separate synods. Given the role that these
churches have played in creating and sustaining the Afrikaner
identity, it is not surprising that they should support the
government policy on the separation of ethnic groups. Again,
not surprisingly given the conflict between the Afrikaners
and the English-speaking settlers, the English-speaking
churches are by and large opponents of the policy of the

government. The Anglican church in particular has an honourable history of opposition to discriminatory policy. Many of its leaders - Clayton, Reeves, Gonville ffrench-Beytagh, Trevor Huddleston, David Russell - have earned themselves censure, harassment and expulsion for their stand. The old and new dissenting churches - Methodist, Presbyterian, Baptist, Congregationalist - also oppose apartheid. In terms of organisation, the churches affiliated to the South African Council of Churches (SACC) are hostile to apartheid. In 1961, the last of the white Dutch churches left the SACC in response to criticism about the government's action in violently suppressing demonstrations in Sharpeville. The black synods remained, however, and their continued membership of the SACC is a useful corrective to the assumption of a direct and simple connection between Calvinism and conservatism.

Calvinism and Afrikaner nationalism are not logically or necessarily connected[5]. The connections are socio-psychological. There are some basic ideas in Calvinism which 'make plausible' some ideas in nationalism. The notion of an 'elect' is one such idea. The idea that only a small number of people are destined to be saved can reinforce the determination of a small ethnic minority and the Old Testament with its theme of a special covenant between the people of Israel and God can provide the imagery for full-blown justification of political action with a developed worldview of the ethnic group as the 'new Israel'. The Afrikaners used it in South Africa; the Protestants have used it in Ulster; the Puritans used it in America. The belief that one is part of an 'elect' can lead to the persecution of outsiders. As Max Weber said of the Puritans:

> This consciousness of divine grace of the elect and holy was accompanied by an attitude toward the sin of one's neighbour, not of sympathetic understanding based on consciousness of one's own weakness, but of hatred and contempt for him as an eneny of God bearing the signs of eternal damnation (1976:122).

But as Weber makes clear, the contempt for others is not the only possible reaction to a belief in one's own election. Apartheid is not the result of Calvinism but rather the result of a particular interpretation of Calvinism that was worked out in Holland in the early years of the 19th century, where an aristocracy combined with the lower working class to oppose the modernising tendencies of the liberal middle classes of the period. This populist alliance produced an ideology known as 'Christian-nationalism' in which Calvinist beliefs were used to justify conservative nationalist politics. This movement was introduced into South Africa through its impact on the small schismatic Gereformeede Kirk and the Kirk's main supporters, the Doppers. The Doppers were the most conservative and educationally backward section of the Boers and - until their policies triumphed in the platform of the National Party - they were ridiculed even by other Boers. The rhetoric of Christian-Nationalism confirmed the isolationist tendencies of the Doppers. The success of the National Party under Malan and the rise and consolidation of Afrikanerdom 'confirmed' Christian-Nationalism, and the increasing hostility of the rest of the world to South Africa since the 1950's has reinforced the Afrikaners' self-image as a new Israel.

The important point about religious legitimation is this: while the Afrikaners use Calvinism to justify their politics, the <u>Black</u> Dutch Reformed Churches use the same doctrines to legitimate their desire for a more equal society. There are committed, articulate and well-educated Calvinists on both sides of the apartheid debate. As I shall make clear in my conclusion to this chapter, there are values and ideas in conservative Protestantism which have an affinity with certain basic conservative political ideas but this political conservatism is not inevitably produced by the religion. Conservative Protestantism, when allied to certain interests and interpreted in certain ways, <u>may</u> produce or reinforce conservative politics, but it does not have to do so.

The South African regime has always sought alliances with conservative groups in other countries. In the late forties there were exchanges between J.D. Vorster and Ed Bundy's Church League of Aerica. Bundy spoke in favour of the South African government in South Africa and sponsored Vorster when he visited America. Bundy has since maintained these links and his organisation has sponsored Fred Shaw. Shaw was a minister in the Methodist Church in South Africa when he founded his Christian League of South Africa organisation and wrote an attack on the ecumenical movement and the World Council of Churches, entitled <u>The Fraudulent Gospel</u>. The book, which argues that the WCC is a communist front, enjoys wide popularity in British conservative circles. In America it is distributed by Bundy's Church League. Shaw has also been promoted by the large American evangelistic organisation, Campus Crusade for Christ (which numbers amongst its supporters, Roy Rodgers and Nelson Bunker Hunt, the texas oil millionaire and Council member of the John Birch Society).

In the investigations of the running of the South African Ministry of Information that followed charges of corruption made by ranking officials against each other, it became clear that Fred Shaw's organisation had been heavily funded by South African government money. It might seem that this money was a poor investment because Shaw has contacts only with the extreme right in Britian and there is little evidence that many conservative Protestants are connected with extreme right-wing organisations. The one exception is Brian Green, the colleague of Ian Paisley, who is secretary of the re-constituted British Council of Protestant Churches. Green was actively supported by the National Front when he stood for parliament in the early seventies and seems to have acted as their chaplain on a number of occasions[6]. But while there is little direct impact of South African propaganda on identifiable Protestants, the investment does seem to have paid off in terms of reinforcing a generalised dislike of the World Council of Churches among Christians who would not dream of being associated with the National Front or the British Movement.

The World Council of Churches (WCC) is anathema to conservative Protestants because of its cooperative ecumenical attitude towards non-Protestant churches. Since the early sixties, it has opposed racism and apartheid and in 1971, it launched a specific 'Program to Combat Racism' (PCR). One of the best known actions of the PCR was to give sums of money to various African liberation movements. Although the funds were specifically designated for humanitarian projects and not for the purchase of arms, political conservatives were quick to characterise this as 'money for terrorist guns'. This confirmed the view of many religious conservatives that the WCC was evil and that support for continued white supremacy in Rhodesia and South Africa was the 'christian' policy. There is also the more mundane but no less important point that many British evangelicals have relatives in Rhodesia and South Africa. Thus, support for South Africa became an issue (in as much as any political matter is an issue) for English evangelicals. The PCR is also used by conservatives in other contexts. Paisley and others in Ulster argue that the WCC supports terrorists; the WCC contains liberal churches; the IRA are terrorists; therefore liberal Protestantism is similar to the IRA and the two must be opposed simultaneously.

Nothing I have said this far should be taken to imply that English evangelicals are by and large racists[7]. It is true that many with a history of involvement in the missionary movement have a very paternalistic approach to blacks and it sometimes happens that people slide from thinking that 'these people cannot fend for themselves' to thinking 'we will stop these people fending for themselves'.

In the main, however, evangelicals show greater practical concern for the well-being of the poor in other countries through their medical missionary work than do the liberals and marxists who berate their conservatism. The politics of the conservative Protestant in England are the politics of a non-doctrinaire conservatism. As one person put it: 'I suppose I've always tottered a little to the right of centre and preferred a paler shade of blue to any other political colour, but I have to face up to the fact that no party has the answer to our moral and social decline' (Fulness, 12:2).

In general the evangelical attitude is one of conservatism with a small 'c'. This can be seen in the view of trade unions. Most evangelicals are against them. A recent book published by the Inter-Varsity Press has the title A Better Way: The Case of a Christian Social Order. Sir Frederick Catherwood, life-long supporter of the evangelical student movement and European MP, argues for a socially concerned laissez-faire capitalism. For all the title, there is little in this book that is particularly 'Christian'. Catherwood is against trade unions which, he feels, improve the lot of their members at the expense of other workers; 'one man's wage increase is another man's price increase' (1976:116). However, the Inter-Varsity Press has also published Deeks' Shopfloor Christianity (1972), which is a plea for greater involvement by evangelicals in trade union activities.

A majority of evangelicals would probably support the idea that unemployment is caused by the sinfulness of those who are without work, but there are some who oppose government policy because they see it as producing conditions that hinder conversionist work. It is not surprising that evangelicals should agree with the Daily Telegraph's editorials on the 'loss of will to work' (a regular columnist of the Life of Faith happily quoted from and endorsed one such editorial). In contrast to Catholicism and Judaism, Protestantism is a highly individualistic faith. Although one finds occasional periods and places in which the fate of a nation is interpreted in an almost Jewish way as embodying the will of God (the cases of Ulster and South African Protestantism discussed above are examples), the basic thrust of Protestantism is the need for a covenant between each and every individual and God. Whole communities and groups cannot be saved; only individuals who personally accept that Christ died for their sins can be saved. Thus there is, right at the heart of Protestantism, an individualistic emphasis which produces a dislike for collectivism, and this is reinforced in the present day by the avowed atheism of many Marxist governments. The rampant hysterical anti-communism of American fundamentalists has never been popular among English evangelicals but there is an anti-communist consensus that is reflected and reinforced by the support for organisations that 'smuggle' Bibles into communist countries. The leader in this field is Brother Andrew who, from 1977 to 1980, wrote a regular column for <u>Life of Faith</u> on the problems of Christians in Eastern Europe. Exiled church leaders and evangelists from these countries are popular speakers on the English evangelical circuit. Many evangelicals then take the state of the churches under present-day communist countries as being representative of the future of religion under any leftist government. 'Communism' becomes 'socialism' and, for some evangelicals, is taken as an accurate description of the form of welfare state found in post-war Britian. One <u>Life of Faith</u> reader wrote: 'Fruits of Socialism? Drug-addicts, hippies, murderers, thieves, liars, muggers in ever-increasing numbers - fostered, encouraged, and well-cared for at the expense of those who work!' (April, 1978:7).

Unlike the American fundamentalists, however, few English evangelical leaders offer clear political direction to their followers. When a political lead is given, it tends to be in a subtle form and one good example of this is the 'prayer request'. Many missionary organisations use a letter listing matters for prayer as a means of communicating with and among their supporters. Whether or not God really does answer such prayers is something that the social scientist must remain neutral about, but it is clear that such requests 'work' in the sense of forming the opinions of the followers and directing their actions. For example, asking one's followers to pray earnestly about the financial problems of one's mission is tantamount to asking them for donations and, if they feel so disposed, has the required effect of producing income. Now one national prayer fellowship, Intercessors for Britain, exists to persuade people to pray for the moral and spiritual state of the nation. It is clear from their judgements on the health of the nation which political party they support:

> party politics apart, we now have a very dangerous position in the House of Commons, for not only is Mr Foot an avowed atheist, but also a member of a society which is determined to destroy Christianity in Britian ... Let us pray for the conversion of Mr Foot to Christ. At least the battle lines are now being more tightly drawn, and this enables us to be more specific in our prayers (quoted by Hutchings, October, November, 1981:20).

The implication is clear. If Foot does not convert, vote Tory. In case the message escapes his readers, Eric Hutchings, who reprinted the above in his Hour of Revival Association prayer letter, adds that 'those who take this news bulletin in Canada, USA, Africa and Australia should specifically be concerned about this and the added threat of Mr Wedgewood Benn's contention for the Deputy Leadership which might well circumvent the authority of an elected government'. Finally, for those who have missed the boat altogether, Hutchings adds a request for the following specific prayer: 'Lord, save Britain from Totalitarian Atheistic Dictatorship (masquerading as democracy)'.

Another prayer fellowship, this time for women, the Lydia Fellowship, shares similar views although it is less specific and articulate about them. The association of conservativism and piety is strengthened in this case by the fact that Mrs Sylvia Allison, the wife of a junior minister in the Thatcher Tory government, is a supporter of the movement. One of the fellowship's leaders claims that Mrs Allison said 'our prayers open windows and doors and our prayers go right into the Houses of Parliament' (Lydia, 1980).

These examples have been offered to show the political attitudes common among evangelicals. The important point to note is that, although the typical position is one of conservatism, this is not made a vital feature of orthodoxy. Life of Faith, for example, while publishing letters like the one above from the person who associates all problems with a welfare state, and reprinting Daily Telegraph editorials, also published a letter from a Christian socialist. While the Inter-Varsity Press published Catherwood's apologia for laissez-faire capitalism, it also published Shopfloor Christianity. While many evangelicals support Brother Andrew in his Bible smuggling escapades, the Bible Society and the Evangelical Alliance eschew such methods, preferring to confine themselves to working through the governments of Eastern European countries.

One remains with the interesting question of direction of cause in the relationship between religion and politics. Are the English evangelicals attracted to their religion because it conforms with their already existing political values, or are they attracted to political conservatism by their religion? Perhaps the two sets of beliefs are arrived at independently of each other? I am not sure what one would have to do to answer that question. Probably the best that can be said by way of general statement is that there are fundamental themes which are 'at home' in both political conservatism and conservative Protestantism. Both are individualistic rather than collectivist. Both are elitist. Both have a tendency to dichotomise. The world is dealt with in terms of simple categories, often reduced to opposites; good and evil; sinner and saved; patriot and traitor; black and white. A similar simplicity can be seen in the solutions offered by both conservative Protestants and political conservatives to what troubles them. Complex and difficult problems such as the contractions in the world economy are solvable simply by the right attitude and a willingness to kick out the communists and communist sympathisers who are selling out America. Unemployment will disappear when the unemployed get saved and acquire the will to work.

At this stage I am making two points. Firstly, there are values (such as individualism) that are common to both conservative Protestantism and political conservatism. Secondly, there are ways of looking at the world (such as dichotomising) that are common to both. These common elements make the two cultures 'natural' allies. One still has the problem of the origins of these values and the status of the 'ways of looking at the world'. In particular, there is the difficult but crucial question of whether or not conservatives (of the theological and political type) have some peculiar psychology, some abnormal personality, which explains their attraction to such ways of thinking about the world. The next chapter will examine the thesis that conservatism in religion and politics is attractive to a certain type of personality.

Notes

1. The new Christian right in America is discussed in detail in my pamphlet <u>One Nation Under God</u>? which is available from the Department of Social Studies, The Queen's University of Belfast, Belfast, BT7 1NN.

2. David Taylor has been doing doctoral research on Paisleyism which will be submitted to Queen's University in 1983. I am grateful to David Taylor for a considerable amount of information on Ian Paisley and for long hours of conversation on protestant politics.

3. Militant Protestantism in Scotland is the subject of my forthcoming book <u>No Pope of Rome: anti-Catholicism in modern Scotland</u>.

4. Pastor Jack Glass informed me that Paisley disputed the accuracy of this statement at the time it was made. Whatever the truth of that particular attribution, Paisley's actions in forming a paramilitary 'third force' in the aftermath of the assassination of the Reverend Robert Bradford, MP, makes it clear that he is prepared to countenance paramilitary co-operation with 'non-saved' Protestants.

5. Irving Hexham's doctoral thesis (1981) is very useful on this topic.

6. It ought to be noted that Green's racism was not supported by Paisley and Glass. Glass disagreed with Green over this issue during their association and rejected overtures made to him by Martin Webster of the National Front in the early seventies. The Orange Lodges have also been generally opposed to attempts to tack fascist and racist themes on to their traditional loyalist politics. (<u>Glasgow Herald</u>, 12th February 1980).

7. While the late Eric Hutchings was opposed to majority rule in South Africa, Dick Saunders makes a point of only preaching to integrated crusade audiences. Historically, the Evangelical Alliance has opposed racism; when it was founded slave owners were barred from membership (Smith, 1965:4). In the United States, some of the more conservative evangelists still exhibit racism. Bob Jones University has very few black students but Oral Roberts University is integrated and even when he was still a supporter of right-wing politicians, Graham went out of his way to schedule an

integrated rally in Selma, Alabama in 1963, at the
height of the south's racial violence.

8 Conservative thought: science and conspiracies

The belief that religion is in decline in the modern world is now so commonly held as to be almost an orthodoxy. There are disagreements between writers about precisely what this means. Some critics of the secularisation thesis argue that we have unwittingly fallen for a mythical picture of the religiosity of previous ages[1]. They point to instances of scepticism and doubt in the medieval ages as proof that things have really not changed that much. Such an argument is misplaced. The pre-industrial world may have had its lonely free-thinkers and the Church may have had trouble getting its people into the buildings for the services. As Laslett says: 'much of their devotion must have been formal, and some of it mere conformity. But their world was a Christian world and their religious activity was spontaneous, not forced on them from above' (1965:71-72).

The decline of religion has many roots. As with the discontinuation of anything, an important part of the explanation concerns mobility. The very fact of movement breaks up the social worlds that supported a particular belief system and provides people with opportunities to reconsider their commitment to particular beliefs and practices. The rapid urbanisation of Britain, with millions leaving their rural homes, played a large part in eroding traditional religious loyalties. However, social dislocation only accounts for the opportunity to change; it does not itself explain why that change actually occurred.

To do that, one must account for the decline in plausibility of religious beliefs. A full account would obviously be beyond the scope of this discussion, but certain elements can be mentioned. One of the main consequences of industrialisation is the intrusion of rationality into many spheres of the social world. Bureaucratic organisation, mass production, an extensive division of labour, and a constant search for increased efficiency produces a type of consciousness in which predictability and technical manipulation become dominant. There is no place for the supernatural in the modern productive world and where religion does retain influence, it is in the residual area of personal and interpersonal problems; what Bryan Wilson calls 'the recessive side' of human activity (1976:7). Religion remains strongest in those parts of our biographies furthest away from the world of industrial production: our private lives. At the social level, it remains strongest in those geographical areas most remote from the centres of industrialisation, the Highland and Islands of Scotland and the Appalachian mountains of the United States - and in those groups least involved in modern production; amongst women rather than men and the traditional professions rather than the industrial working class (Berger 1973).

To talk of the 'recessive side' of life is not to suggest that we are in any way the intellectual superiors of our forebears with their 'primitive' supernatural beliefs. One of the mistakes of some accounts of secularisation is the arrogant and misguided thesis that we have educated ourselves out of Gods. Some scholars (eg. Symondson 1970) give far too much influence to scientific thought and the intellectual problems of that small minority who (a) knew about Darwin and (b) believed that his work made Christianity redundant. To explain a phenomenon as widespread as secularisation one must go beyond the anxieties of one small section of the society and look instead at the general features of consciousness in that society. From the above description of the consciousness of the modern industrial society one might expect that traditional religions that continued to advertise the supernatural would provoke crises for their followers in requiring beliefs and casts of mind that are difficult in modern society. One would expect that (a) religion would decline, and (b) those religions which were most supernaturalist - that is, most committed to traditional beliefs and practices - would suffer the most rapid and severe decline. If liberal Protestantism is 'impossible' in the modern world, then surely the Neanderthal-like conservative variety should be even more vulnerable.

In this book so far I have attempted to show by looking separately at different aspects of conservative Protestantism why, far from the expected vulnerability, one finds every appearance of increased resilience.

I now want to look at the rather abstract question of consciousness, of thought styles, of ways of understanding the world. I will argue that the concentration on the conflict between science and religion over questions like the age of the earth and the origins of species has blinded people to an underlying similarity between the thought styles of the conservative Protestants and a certain type of science. In a discussion of science, medicine, devils and conspiracies I will argue that, in a curious way, the conservative has a rather modern method of thinking about the world.

EVANGELICALS, SCIENCE AND MEDICINE

I had always supposed that science and conservative Protestantism were fundamentally opposed and research supports such a supposition (Stark 1963; Vaughan et al 1966). For that reason I was surprised to find that there were scientists and doctors who were evangelicals. That there were any scientists at all who continued to believe that Genesis 1-12 was an accurate account of the origins of life struck me as interesting; when I began to pay attention to this phenomenon I found that there seemed to be more scientists in evangelical circles than one should expect on the basis of random sampling. That is to say, there were even more scientists in evangelical circles than there should have been if their science had no impact at all on their religion. Thus, not only was science not an obstacle to conservative belief; it almost seemed to be an encouragement. In his history of the Inter-Varsity Fellowship (IVF), Johnson mentions 16 important patrons; one was in business, three were theologians, four were university teachers in various disciplines and eight were involved in some branch of medicine (1979:235). In the period from 1900 to 1910 when there was much unfocused discontent in the SCM about its liberal direction, the strongest protests came from the medical students. The Christian Unions in London, Edinburgh, Birmingham, Bristol, Newcastle, Sheffield, Aberdeen, Glasgow, Belfast and Dublin were all started by medical students. Of the first eight pamphlets published by the IVF, three were by Sir Ambrose Fleming FRS and three were by Professor Albert Carless FRCS. Two of the most influential senior men in the world of the Inter-Varsity Fellowship were professors of medicine: Rendle Short of Bristol and Duncan Blair of Glasgow. Martyn Lloyd-Jones, minister of Westminster Chapel and a leading conservative preacher, was a consultant before he felt called to the ministry. There seemed to be an over-representation of medical men and scientists in the IVF.

One can think of a number of explanations for this affinity. In the first place, one can note the connection between medicine and missionary work. The short-lived Students Foreign Missionary Union (a forerunner to the successful Students Volunteer Missionary Union; see Bruce, 1980), founded in 1899, drew its members almost entirely from the medical students of Edinburgh and London. Many of these students were studying medicine because they intended to become missionaries and medical skills were, and still are, valuable assets for foreign missionaries. This connection is less important now because it does not account for the fact that the number of conservative evangelical medical students is considerably higher than the number who become missionaries. This observation does not, of course, totally invalidate the missionary argument; it may well be that some students feel that they want to become missionaries, study medicine for that reason but then are either not accepted for missionary work or change their minds.

A more general version of the same theme would argue that the connection between medicine and evangelicalism lies in the notion of <u>service</u>. Here the suggestion is that the young evangelicals choose a career which allows them to serve other people because service is an important consequence of their faith. Again, I would acknowledge that there are elements of this in the biographies of many evangelicals, but it cannot serve as an adequate explanation because it does not tell us why evangelicals in particular, rather than Christians in general, experience this motivation to pursue a life of service.

These two suggestions concern the idea of vocation. There is another possible explanation and that concerns status and prestige. As I have already noted, conservative Protestantism is located on the edges of the modern world, in the geographical peripheries of industrial societies.

Where it is found in the centre of a society, it is usually the creed of the bourgeoisie. There are exceptions of course. Some circumstances (such as political divisions in Ulster) provide the working classes with reasons for maintaining some of their allegiance to conservative Protestantism, and some varieties of Protestantism (the first generation holiness churches, for example) appeal to the lower classes, but by and large it is a faith for the comfortable. There are two obvious reasons why this should be the case. I made the point in the last chapter that there are clear possibilities for evangelicalism to be used to legitimate and justify conservative politics. But it is also possible for the type of religious belief to raise the standard of living of its adherents. As Wesley noted of his

Methodists, ascetic religion often improves the status of its members. If one abandons the sins of the flesh, one saves money. Thus evangelicalism both appeals to those who are middle class _and_ raises those from lower socio-economic positions into the middle class.

Medicine offers a worthwhile professional career and hence appeals to the evangelical parent as the right sort of job for the children. It may well be that it is the status and prestige of medicine that makes it popular among evangelicals. There is one further point. Medicine has status but it is also 'serious'. Evangelicals have a profound distrust of the frivolous, which distracts from the glorification of God. Before the second world war, books with titles such as Twenty reasons why I will not dance were commmon evangelical fare. Even today one finds people such as the Christian Herald reader who took seriousness to the extent of reading only certain part of the paper:

> 'I have read the Christian Herald for nearly fifty years. In all that time I have read the religious parts avidly, but have never read the fiction serial or short story yet. I am the most avid reader I know, loving books such as those ... which are based on personal experiences ... To sum up, more solid food and less desserts' (Christian Herald, 31st January, 1981).

These themes – vocation, status concerns, seriousness – go some way to explaining the appeal of medicine and science for evangelicals, but the following quotation, in which Douglas Johnson talks about the attempts of the evangelical students to produce a doctrinal basis, suggests another explanation:

> 'some of the leading clergy and ministers of London were repeatedly put on the spot by deputations of ... students who were suspicious of any ambiguity when reference was being made to the authority of the Bible or the central facts of the Gospel. They wanted no stone left unturned in order to find out what was _essential_' (1979:112 emphasis in original).

The reference to a distrust of 'ambiguity', 'central facts', and that which is 'essential' suggest a certain style of thought. In the rest of this chapter I will look at certain features of the way in which conservative Protestants think about the world, suggest that such a 'cognitive style' has some major similarities with the cognitive style of basic science, and then examine the psychological literature that goes on from that to argue that conservative Protestants possess a special type of personality.

COGNITIVE STYLE

We are all in the business of making sense of the world around us. We all need to know whether this or that is true or false. Thus, although epistemology - the theory of knowledge - is the professional concern of only a small handful of people, we all have an epistemology. We all have means of finding out 'what is going on' and what it means. I want to describe how these things are done by conservative Protstants. There is, of course, the possibility that we all have more than one cognitive style, and there are within conservative Protestantism some differences in epistemology. The following characterisation does, however, capture the essence of the cast of mind that distinguishes conservatives from liberals.
    For the evangelical and the fundamentalist, the Bible is the supreme source of knowledge. Every idea in the world is either derived from the Bible, or must be in accordance with it. To understand the epistemology of the conservative Protestant is to understand how the Bible is perceived and used. My second preliminary point concerns two broadly alternative positions on the problems of perception and understanding. There is firstly an empiricist view in which the person doing the perceiving and understanding adds nothing to the process. The mind is seen as 'the initially empty and passive receptor of impressions or "ideas" through the organs of sense' (Benton, 1977:22). The world simply flows into the mind of the observer. In such a view the meaning of an object is contained in the object itself. Trees are trees by virtue of containing within them 'treeness'. An alternative theory of meaning would argue that we are not passive in perception. Perception is an action in which we confer meaning on objects. We do not 'perceive' so much as create an interpretation.
    We interpret in terms of our interests and schemes. What things mean depends largely on what we intend to do with them. In such a view, the same object could mean a number of diffrent things to different people. To use Blumer's example, a tree will not mean the same thing to a lumberjack, a botanist, a painter and a fugitive from a search party (1966:10-12).
    The cognitive style of the conservative Protestant is very much like the empiricist view of the world. They do not

186

see themselves as 'interpreting' the Bible. Instead they believe that 'the semantic effect of these words as directly formed in the mind of the English reader formed a direct and not a mediated transcript of God's intention' (Barr, 1977:210). The Word literally carries its own meaning. The reader does not interpret or confer meaning on the words; they simply leave impressions on the mind, like animal tracks in mud. This particular view of perception explains the common conservative obsession with one particular translation of the Bible, the King James (or Authorised) Version. Ian Paisley's church announces its use of the Authorised Version on its sign. American fundamentalists believed the alternative Revised Standard Version to be a product of a Jewish conspiracy (Gasper, 1963:72). Paisley sees modern translations as products of Popish plots. Even single word changes produce a strong conservative reaction (Roy, 1953:208). This preservationist attitude to specific verbal forms is not shared by liberal Protestants. The liberal is already committed to an interpretive epistemology. Meaning is at least partly conferred by the perceiver. Hence what the Bible means for different cultures will be something quite different. This is the justification for 'modernising the Gospel' and 'demythologising' theology. The following preface to a book, calling itself <u>A Modern Restatement of the Christian Faith</u>, offers a clear example of such a rationale:

> the scriptures ... are a translation into English of certain preserved Greek manuscripts that gave an early interpretation of the life and teachings of Jesus. But since these manuscripts were written considerable research has been made, not only into the validity of their contents, but also into the identity and authority of the writers ... the result of this has been that we now find it impossible to put full reliance on what they wrote ... to overcome this it will be necessary to restate the revelation Jesus made so that it will be in keeping with the findings of research but also to show that it is in harmony with modern knowledge (Duff, 1963:7).

There are, of course, disagreements amongst conservatives about how literal to be on any particular occasion. They allow that some passages should be read as myths and then disagree over precisely which ones. They clearly differ in their interpretations of certain stories, but that does not alter the basic fact that <u>they deny that they are interpreting</u>. They maintain that the meaning of the Bible is fixed and accessible to a common-sense reading. This process of reducing the role of the reader in understanding what he is reading can be taken to some curious extremes. On some occasions the reader is placed in such a passive position tha the Word is imbued with apparently magical powers of action. In a recent sermon in Oxford, Billy Grahan offered an epistemology in which the reader was almost irrelevant. He challenged the members of the audience simply to sit down with the Gospel of John, read it through five times, and then ask the Lord for salvation. It no longer matters what previous interests and interpretations might be brought to that reading; just read, ask and be saved! Understanding is not a problem; reading is all. It is only then a short step to believing that it does not even matter whether the potential convert can read at all! And sure enough, such a view has been voiced by Anita Bryant, a leader of the anti-Gay Rights movement in America: 'I've heard wierd stories all over the world about where missionaries have gone to odd places and where people have been saved just by seeing a torn page of the Bible on the floor' (1978:92). It is not being suggested that this view is common among evangelicals but it does show, in its extreme form, the lack of an interpretive element in their view of perception.

Patterns: Creation or Discovery

One of the most common themes of suspense novels is paranoia and the creation of a spurious order. The victim begins to perceive trends and patterns. Isolated events are interpreted in a larger scheme and are taken as confirmation of the existence of that order. In the best writing of this form, one is never sure whether there is 'really' a conspiracy out there in the world or whether the apparent pattern is the production of the mind of the paranoid victim. Thomas Pynchon's The Crying of Lot 49 has as its central character a woman who 'discovers' the existence of a slightly sinister organisation which acts as an alternative postal system. Pynchon never gives us overwhelming evidence for the existence of the organisation; the evidence is always merely suggestive and the riddle is never solved. The novel ends in such a way as to leave the reader undecided as to whether the order of the conspiracy actually existed outside the head of the central character, or whether it was produced by an ordering mind linking together things that were 'really' isolated. For the philosopher this is a persistent problem. When we think that we perceive a pattern to events, is that pattern being discovered or are we creating it? The conservative Protestant believes in a creator God who made the world and all that it contains. Hence for the conservative, the patterns are usually seen as being 'out

there'. The liberal Protestant tends to the second view;
that apparent order is a product of our patterning minds
rather than the discovery of a real order. This is why the
liberal tends to remove the God from out there and replace
him with some sort of inner spirit. The old supernatural
deity is replaced by 'being truly human', or 'the essence of
our being'; things that are inside rather than outside us.

One feature of an epistemology that sees meaning as
being embedded in objects is that it allows an <u>arithmetic</u>
system of imputing importance. I will try and make this
clear by making a comparison with an interpretive worldview.
The person with an interpretive style may see a certain
object in one light one day because it is slotted into one
particular scheme or context, and then see the same object in
quite a different light the following day when another scheme
or context is in play. The meaning of any object or event
can vary from scheme to scheme and context to context. This
variation prevents one making the simple association that
this plate is the same as that plate. To give a very simple
example, it is obvious that what a word means is largely
dependent on the sentence and general context in which it is
used. 'Plate' is a good case, for it could refer to things
we eat off, surfaces coated with light sensitive material (a
photographic plate) and so on. We can see the variation with
the meaning of words quite easily but actual objects and
events have the same potential to vary according to context.
My wife in bringing me a cup of tea may be acting out of
innocent affection, preparing me for a nasty surprise, or
apologising for some earlier display of ill-feeling.

In contrast, an epistemology that asserts that the
meaning of things is embedded in them has no problem with
contextual variation. Each thing in the world is a finite
unit with its own significance. This allows one to assume
equivalence between units (this plate is the same as that
plate), and to perform simple arithmetic exercises such as
addition. This in turn allows people to work out the
relative importance of things by simply counting them up.
This is precisely what one finds among conservative
Protestants (though I am sure that they are not unique in
this). Things that are mentioned twenty times in the Bible
are seen as twice as important as things that only get ten
mentions. In one sermon Billy Graham demonstrated the
importance of bread by telling the audience that the word
'bread' was used nineteen times in one chapter of John's
gospel. In another sermon Graham said 'the end is coming.
Jesus predicted it 318 times in the New Testament' (Coomes,
1973:76). Another fundamentalist preacher said there are
'now twenty million people practising demonology'. The
fascinating feature here is the use of <u>exact</u> numbers. Graham
is not content to argue the importance of a concept from its

189

significance for him, or its place in the tradition of reformed theology, or even from its prominence in the scriptures. He has to know the number of times it appears and by implication, something that appears 318 times is more important than something that only appears 280 times.

The Campus Crusade for Christ evangelistic material shows just such a view of the world. One booklet says that there are _four_ spiritual laws (not three or five). Once one has the hang of those, one is told that there are _four_ steps to 'being filled' (with the Spirit). Now dividing the complex mass of reality into easy-to-handle packages is something that is done by all of us, and even liberal preachers will present their material under some such division but my reading of evangelical and fundamentalist literature convinces me that there is a critical difference between the liberal's use of such devices and the way in which the conservative employs them. For the liberal this sort of ordering of material is a convenience, a technical device that is chosen for its end: ease of comprehension. In the hands of the conservative this device signifies a particular mode of thought; a particular way of thinking about the world and a particular way of divining knowledge about the world. While the liberal sees _himself_ dividing up the world into convenient units, the conservative sees himself _discovering_ the real and actual divisions that already exist.

One further feature of the evangelical cognitive style is reification: treating abstractions as if they were 'things'. It follows logically from a belief in a creator that one views the world as 'thing-like', as 'created', and if one attributes to one's creator the dynamic force not only for the material world but also for the social, and reintroduces the miraculous into the world, then one has the basis for reifying what could be seen as human and social productions. Reification thus parallels the move to empiricism in that it takes away from the actor and the perceiver the creative _dynamic_ force, and locates it elsewhere. This removal of action and meaning from the human being is the necessary condition for the massive simplification one finds in 'extremist' belief systems. A feature of any strong belief is its ordering of the complexities and ambiguities of the world into simple categories (which is the basis of dogmatism). For example, the American radical right does not conceive of Maoism, Yugoslavian cooperatives, Italian 'Eurocommunism', Russian expansionism, Albanian retreatism, and the social democracy of the British Labour Party; they are all subsumed under the umbrella of 'Communism'. The capital letter is frequently used, and is important. It is the clue to a process of simplification and reification that makes a multi-faceted reality comprehensible by making it into a discrete entity whose homogeneity is recognised by regarding it as a proper noun.

Of course the above applies to all of us at some times, and to most of us much of the time. My argument is that it applies more often and more acutely to conservative than to liberal Protestants. The case could be reinforced with many more examples from the literature and conversation of conservative evangelicals, were there scope. Instead I will mention one aspect of evangelical thought that both illustrates my point, and in its popularity, offers evidence for my argument. Despite its obvious and well-known philosophical flaws, the argument from design – if there is a watch, there must be a watchmaker – is still a very popular evengelical argument for the existence of God and a reductio-ad-absurdam of its converse – it is silly to believe that an organ as complex as the human brain could be an accident – is frequently used as a device for showing the ludicrous nature of atheism. Almost all of the 200 or so evangelicals I have interviewed have at some point asked me how I can explain the order in the world without a creator. An anonymous medical professor said:

> Of course accurate factual knowledge is important ... but having said that, we often forget the fascination of studying the structure and function of the human body for its own sake. We have no sense of wonder because we have no sense of creation. Our thinking has been so dominated by a theory of purposeless forces working on chance mutations that we fail to see the beauty and plan behind the mechanism. When we are discussing the incredible chemical reactions that happen in every cell ... we are not inventing them ... but we are, in Kepler's words 'thinking the thoughts of God after him' (CMF, 1980:7).

The major flaw in this sort of argument is given by Hume in the same discourses in which he presents the argument from design; there is always the possibility that the apparent 'order' we see in the world is not actually 'out there', but is rather a product of our interpretation. Two men might disagree over some plants in a clearing in a wood; one sees a 'garden' and thus infers a gardener, the other sees only chaos. By this use of the argument from design the evangelical constantly reaffirms an essentially empiricist epistemology that, in the final analysis, seperates him from the liberal and modernist believer who has an epistemology that is interpretive.

Any doubts on this point could be assuaged by an extensive review of conservative literature, but such a display would be tedious and would not add to the main point of my argument. To close this section I will refer to two statements from conservatives. An article in the Free Presbyterian Church of Scotland magazine says 'Dwell upon the facts recorded in the New Testament' (James, 1980:236) and a creationist scientist said 'Evolution is a faith, not a fact' (Barker, 1979:5). The conservative Protestant world is one of hard reality, facts that can be separated from theories, meanings that inhere in the objects themselves and hence are not imposed by our interpretations.

So described, the epistemology of the conservative seems to be very similar to the classical rationalism of 19th century science. It is true that the central beliefs relate to the realm of the supernatural, but the underlying cognitive style of conservative Protestantism seems to have a deep resonance with empiricism and rationalism. The mistake in previous analyses of the conflict between science and religion has been to take the continued existence of the supernatural in conservative thought to be a sign of mysticism. Far from being mystical, the conservatives think about the world in a style similar to that of routine natural scientists. George Marsden captured this feature of conservative thought well in describing it as 'supernatural empiricism': 'Far from emphasising the irrational, fundamentalists characteristically presented their faith as being the exact representation of biblically revealed matters of fact for which could be claimed the highest positive standards of scientific objectivity' (1977:138).

Herbert W Armstrong, founder of the Worldwide Church of God, said of his magazine: 'the purpose of Plain Truth is to inform, to challenge, to stimulate thinking, checking and proving what you believe ... listen without prejudice, check, verify, PROVE – and then believe waht you find PROVED' (Plain Truth, October, 1981:1). Armstrong here expresses a theory of knowledge identical to that of a Baconian natural scientist, in which advance is made by collecting enough 'facts' to verify a theory, which then becomes part of an accumulating body of true knowledge. At least one reader seems to share such an approach. In his general comments on the magazine, he wrote 'All is well-written, and the logic of your arguments I find quite acceptable (I have an analytical mind)' (March, 1981:29).

To return to the starting point of this discussion, I think I have done enough to show the basic symmetries between the cognitive style of conservative Protestants and the epistemology common to an old-fashioned natural science. The cognitive style is both evidenced in, and reproduced by, the teaching styles of these enterprises. Both are transmitted to neophytes as an authoritative body of accepted 'facts'; a basic canon that has to be acquired (this is especially true of the science components of medical degrees). My case is that these similarities are normally overlooked in a concentration on the conflict between the content of propositions about the world. It is true that the evangelical student will, in the course of study, comes across statements which offend. Any study of biology is bound to bring the evangelical into contact with evolutionary ideas, but these can be handled by mastering the creation science literature; there are 'antidotes' to harmful propositions. What would be more damaging to the evangelical would be to be confronted with an alternative cognitive style, a different way of thinking about the world; antidotes are not so readily available here. Such a confrontation does not arise, for underneath the surface conflicts there is a basic resonance between the cognitive styles of medicine and traditional natural science on the one hand, and conservative Protestantism on the other.

CONSPIRACY THINKING

I now want to take up a point raised in the last chapter: the popularity of conspiracy thinking among conservative Protestants. The world of the conservative abounds with plots. Anita Bryant believes that the hostile media reception given to her campaigns against various homosexual groups was the result of a conspiracy by homosexuals in the media. The television preacher, Jim Bakker, sees organised groups of liberals, communists and perverts behind every part of the modern world he dislikes. For Ian Paisley, it is Rome that is the coordinator, the moving hand. In the period leading up to the first direct elections to the Parliament of the European Economic Community (an election which was, incidentally, won by Paisley in Northern Ireland), Paisley delivered a series of sermons on 'The Common Market Prophetically Considered' in which he argued that the EEC was a plot by the the Catholic Church to dominate the Protestant countries of Europe. One of his proofs was the name of the document that laid the basis for the EEC: the Treaty of Rome. For Paisley, the IRA and the Catholic church are almost identical: 'the Roman Catholic Church's objectives and the objectives of the Provisional IRA are one and the same' (Protestant Telegraph, August, 1979;2). An early pamphlet on the Jesuits argues that the whole of the ecumenical movement is a Jesuit plot. Furthermore, he asserts that the Jesuits are 'really' pagan and as evidence for this says that the IHS sign of the Jesuits (Jesus Homum Salvator) really stands for Isis, Horus, Seb. Like Bryant, Paisley attributes unfavourable media coverage to an insidious conspiracy with the BBC 'riddled with the Romanists, absolutely riddled' (Guardian, 9th September, 1980).

Florid conspiracy thinking can be found in the views of Robert Welch, the founder of the John Birch Society (Grove, 1961). Every change in the world that can be interpreted as being against the interests of America and laissez-faire capitalism is attributed to an undifferentiated body of 'communists'. Welch's discovery of communist traitors went further than Senator Joseph McCarthy's revelations; Welch believes that Eisenhower was a communist spy. Catholics rank with communists as the right's favourite conspirators, and Jews are frequently invoked as powerful underminers of that which conservative Protestants hold dear. Of course, the notion that all of one's problems are the result of 'International Zionism' is not novel. For centuries, the Jews have been used as scapegoats, and although the so-called Protocols of the Elders of Zion were exposed as forgeries within months of their publication, they are still sold, bought and believed in by many conservative Protestants.

In addition to the conspiracies that are attributed to major ethnic, political and religious groupings, there are also interesting conspiracies that are thought to be the work of secret societies such as the Masons and the Illuminati. This latter organisation was formed in 18th century Bavaria as a secret educational order by a young university teacher. The Illuminati transmitted what would now be regarded as rather unremarkable egalitarian and republican ideas. Much of the ritual and mythology was borrowed from the Masonic tradition (Roberts, 1974;136-7). There is no evidence that the Illuminati were ever influential or that they continued into modern times, but this does not stop them figuring in conspiracy mythology. Not only do people attribute influence and power to them, but others (such as the anti-rock music ex-Druid evangelist John Todd) claim to have been members. As prime-movers in a conspiracy, the Illuminati do seem more plausible than the Masons, if only for the reason that nothing is known of them (probably because they no longer exist). If nothing is known, then anything might be known. In contrast, the Masons seem poor conspirators. The activities of the Masons are only too well known. They operate a fraternal self-help organisation which occasionally has considerable local influence and power, as was demonstrated in the recent Italian government corruption stories involving the P2 lodge. Knowing that the Masons are involved in discrimination in business dealings and in seamy financial affairs makes them unlikely candidates for the world-dominating aspirations that conspiracy theorists attribute to their bogeymen. Nevertheless there are many conservative Protestants who are willing to see the Masons in this way. Such a view is also common among Roman Catholics (the Catholic Church has always been more actively opposed to the Masons than have the Protestant Churches); which raises the fine irony of the conservative Protestant's favourite candidate for conspirator status believing that it is being undermined by a secret conspiracy!

Finally one might note that not all those conservative Protestants who believe in conspiracies have actually arrived at a clear understanding of who it is that is doing the conspiring. One often finds vague references to 'forces' that are never unambiguously identified. Thus Eric Hutchings could ask for prayer about civil unrest and ask whether: 'the fighting in the streets etc. is financed by some foreign power?' (January/February, 1981), without being more specific about the identity of the power. He probably meant the Soviet Union, but he might well have had Libya or some other Islamic state in mind. In other writings, the belief does not go beyond the suspicion that things are not as they seem; that there is some hidden purpoe and meaning to events; that there is more to reality than meets the eye, and that the 'more' in question is active, conscious and deliberate.

Conspiracy thinking is simply one form of a style already mentioned which assumes that there are underlying patterns to the confused mass that is social reality, which are the results of the actions of some conscious force. Such thinking is sometimes accompanied by the belief that there are special techniques that will allow access to this underlying and normally hidden reality. There are ways of finding out what is 'really' going on. For someone like the average John Bircher, the knowledge is not especially esoteric. Once one has read Robert Welch's writings and realises that there are communists all around, then one has the knowledge to see the true state of affairs. But in some cases the method for gaining true insight is decidely esoteric. The popular English evangelical magazine <u>Life of Faith</u> published a letter from a reader whuch showed that the name 'Kissinger' could be converted into the number '666'. One takes each letter of the alphabet and assigns it the numerical value of the next ascending multiple of six. Thus A = 6, B = 12, C = 18, and so on. The separate letters of 'Kissinger' are then given the appropriate number, and the total adds up to '666'. The writer suggested that this meant that Henry Kissinger would somehow be instrumental in the hastening of Armageddon (<u>Life of Faith</u>, January, 1980:5). This reasoning is not, of course, typical of the English conservative evangelicals. The next issue of <u>Life of Faith</u> contained two very humourous responses. But although not typical, this mode of reasoning is common among conservative

Protestants, especially among those who are influenced by the attempts of millenialists to divine the meaning of the apocalyptic parts of the books of Daniel and Revelations.

The Occult and Spiritualism

Conspiracy thinking consists of attributing inordinate power and implausible motivation to an unlikely (and usually non-existent) agent. This definition, of course, involves the judgement that there is, in fact, no such unified body as 'Communism' that does the things that Welch attributes to it, and that judgement may turn out to be wrong. What distinguishes conspiracy thinkers from the rest of the world is that they attribute power where others do not; they attribute conscious motivation where others do not; and they regard as 'agents' things which the rest of us regard as abstractions. Conservative Protestants appear to those of us who do not share their views to take things like communism too seriously. Most of us would recognise that the term 'communist' covers a vast array of groups who rarely agree on anything and who rarely act in concert; when they do act in concert, they do not sweep before them all the social orders because they do not have sufficient power. Most of us would have similar reservations about the conservative Protestant's concern about the occult and spiritualism. For the same reasons that they do not take the supernatural parts of 'normal' religion seriously, liberal Protestants and atheists do not take the occult seriously. The common reaction to Satanism and the 'black arts' is to treat such things as the pursuits of the eccentric, and to psychologise its impact, so that there might be concern about the effects of black magic on the mental stability of the practitioners, but there is little expectation that these techniques will actually 'work'. In contrast, conservative Protestants tend to take the occult very seriously. The topic is commonly the subject of lengthy articles in the evangelical press, and there are many books that warn evangelical parents of the dangers of allowing their children to have contact with even the more 'legitimate' fringes of the occult, such as Halloween. One writer says:

> 'in my experience, which agrees with biblical teaching, I have found the following to be occult activities which can lead to involvement with evil spirits ... the use of charms ... astrology ... fortune telling ... yoga and kung fu ... fetishes ... levitation ... drug addiction and alcoholism' (Dearing, 1978:24).

As with secret societies, the willingness to believe in the efficacy of occult practise is matched by the presence of those willing to claim that they were effective satanists and witches. The already mentioned John Todd claims to have been a leading Druid. Doreen Irvine claims to have been a witch and a good one at that: 'my ability to levitate for four or five feet was very real ... killing birds in flight after they had been let loose from a cage was another feat I performed as a witch. I could make objects appear and disappear' (1973:94).

It might appear that much of the above - especially the case of divining meaning by a code based on multiples of six - undermines my earlier argument about the fundamental resonance of conservative Protestant thought with the cognitive style of natural science. I would argue that it is a mistake to see conspiracy thinking as something magical or pre-logical. Far from it, such thought can be seen more accurately as a 'perverted' positivism; empiricism taken to extremes. Billy Graham said: 'mathematics has its inviolable rules, formulas and equations; if these are ignored, no provable answers can be found ... Music has its rules of harmony, progression and time ... to break the rules is to produce discord ... to ignore the laws of music is to make no music' (Christianity Today, 15th October, 1956).

What Graham misses is that, for mathematics and music, the rules and laws are social products and are culturally confined. The 'laws' of trigonometry are elaborate tautologies that are 'true', not because they accord with the real world, but because they are correctly deduced from the theorems. The question of 'proof' is irrelevant. Likewise the 'laws' of music are human conventions which could be different (and actually are different in different cultures). Having said that, Graham's statement is useful as an example of the cognitive style of conservative Protestants. Where they see patterns, and where the pattern could be seen as either 'really' existing out there in the world or existing in our consciousness, the conservative seems far more likely than the liberal to locate the pattern 'out there'. That some of their patterns sound implausible, that some of them should believe that the significance of the patterns can be unlocked through curious gnostic teachings should not obscure the basic resonance between this patterning and the view of the world held by traditional scientists.

THE ABNORMAL PSYCHOLOGY OF CONSERVATIVE PROTESTANTS

The discussions of cognitive styles in this chapter and of the dogmatic nature of the belief system of conservative

Protestantism in chapter 4 raise the possibility that there might be something fundamentally different about the psychology and personality of people attracted to such beliefs. There is a long and honourable tradition in experimental psychology that argues precisely that; certain sorts of conservatism (religious and political) are related to distinct personality types.

Such work began with the problem of explaining (and hence hopefully learning to prevent) fascism. Wilhelm Reich's The Mass Psychology of Fascism (1975) and Erich Fromm's Fear of Freedom (1972) were early texts in a basically psychoanalytical tradition. Adorno, Frenkel-Brunswick and their colleagues were responsible for the Authoritarian Personality studies (1950), which attempted to identify and explain authoritarian psychology. This work, and later research in the same vein, claims to identify a person who is unusually submissive to those in authority over him while being punitively hostile to his subordinates; who is brutal to those seen as outsiders; who views outsiders in terms of narrow stereotypes; who tends to be superstitious (in order to be able to blame 'fate' for his own shortcomings); and who is unusually intolerant of uncertainty and ambiguity.

One can see a number of points of contact between this model of the authoritarian personality and the typical conservative Protestant. The type of awesome God favoured by some conservative Protestants suggests a desire to be submissive. Their law and order politics suggest a 'punitive hostility' to outsiders, and the typical fundamentalist's view of 'Communists' is clear evidence of the use of narrow stereotypes for making sense of outsiders. The use of superstition to deflect responsibility for one's own failings could be identified with the conservative Protestant's belief in the work of the devil. The dislike of ambiguity can be seen in the conservative Protestant's use of dichotomies to simplify the world; good and evil, saved and sinner. The obvious similarities between the authoritarian personality model and conservative Protestants have not been wasted on psychologists, and it is common to find fundamentalists identified as authoritarians in the literature (for example Wilkinson, 1972:252).

The explanation of the authoritarian personality is psychoanalytical. As Frenkel-Brunswick (1949) argues, children who have certain types of relationships with their parents in early childhood will develop this special sort of personality; the personality then in turn explains why this sort of person is likely to behave in certain ways (such as joining the John Birch Society or the Nazi party). Relating it to the genesis of conservative Protestantism, the thesis would be that the conservative Protestantism of, for example,

Appalachian fundamentalists (Ford 1960; Jackson 1961) was explained by their childhood relationships with their parents.

Both the theory and method of the authoritarian personality studies have been the objects of much critical comment (Christie and Jahoda 1954; McKinney 1973; Billig 1977). In particular it has been argued that the main research instruments (such as the F-scale) were too narrowly concerned with fascism and anti-semitism to be directly generalisable to conservatism and authoritarianism in general. The work of Milton Rokeach (1956, 1960) purports to be an advance in this respect. Rokeach claims to have developed scales that identify and measure 'dogmatism' and 'opionionation' irrespective of what it is that the subject is dogmatic or opinionated about. In the Open and Closed Mind (1960) Rokeach depicts the features of the typical 'open' and 'closed' belief systems and his models seem remarkably similar to liberal and conservative Protestantism.

There are a number of criticisms that can be made of the experimental psychology tradition of authoritarian personality research. The more technical ones I will leave to one side (but see McKinney 1973). I will concentrate on the two main problems of evidence and theory. Elms (1969;1970) could find no evidence that John Birchers possessed a special identifiable personality type. The evidential problem is simply that, as Billig concludes after an excellent short review of the literture, there is little evidence from non-laboratory studies for any distinct authoritarian personality (1979:319).

The second major problem concerns the way in which the researchers make inferences from what we know about the thinking of certain people to the location of their 'abnormality'. With little or no good evidence for doing so, they assert that odd attitudes and beliefs are a reflection of an underlying odd personality that finds such things attractive and plausible. Rokeach depicts the features of open and closed belief systems but titles the book Open and Closed Mind, without justifying the shift from beliefs to the mind that holds them. Although the reasons why people believe something do not determine whether or not what they believe is true, it is important to understand the cultural and political background to these studies. They come from the same period that produced the 'end of ideology' debates; a period in which many commentators believed that the advanced societies were moving into a new era of enlightened liberalism and pluralism. In a mixed economy there would no longer be any real need for class conflict or racial conflict. In the arena of religious belief, narrow dogmatic beliefs would be replaced by ecumenism and tolerance. In such a climate, it was easy to suppose that anyone who refused to be a tolerant liberal was not just someone who held different beliefs but was rather someone who had a different personality. And the personality was not only different, but also inferior. The racial tolerance of the liberal was treated as the correct product of rational thought, while the bigotry of the Klansman was assumed to be the product of an abnormal psychology.

This is a central point for my argument and I want to make it clear by considering a particular example in some detail. Wilson (1973:10) wishes to show the difference between an attitude that is the result of rational belief, and an attitude that results from an abnormal personality. To do so, he cites the example of someone who wrote to a member of the British Parliament in support of an anti-abortion stance. The letter contained many pages of argument on the principle of the sanctity of life. It closed with the writer in an off-hand fashion expressing support for the same MP's pro-hanging politics. Wilson says: 'in this case, it might be supposed that the argument concerning "sanctity of life" was some kind of secondary rationalization adopted in order to bolster and justify an attitude towards the abortion issue that derived primarily from a generally conservative personality disposition' (1973:10). One might suppose this, but one might also suppose otherwise. Wilson is saying that it is logically inconsistent to be anti-abortion and pro-hanging because the latter involved taking life. It is thus unreasonable to be strong on the sanctity of life, and yet to want to see some people killed. As such a combination of beliefs is unreasonable, then their co-existence in the same person is to be explained by reference to an abnormal personality. Such an argument is nonsense. The lynch-pin is the logical compatibility of wanting to preserve foetuses and to hang some people. If one asked the letter writer about this, he would probably say that hanging certain types of criminals would deter others, and hence reduce the incidence of violent crime which would in turn save lives. This is an entirely reasonable thesis. It may well be wrong, but there is as yet no evidence of such incontravertibility that anyone who continues to hold the thesis can be safely assumed to be odd. Whether one accepts it or not (and I do not), the pro-hanging position is not logically incompatible with a commitment to the sanctity of life. Certainly there is not a sufficient conflict between the two to justify assuming that the sanctity of life argument is a 'secondary rationalization'. There is thus no need to suppose that there is a conservative 'personality' at work here.

What is known is that conservative Protestants believe some things which many of us do not believe. They believe particular propositions, such as 'God made the world in six days' and 'the EEC is a Roman Catholic plot for world domination', that are not commonly believed by non-conservative Protestants. In addition to specific propositions, one can identify general themes - such as a belief in there being a basic objective (but hidden) pattern and purpose to the world - that are not shared by liberal Protestants. The further one moves from concrete propositions to general themes, the more appealing it is to think that one is now talking, not about beliefs and attitudes, but about the 'mind' of the believer. I do not believe that such a shift is either necessary or justified. The case of the occult can be used to make my point. My first inclination was to suppose that people who believed that playing with the tarot cards was dangerous were deranged. However, a common-sense reading of the Bible makes it clear that (if one believes the Bible) there is a devil who does have power and who can achieve things; hence even playing at Satanism and dabbling in the occult may give Satan an opening. <u>Conservative Protestants believe in the occult because they believe in God</u>. Their apparently strange views on Halloween follow quite reasonably from other beliefs they hold. Likewise, the 'supernatural empiricism' that I have depicted above follows quite sensibly from the idea that there is a person who created the world. The point here can be made with a simple example. We would think that a man who waxed lyrical about the meaning and symbolism of a painting was an art critic. We would suppose that someone who did the same for a random scattering of bird seed was a fool. The difference between the two cases lies simply in our belief that the painting was created in order to communicate something to the viewer, while the bird seed just fell like that. One can discover meaning in the painting because it was <u>intended</u>. Thus behaviour that would appear strange coming from an atheist or a liberal Protestant, makes sense for the conservative Protestant because he holds a set of beliefs that assert that the world <u>was</u> intended; it was created by God. The conservative Protestant's willingness to identify hidden patterns, orders and conspiracies in the world is entirely reasonable and consistent with beliefs about the world that make him a conservative Protestant.

One must be clear that the claim that conservative Protestants have an abnormal psychology rests on the researcher's unstated claim to a more accurate grasp of how the world really is. For example, the idea that 'intolerance of ambiguity' is a feature of, and a product of, a certain type of personality, rests on the implied assertion that (a) there is ambiguity in the world and (b) that all normal people should tolerate this situation. To offer as evidence of 'intolerance of ambiguity' the fact that John Birchers tend to see communist conspiracies behind everything they do not like is to deny that Birchers have got it right. It is to say that there is no communist conspiracy. Thus such research begins with the claims that Birchers are basically wrong and that they do not hold their false beliefs on good grounds. The analyst does not usually even discuss these problems, let alone offer good evidence for such claims.

At its most general, what this process involves is the researcher substituting his own explanation of certain beliefs for the explanation that would be offered by the actor. The John Bircher sees conspiracies everywhere because he believes communists to be clever, skilled and devious creators of mayhem. The authoritarian personality researcher denies that source of motivation and asserts that Birches believe the things they do because they have a personality that cannot tolerate ambiguity and requires simplification. Of itself there is nothing wrong with a researcher claiming greater insight than the actors whose behaviour he is trying to explain; that is the essence of social science. But there have to be good grounds for doing this and one has to be careful that one is not allowing prejudice to intervene. Wilson (1973:9) offers a good case of one-sided and prejudiced substitution. He offers superstition as one of the basic characteristics of a conservative personality. Conservatives are superstitious because they do not want to accept the responsibility for their mistakes. Hence they use some motion of 'fate' to explain things that go badly rather than consider that they might be deficient themselves. Firstly, I wonder to what extent such a process of reasoning is more common with conservatives than with any other group of people. In the second place, Wilson is missing a vital observation that undermines his interpretation of the reasons for believing in fate. Conservative Protestants use the Devil and evil to explain things that go wrong. But they also use the related principles of God and his providence to explain things that go well. They thus displace blame for their own failings and deny responsibility for their successes. Both failure and success are to some extent attributed to agencies other than themselves. One wonders what story personality researchers could offer for conservative Protestants displacing their successes.

An Alternative to Personality

The conclusion of this discussion has to remain open-ended. The sort of research that would firmly establish the value of an idea of a distinct personality type with its roots in early childhood experiences has not been done for the simple reason that it would be extremely costly and difficult. One would have to take a large sample of children, study their childhood experiences and at that stage predict which are liable to develop an authoritarian personality or a 'closed mind'. One would then have to follow them as they developed into adulthood and see whether or not those so identified showed a significantly higher attraction to fascism, radical movements or conservative belief systems.

All that we know at present is that conservative Protestants believe things about the world that liberal Protestants and atheists do not. In my discussion of cognitive styles I have suggested that this difference goes deeper and broader than simple failure to agree about the truth or falsity of specific stories about the world. This recognition brings me close to a particular tradition within psychology but although there is a superficial similarity I want to distance myself from the authoritarian personality research and its various heirs. I do not believe that there is as yet good evidence for the existence of either a particular personality type or particular traits that are more common among conservatives than they are among liberal Protestants. The conservative cognitive style is entirely consistent with certain fundamental religious beliefs held by the conservative Protestants. Conspiracy thinking, for example, seems to be entirely reasonable in the context of other beliefs about the created order of the world. To suppose that such beliefs need to be explained in terms of their fit with a certain type of psychology one needs to be ignorant of the web of beliefs that make such view of the world perfectly sensible. The conservative's cognitive style can be seen simply as a generalised abstraction from the core beliefs of his religion.

The idea of a conservative personality would be more appealing if it were the case that there was a great difficulty explaining why people became conservative Protestants. But there is no such problem. Conservative Protestants are created in the same way as are other kinds of people. They acquire their beliefs in the main from their parents. In the comparatively rare cases of adult conversions, the beliefs are usually acquired through interaction with existing believers. Beliefs communicated through pleasing social interaction have a greater plausibility than those presented through some impersonal medium, because they are seen to be held by people we can come to trust. I could continue to put detail into this account, but the main point is simple. There is no need to abandon the notion that most people are rational most of the time. There is no need to assume that people who hold what seem to us abnormal beliefs must have come about them in an abnormal fashion. One does not need to create the lengthy and implausible thesis that certain types of child-rearing practices create certain relationships between parent and child which then produce an authoritarian or conservative personality, which in turn is especially susceptible to conservative Protestantism. There is a much more economical, and much more plausible account: most of what any of us know about the world is acquired from our parents and early acquaintance; hence conservative Protestant parents beget conservative Protestant children.

CONSERVATIVE PROTESTANTISM: A SUMMARY

The obituary of conservative Protestantism has been written many times, but never with as much conviction as in the period shortly after the second world war, when the establishment of the World Council of Churches confirmed the view of the many observers who argued that the survival of religion in modern industrial societies depended on the strategies of accommodation and compromise. The reduction of differences, firstly between denominations, and then between the Churches and the secular world, was pursued with enthusiasm by many well-meaning Protestant leaders who believed that there was no longer a market for supernaturalist religion. Those who attempted to reconstruct their religion along lines acceptable to its cultured despisers, and who later preached the 'death of God' theology, clearly believed that they were also announcing the shortly forthcoming death of any religion that continued to claim that the Bible was the verbally inspired word of God, that Christ was the God Incarnate, and that his death was in atonement for our sins.

The obituaries were exaggerated. As I demonstrated in chapter 3, conservative forms of Protestantism have endured in a period when liberalism has declined in popularity. The reasons for this conservative success are many. There are major differences between English evangelicals, Scottish Presbyterians, and American fundamentalists, and where appropriate I have tried to maintain the distinction, but in this concluding review I will pass over internal conservative differences and concentrate on a broad comparison with liberal Protestantism. The main themes in my explanation of conservative resilience can be dealt with under two headings; those that are concerned with the relationship between conservative Protestantism and the wider society, and those that refer to internal features of conservatism.

There are a number of ways in which conservative Protestantism 'fits' with the modern world. At the most abstract level of cognitive style one finds a basic resonance between the ways of thinking about the world that are common to conservative Protestants, and the rational and empiricist epistemology of a Baconian natural science. While the belief system of the conservative Protestant contains propositions about a supernatural realm, the style of reasoning is similar to the rationalism of the secular world. Thus, provided the believer can neutralise actual propositions that conflict with his beliefs, he can continue to work within a scientific worldview, as the large number of English evangelicals to be found in medicine and natural science demonstrates.

Unlike its major competitors, Protestantism is a faith for the individual. Nations and societies are not saved; only individual repentant sinners can attain salvation. The primacy of the individual allows Protestantism to adapt to the shift from the public and the social to the private and the familial that one finds in modern societies. The move of the main source of identity from the public to the private that one can see in the recent interest in psychotherapies poses no serious problems for Protestantism. But of the two main varieties, it is the conservative form that most easily fits such new concerns. Liberal Protestantism has a tendency to focus on the social rather than the personal. This can be seen both in the tendency to left-wing politics and in the notion of relevance. The thrust of liberal Protestantism is its concern to make the faith relevant for modern man and although this is sometimes concerned with the question of 'what modern man will <u>believe</u>', it often becomes a matter of 'what <u>concerns</u> modern man'. Such concerns are usually taken to be social and political and hence the liberal tends to have interests that go beyond the individual.

There is another way in which conservative Protestantism has an advantage over liberalism and that is in its underlying pessimism. Liberalism involves an essentially hopeful and optimistic picture of man and his ability to improve himself and his world. Conservative forms of Protestantism tend to assert the total sinfulness and depravity of man. In a world of nuclear weapons, apparently uncontrollable economies, pollution and terrorism, the notion that man is innately sinful has considerable appeal. The last decade seems to have been characterised by an increase in general conservatism in the Western world and such a change in political climate adds to the general 'plausibility' of conservative Protestantism. A second related observation concerns the theme of individualism. Part of the widespread pessimism has been concerned with the apparent failure of the welfare state to 'solve' major social problems. The right has been able to capitalise on a loss of faith in government and the increase in popularity of right wing individualism again aids conservative Protestantism. In the first place this aid comes through the similarity of the root image of man involved in both religious and political conservatism, but there is a second historical connection. The time to which conservatives wish to return is taken, rightly or wrongly, to have been a time in which preachers preached that 'old time religion'. Conservative

Protestantism is seen as one of the features of the golden age and as such a potent symbol for conservatives in a dismal time.

Such resonances with the themes and interests of the surrounding secular world have advantages for conservative Protestantism. The presence within the religion of things found outside it increases the plausibility of the belief system. But there are potential dangers. To use a metaphor much loved of the liberal, 'building bridges' to the secular world is a precarious business. Bridges carry two-way traffic and can as readily transport defectors as they can recruits. Minimising the differences between the minority belief system and the beliefs of the secular may well make the minority beliefs appear more legitimate but such compromise undermines the attraction of the religious beliefs. If everyone is really 'saved' and all religions really have some of the truth and there is no price to pay for getting it wrong, why should I leave the secular world for your religion? The success of conservative Protestantism lies in its ability to resonate with the interests of the secular world while still preserving its own distinct identity. This is possible because of the nature of conservative beliefs. Liberal Protestantism has a form which makes it highly precarious. Conservatives can know what they believe, enforce membership tests, identify and expel heretics, and thus maintain consensus and cohesion anong large numbers of believers and over long periods of time. This allows the construction and preservation of an alternative milieu, a world of distinctly conservative Protestant activities and institutions, and such a milieu helps to reproduce the belief system.

It is thus the relationship between the form of the beliefs and social organisation, discussed in chapter 4, which gives conservative Protestantism its ability to accommodate to the secular world without being assimilated. It is the ability of the ideology to be embodied in institutions and practices that accounts for both its survival in extended periods in the ecclessiastical wilderness and its revival in more promising 'perilous times'.

Notes

1. The best works on secularisation are Martin (1978), Wilson (1976), Macleod (1981), and Gilbert (1980).

Bibliography

Aberle, David, (1966), <u>The Peyote Religion Among the Navaho</u>, Chicago: Aldine.

Adams, Jay E., (1974), <u>The Christian Counsellor's Casebook</u>, Nutley, NJ: Presbyterian and Reformed Publishing Co.

Adams, Jay E., (1976), <u>Coping with Counselling Crises</u>, Grand Rapids, Micnigan: Baker Book House.

Adams, Jay E., (1977), <u>Your Place in the Counselling Revolution</u>, Nutley, NJ: Presbyterian and Reformed Publishing Co.

Adams, Robert L. and Fox, R.J., (1972), 'Mainlining Jesus; the new trip', <u>Society</u> 9 (4), pp 50-56.

Adorno, T.W., Frenkel-Brunswick, Else, Levinson, D.J. and Sandford, R.N., (1950), <u>The Authoritarian Personality</u>, New York: Harper.

Ahlstrom, Sidney E., (1972), <u>A Religious History of the American People</u>, New Haven: Yale University Press.

Allan, John, (1980), 'Christian Rock Today' in Tom Morton, <u>Solid Rock?</u>, Glasgow: Pickering and Inglis/British Youth for Christ.

Allen, Tom, (1956), <u>Crusade in Scotland</u>, Glasgow: Pickering and Inglis.

Allen, William E. (n.d.), <u>The '59 Revival in Ireland</u>, Belfast: Revival Publishing Co.

Allport, G.W., (1970), 'The religious context of prejudice', in W. Sadler, <u>Psychology and Religion</u>, New York: Harper and Row.

Altheide, David L. and Johnson, J.M., (1977), 'Counting souls: a study of evangelical crusades', <u>Pacific Sociological Review</u> 20 (3), pp 323-348.

Andrews, Edgar H., (1978), 'Creation and Evolution' in Roland Lamb, <u>The Bible Under Attack</u>, Welwyn: Evangelical Press.

Argyle, Michael and Biet-Hallahmi, B., (1975), <u>A Social Psychology of Religion</u>, London: Routledge Kegan Paul.

Ashma, Chuck, (1977), The Gospel According to Billy, Secaucus, NJ: Lyle Stuart Inc.

Bainbridge, W.S., (1978), Satan's Power: a deviant psychotherapy cult, London: University of California Press.

Barkley, John, (1960), A Short History of the Presbyterian Church in Ireland, Belfast: Presbyterian Church in Ireland.

Barker, Eileen, (1980), 'Science and Theology: diverse resolutions of an interdisciplinary gap by the new priesthood of science', Inter-Disciplinary Science Review 5 (4) pp 281-291.

Beggs, R.J., (1977), Great is thy faithfulness: an account of the ministry of Pastor James Kyle Paisley and the separatist movement in Ballymena, Ballymena: Ballymena Free Presbyterian Church.

Bellah, Robert and McLoughlin, W., (1967) 'Religion in America', special issue of Daedalus: the Journal of the American Academy of Arts and Sciences, 96 (1-2).

Benton, Ted, (1977), Philosophical Foundations of the Three Sociologies, London: Routledge Kegan Paul.

Berger, Peter L., (1963), 'A market model for the analysis of ecumenicity', Social Research 30 (1), pp 77-93.

Berger, Peter L., (1965), 'Towards an understanding of psychoanalysis', Social Research 32 (1), pp 26-41.

Berger, Peter L., (1967), 'A sociological view of the secularisation of theology', Journal for the Scientific Study of Religion 6 (1), pp 3-16.

Berger, Peter L., (1973), The Social Reality of Religion, Harmondsworth, Middx.: Penguin.

Berger, Peter L., (1979), Facing up to Modernity, Harmondsworth, Middx.: Penguin.

Berger, Peter L., Berger, Brigitte, and Kellner, Hans, (1973), The Homeless Mind, Harmondsworth, Middx.: Penguin.

Berger, Peter L. and Luckmann, Thomas, (1973), The Social Construction of Reality, Harmondsworth, Middx.: Penguin.

Best G.F.A., (1964), Temporal Pillars, London: Cambridge
University Press.

Bestic, Alan, (1971), Praise the Lord and Pass the
Contribution, London: Cassell.

Bibby, R. and Brinkerhoff, M., (1973), 'The circulation of
the Saints: a study of people who join conservative
churches', Journal for the Scientific Study of Religion,
12, pp 2/3-285.

Bibby, R., (1978), 'Why the conservative churches really are
growing: Kelley revisited', Journal for the Scientific
Study of Religion 17 (2), pp 129-137.

Billig, Michael, (1977), 'The new social psychology on
fascism', European Journal of Social Psychology 7, pp
393-432.

Billig, Michael, (1978), Fascists: a socio-psychological view
of the National Front, London: Harcourt Brace Jovanovich.

Blumer, Herbert, (1969), Symbolic Interactionism, Englewood
Cliffs, NJ: Prentice-Hall.

Bowden, John, (1970), Who is Christian?, London: SCM Press.

Box, Steven, (1981), Deviance, Reality and Society (2nd Ed.),
London: Holt Rinehart and Winston.

Brabant, F.H., (1949), Neville S. Talbot 1879-1943: a memoir,
London: SCM Press.

Brady, D.W. and Tedin, K.L., (1976), 'Ladies in pink:
religion and political ideology in the anti-ERA
movement', Social Science Quarterly, 56 pp 564-575.

Bradley, Ian, (1976), The Call to Seriousness: the
evangelical impact on the Victorians, London: Cape.

Braisted, Ruth Wilder, (1941), In this Generation: the story
of Robert P. Wilder, New York: Friendship Press.

Brierley, Peter, (1978), UK Protestant Missions Handbook Vol.
2: Home, London: Evangelical Alliance/The Bible Society.

Briggs, John, (1979), Report of the Denominational Enquiry
Group to the Baptist Union Council, mimeo (later
published by the Baptist Union as Signs of Hope).

Brown, G. and Mills, B., (1980), The Brethren Today: a factual survey, Exeter: Paternoster Press.

Browne, David G., (n.d.), Hugh Hanna, Belfast: Puritan Printing Co.

Bruce, Steve, (1978), 'A witness to the faith: dilemmas of "evangelism" as reality and rhetoric', Scottish Journal of Sociology 2 (2) pp 163-173.

Bruce, Steve, (1980), 'The Student Christian Movement and the Inter-Varsity Fellowship: a sociological study of two student movements', Ph.D thesis, Stirling University.

Bryant, Anita, (1977), The Anita Bryant Story, Old Tappen, NJ: Revell.

Bryant, Anita, (1978), 'Playboy interview: Anita Bryant', Playboy, May 1978, pp 73-96 and 232-250.

Budd, Susan, (1967), 'The Humanist societies: the consequences of a diffuse belief system' in B.R. Wilson, Patterns of Sectarianism, London: Heinemann.

Buis, Robert P.D., (1979), 'The relationship between the dogmatic teachings and attitudes towards race relations of two South African religious denominations' in Hare, A. Paul, Wiendieck, Gerd and Von Broembsen, Max H., South Africa: sociological analyses, Cape Town: Oxford University Press.

Cairns, D.S., (1919), The Army and Religion, London: Macmillan.

Cameron, N.M. de S., (1980), In the Beginning: a symposium on the Bible and Creation, Glasgow: Biblical Creation Society.

Carroll, Jackson W., (1978), 'Understanding church growth and decline', Theology Today, April 1978.

Carroll, Jackson W., Johnson D.W. and Marty M.E., (1979), Religion in America: 1950 to the present, New York: Harper and Row.

Carroll, Jackson W., and Roozen, David A., (1979), 'Continuity and change: the shape of religious life in the United States, 1950 to the present' pp 1-46 in Carroll et al 1979.

Carwardine, R., (1978), 'Religious revival of 1857-8 in the United States' in D. Baker, Religious Motivation: biographical and sociological problems for the church historian, Studies in Church History 15, Oxford: Basil Blackwell.

Catherwood, Frederick, (1975), A Better Way: the case for a Christian social order, London: Inter-Varsity Press.

Chapman, Colin, (1968), 'Modern music and evangelism' in Evangelical Alliance, Background to the Task, London: Evangelical Alliance.

Chomsky, Noam, (1973), For Reasons of State, London: Fontana/Collins.

Christian Medical Fellowship/(CMF), (1980), Why did you ever take up medicine?: an open letter from a professor to a medical student, London: CMF.

Christie, R. and Jahoda, M., (1954), Studies in the scope and method of the 'Authoritarian Personality', Glencoe, Ill: Free Press.

Christman, W.J., (1978), The Christman File, Edinburgh: St. Andrews Press.

Church, R.W., (1970), The Oxford Movement, Chicago: University of Chicago Press.

Clabaugh, Gary, (1974), Thunder on the Right: the Protestant fundamentalists, New York: Nelson-Hall.

Clelland, Donald A., Hood, Thomas, Lipsey, C.M. and Wimberley, R., (1974), 'In the company of the converted: characteristics of a Billy Graham crusade audience', Sociological Analysis 35, pp 45-56.

Cohn, Norman, (1970), The Pursuit of the Millenium, St. Albans: Paladin.

Condren, Mary, (1979), 'The widening gyre: reflections on the SCM in transition', Movement 38 pp 2-4.

Coomes, David, (1973), Spre-E 73, London: Coverdale.

Corkey, William, (1962), Glad did I live: memoirs of a long life, Belfast: Belfast Newsletter.

Cummings, E. and Harrington, C., (1963), 'The clergyman as counsellor', American Journal of Sociology 69, pp 234-243.

Currie, Raymond F., (1976), 'Belonging, commitment and early socialisation in a western city', pp 462-478 in S. Crysdale and Les Wheatcroft, Religion in Canadian Society, Toronto: Macmillan.

Currie, Robert and Gilbrt, Alan, (1974), 'Religion' pp 407-450 in A.H. Halsey, Trends in British Society since 1900, London: Macmillan.

Currie, Robert, Gilbert, A. and Horsley, L., (1977), Churches and Churchgoers: patterns of church growth and decline in the British Isles since 1700, London: Oxford University Press.

Dearing, Trevor, (1978), 'In search of the supernatural', Life of Faith, August 1978, pp 22-25.

Deeks, H. Frank, (1972), Shopfloor Christianity, Leicester: Inter-Varsity Press.

Dike, Samuel W., (1909), 'A study of New England revivals', American Journal of Sociology, pp 361-378.

Dollar, George, (1973), A History of Fundamentalism in America, Greenville, S.C.: Bob Jones University Press.

Drummond, Andrew L. and Bulloch, James, (1973), The Scottish Church 1688-1843; (1975), The Church in Victorian Scotland 1843-1874; (1978), The Church in Late Victorian Scotland 1874-1900, Edinburgh: St. Andrews Press.

Duff, Henry, (1963), A Modern Restatement of the Christian Faith, Belfast: Henry L. Duff.

Dylan, Bob, (1973), Writings and Drawings, London: Panther.

Eister, Alan, (1950), Drawing Room Conversion, Durham, NC: Duke University Press.

Ellwood, Robert S., (1973), One Way: the Jesus movement and its meaning, Englewood-Cliffs. NJ: Prentice Hall.

Elms, A.C., (1969), 'Psychological factors in right-wing extremism' in R.A. Schoenberger, The American Right Wing, New York: Holt, Rinehart and Winston.

Elms, A.C., (1970), 'These little old ladies in tennis shows are no nuttier than anyone else, it turns out', Psychology Today (Feb), pp 27-59.

Evangelical Alliance, (1968), Background to the Task, London: Evangelical Alliance/Scripture Union.

Fielding, Nigel, (1981), The National Front, London: Routledge Kegan Paul.

Firebaugh, Glenn, (1981), 'How effective are city-wide crusades?', Christianity Today XXV (6), pp 412-417.

Ford, T.R., (1960), 'Status, residence and fundamentalist religious beliefs in the Southern Appalachians', Social Forces 39(1), pp 41-49.

Frady, Marshall, (1979), Billy Graham: a parable of American righteousness, London: Hodder and Stoughton.

Fraser, Agnes R., (1934), Donald Fraser of Livingstonia, London: Hodder and Stoughton.

Frenkel-Brunswick, Else, (1949), 'Intolerance of ambiguity as an emotional and perceptual personality variable', Journal of Personality 18, pp 108-143.

Fromm, Erich, (1972), Fear of Freedom, London: Routledge Kegan Paul.

Fulton, Austin, (1970), J. Ernest Davey, Belfast: Presbyterian Church in Ireland.

Gasper, Louis, (1963), The Fundamentalist Movement, The Hague: Mouton and Co.

Gay, John, (1971), The Geography of Religion in England, London: Duckworth.

Gehlen, Arnold, (1980), Man in the Age of Technology, New York: Columbia University Press.

Gerlach, Luther P. and Hine, V., (1968), 'Five factors crucial to the growth and spread of a modern religious movement', Journal for the Scientific Study of Religion 7, pp 23-40.

Gerlach, Luther P. and Hine, V., (1970), People, Power and Change: movements of social transformation, New York: Bobbs-Merrill.

Gibson, William, (n.d.), The Year of Grace: a history of the Ulster revival of 1859, Edinburgh: Oliphant, Anderson and Ferrier.

Gibbon, Peter J., (1975), The Origins of Ulster Unionism, Manchester: Manchester University Press.

Gilbert, Alan D., (1980), The Making of Post-Christian Britain: a history of the secularisation of modern society, London: Longman.

Glasner, Peter, (1977), The Sociology of Secularisation, London: Routledge Kegan Paul.

Goffman, Erving, (1974), Stigma, Harmondsworth, Middx.: Penguin.

Gray, Tony, (1972), The Orange Order, London: Bodley Head.

Greil, Arthur L., (1977), 'Previous dispositions and conversion to perspectives of social and religious movements', Sociological Analysis 38 (2), pp 115-125.

Grier, W.J., (1945), The Origin and Witness of the Irish Evangelical Church, Belfast: Evangelical Bookshop.

Grove, Gene, (1961), Inside the John Birch Society, New York: New York Post/Fawcett Publications.

Grubb, Norman P., (1933), CT Studd: cricketer and pioneer, London: Religious Tract Society/Lutterworth.

Guinness, Howard W., (1978), Journey Among Students, Sydney: Anglican Information Office.

Hale, Leslie, (n.d.), The Chrysalis, Belfast: Leslie Hale.

Hanke, Gerald L., (1977), American Revivalism and the Convert Role, Ph.D thesis, University of Pennsylvania.

Harford, Charles P., (1907), The Keswick Convention, London: Marshall Brothers.

Hawthorn, Mary B., (1980), The Doukhobors of British Columbia, Westport, Conn.: Greenwood Press.

Herink, Ritchie, (1980), The Psychotherapy Handbook, New York: New American Library.

Hexham, Irving, (1980), 'Christianity and Apartheid: an introductory bibliography', supplement to the Reformed Journal, April 1980.

Hexham, Irving, (1981), The Irony of Apartheid: the struggle for national independence of Afrikaner Calvinism against British Imperialism, New York: Edwin Mellen Press.

Highet, John, (1950), The Churches in Scotland Today, Glasgow: Jackson Son & Co.

Highet, John, (1960), The Scottish Churches, London: Skeffington.

Hill, Michael, (1973), A Sociology of Religion, London: Heinemann.

Hill, Samuel S., (1972), Religion and the Solid South, Nashville: Abingdon.

Hostetler, J.A., (1963), Amish Society, Baltimore: John Hopkins Press.

Hoge, Dean R. and Roozen, D.A., (1979), Understanding Church Growth and Decline: 1950-1978, New York: Pilgrim Press.

Hulse, E., (1966), Billy Graham: the pastor's dilemma, Swengel, PA: Reiner Publications.

Humbard, Rex, (1971), Miracles in my life, New York: New American Library (Signet).

Hunter, J.D., (1981), Contemporary American Evangelicalism: conservative religion and the quandary of modernity, Ph.D thesis, Rutgers Univeristy.

Hutchings, Eric, (n.d.), International Daily News Bulletin, Bimonthly, Eastbourne: Hour of Revival Association.

Hutchinson, Matthew, (1893), The Reformed Presbyterian Church in Scotland: its origin and history, 1680-1876, Paisley: J. and R. Parlane.

Irvine, Doreen, (1973), From Witchcraft to Christ, London: Concordia Press.

Jackson, A.K., (1961), 'Religious beliefs and expressions of the Southern Highlander', Review of Religious Research 3 (1), pp 21-39.

James, John Angell, (1980), 'The dangers of self-deception', Free Presbyterian Magazine 85 (8), pp 234-7.

Johnson, Douglas, (1979), Contending for the Faith, Leicester: Inter-Varsity Press.

Jones, Bob Jnr., (1980), Sermon at Dr Paisley's Martyrs Memorial Church, 5th October 1980.

Jones, Charles Edwin, (1974), Perfectionist Persuasion: the Holiness movement and American Methodism, 1867-1936, Metuchen, NJ: the Scarecrow Press Inc.

Jones, Hywell, (1978), 'The inerrancy of scripture', in R. Lamb, The Bible Under Attack, Welwyn, Herts.: Evangelical Press.

Jorsted, Erling, (1970), The Politics of Doomsday: fundamentalists of the Far Right, Nashville: Abingdon.

Kanter, Rosabeth M., (1968), 'Commitment and social organisation: a study of commitment mechanisms in utopian communities', American Sociological Review 33, pp 499-517.

Kanter, Rosabeth M., (1972), Commitment and Community, Cambridge, Mass.: Harvard University Prss.

Kelley, Dean, (1972), Why the Conservative Churches are Growing: a study in the sociology of religion, New York: Harper and Row.

Kelley, Dean, (1978), 'Why the conservative churches are still growing', Journal for the Scientific Study of Religion 17, pp 165-172.

Kennedy, John, (1979), The Days of the Fathers in Ross-shire, Inverness: Christian Focus Publications.

Kent, John, (1979), Holding the Fort: studies in Victorian revivalism, London: Epworth.

King, Larry, (1966), 'Bob Jones University: the buckle on the Bible belt', Harpers, June 1966, pp 57-58.

Kitching, Robert J., (1976), The Conservative Evangelical Influence in Methodism, 1900-76, MA thesis, Birmingham University.

Koestler, Arthur, (1981), 'The Ratman cometh', Sunday Times Review, 1st November.

Kornhauser, William, (1959), The Politics of Mass Society, New York: Free Press.

Lakatos, I. and Musgrave, A., (1970), Criticism and the Growth of Knowledge, London: Cambridge University Press.

Lake, Frank, (1966), Clinical Theology, London: Darton, Longman and Todd.

Lamb, Roland, (1975), 'Yesterday, Today and Tomorrow', The Bulwark May/June, pp 10-17.

Lamont, Donald, (1946), God's Word and Man's Response, London: Inter-Varsity Fellowship.

Lang, Kurt and Lang, G., (1960), 'Decisions for Christ: Billy Graham in New York', in Maurice Stein, A. Vidich and L. White, Identity and Anxiety, Glencoe, III: Free Press.

Larson, Mel, (1945), Young Man on Fire: the story of Torrey Johnson and Youth for Christ, Chicago: Youth for Christ International.

Laslett, Peter, (1965), The World We Have Lost, London: Methuen.

Lee, Shu-Ching, (1970), 'Group cohesion and Hutterian colony' in T. Shibutani, Human Nature and Collective Behaviour, Englewood Cliffs, NJ: Prentice-Hall.

Lindesmith, Alfred, Strauss, A. and Denzin, N., (1977), Social Psychology, New York: Holt, Rinehart and Winston.

Lipset, Seymour M. and Raab, A., (1971), The Politics of Unreason, New York: Harper and Row.

Lofland, John, (1966), Doomsday Cult: a study of conversion, proselytisation, and maintenance of faith, Englewood Cliffs, NJ: Prentice-Hall.

Lofland, John and Stark, R., (1965), 'Becoming a worldsaver: a theory of conversion to a deviant perspective', American Sociological Review 30 (6), pp 862-75.

Lydia Fellowship, (1980), Recording of meeting at Westgate, 1st May, 1980.

McBride, James and Schwarz, Paul S., (1980), 'The Moral Majority and the failure of religious legitimation' mimeo, New Religions Research Collection, Centre for the Study of New Religious Movements, Berkeley.

McConnell, James, (1912), Presbyterianism in Belfast, Belfast: Davidson and McCormack.

McFadden, Michael, (1972), The Jesus Revolution, New York: Harper and Row (Harrow Books).

McIntyre, Thomas and Obert, J.C., (1979), The Fearbrokers, New York: Pilgrim.

Mackie, Robert C., (1965), Layman extraordinary: John R. Mott, 1865-1965, London: Hodder and Stoughton.

McKinney, David J., (1973), The Authoritarian Personality Studies, The Hague: Mouton.

Maclaren, A. Alan, (1974), Religion and Social Class: the disruption years in Aberdeen, London: Routledge Kegan Paul.

Macleod, Hugh, (1981), Religion and the People of Western Europe 1784-1970, London: Oxford University Press.

McLoughlin, William G., (1955), Modern Revivalism, New York: Ronald Press.

Mailer, Norman, (1968), Miami and the Siege of Chicago, Harmondsworth, Middx.: Penguin.

Mann, W.E., (1955), Sect, Cult and Church in Alberta, Toronto: University of Toronto Press.

Marsden, George, (1977) 'Fundamentalism as an American phenomenon: a comparison with English evangelicalism', Church History 46 (2), pp 215-232.

Marsden, George, (1980), Fundamentalism and American Culture: the shaping of 20th century evangelicalism, 1870-1925, New York: Oxford University Press.

Martin, David, (1978), A General Theory of Secularisation, Oxford: Basil Blackwell.

Martin, William C., (1970), 'The God-hucksters of radio: "keep those cards and letters coming in"', Atlantic Monthly, June.

Martin, William C., (1974), 'This man says he's the divine sweetheart of the universe', Esquire, June.

Marty, Martin S., (1976), A Nation of Behavers, Chicago: University of Chicago Press.

Marx, John H. and Holzner, B., (1977), 'The social construction of strain and ideological models of grievance in contemporary movements', Pacific Sociological Review 20 (3), pp 411-439.

Matthews, Basil, (1934), John R. Mott: world citizen, London: SCM Press.

Moffatt, John Mecklin, (1963), The Ku Klux Klan: a study of the American mind New York: Russell and Russell.

Meiring, Piet, Van Wyk, J.A. and Giddy, Paul, (1981), 'Religion' in S.T. Van der Horst and J. Reid, Race Discrimination in South Africa, Cape Town, London: David Phillip, Rex Collings.

Miller, David W., (1878), Queen's Rebels: Ulster Loyalism in historical perspective, Dublin: Gill and Macmillan.

Moody, A.F., (n.d.), Memories and Musings of a Moderator, London: James Clark and Co. Ltd.

Moody, W.R., (1937), The Life of Dwight L. Moody, Kilmarnock: John Ritchie.

Morris, James, (1973), The Preachers, New York: St. Martins Press.

Moule, H., (1892), Charles Simeon, London: Metheun.

Munson, J.E.B., (1975), 'The Oxford Movement by the end of the 19th century: the anglo-catholic clergy', Church History 44, pp 382-395.

Munters, Q.J., (1971), 'Recruitment as vocation: the case of the Jehovah's Witnesses', Netherlands Journal of Sociology 7 (2), pp 88-100.

Murray, Paul Beasley and Wilkinson, A., (1980), Turning the Tide: an assessment of Baptist church growth in England, London: Bible Society.

Nationwide Initiative on Evangelism, (1980), Prospect for the Eighties, London: Bible Society.

Nye, Robert D., (1975), <u>Three Views of Man: perspectives from
Sigmund Freud, B.F. Skinner, and Carl Rogers</u>, Monterey:
Brooks/Cole.

Osborne, Alastair, (1980), <u>Focus on Ferguslie: a report on
the St. Ninians Team Ministry, 1974-1980</u>, Paisley: St.
Ninians Team Ministry, Ferguslie Park.

O'Toole, Roger, (1975), 'Sectarianism in politics: case
studies of Maoists and De Leonists' in Roy Wallis,
<u>Sectarianism: analyses of religious and non-religious
sects</u>, London: Peter Owen.

O'Toole, Roger, (1976), 'Underground traditions in the study
of sectarianism: non-religious use of the concept
"sect"', <u>Journal for the Scientific Study of Religion</u> 15
(2), pp 145-156.

Paisley, Ian R.K., (n.d.), <u>The Jesuits: their start, sign,
system, secrecy, and strategy</u>, Belfast: Martyrs Memorial
Publications.

Paisley, Ian R.K., (1977), <u>'The Myth of God Incarnate'
reviewed and refuted by</u> .., Belfast: Martyrs Memorial
Publications.

Peters, Victor, (1971), <u>All Things Common: the Hutterian way
of life</u>, New York: Harper (Torch books).

Peters, Walter G., (1970), 'Fundamentalist scientists oppose
Darwinian evolution', <u>Bioscience</u> 20 (19), pp 1067-9.

Pettigrew, Thomas F., (1958), 'Personality and socio-cultural
factors in inter-group attitudes: a cross national
comparison', <u>Journal of Conflict Resolution</u> 2, pp 29-42.

Pettigrew, T.F. and Riley, R.T., (1971), 'The social
psychology of the Wallace phenomenon', in T.F.
Pettigrew, <u>Racially Separate or Together?</u>, New York:
McGraw-Hill.

Pierard, Richard, (1970), <u>The Unequal Yoke: evangelical
Christianity and political conservation</u>, New York: J.B.
Lippincott.

Pollock, John, (1953), <u>A Cambridge Movement: history of the
CICCU 1877-1952</u>, London: John Murray.

Pollock, John, (1955), <u>The Cambridge Seven</u>, London:
Inter-Varsity Press.

Pollock, John, (1963), Moody without Sankey: a new biographical portrait, London: Hodder and Stoughton.

Pollock, John, (1964), The Keswick Story: the authorised history of the Keswick Convention, London: Hodder and Stoughton.

Pollock, John, (1966), Billy Graham: the authorised biography, London: Hodder and Stoughton.

Pollock, John, (1979), Billy Graham: evangelist to the world, San Francisco: Harper and Row.

Potter, Sarah, (1975), 'The making of missionaries in the 19th century:conversion and convention' in David Martin (ed.), Sociological Yearbook of Religion 8, London: SCM Press.

Popper, Karl R., (1978), Logic of Scientific Discovery, London: Hutchinson.

Popper, Karl R., (1979), Objective Knowledge: an evolutionary approach, London: Oxford University Press.

Pynchon, Thomas, (1976), The Crying of Lot 49, Harmondsworth, Middx.: Penguin.

Redekop, James, (1966), The American Far Right, Grand Rapids, Mich.: W.D. Eerdmans.

Redmond, John, (1965), Church, State, Industry in East Belfast (1827-1929), Belfast: private publication.

Reformed Presbyterian Church of Ireland, (1939), Testimony of the Reformed Presbyterian Church of Ireland, Belfast: John Adams.

Reich, Wilhelm, (1975), The Mass Psychology of Fascism, Harmondsworth, Middx.: Penguin.

Reno, Cora A., (1953), Evolution: fact or theory?, Chicago: Moody Press.

Reymond, Robert L., (1977), A Christian View of Modern Science, Nutley, NJ: Presbyterian and Reformed Publishing Co.

Roberts, David A., (1971), 'The Orange Order in Ireland: a religious institution?', British Journal of Sociology 22 (3), pp 269-.

Roberts, David A., (1975), The Orange Order, Ph.D thesis, London University.

Roberts, J.M., (1974), The Mythology of the Secret Societies, St. Albans: Paladin.

Roberts, Oral, (1970), The Miracles of Seed-Faith, Tulsa, Ok.: Oral Roberts.

Roberts, Oral, (1974a), Twelve Greatest Miracles of My Ministry, Tulsa, Ok.: Pinoak Publications.

Roberts, Oral, (1974b), How to Live Above Your Problems, Tulsa Ok.: Pinoak Publications.

Robinson, Ruth, (1965), 'Spiritual education in a world without religion' in John Robinson, The New Reformation, London: SCM Press.

Rodeheaver, Homer, (1936), Twenty Years with Billy Sunday, Nashville: Cokesbury Press.

Rogers, Carl, (1973), Client-Centred Therapy, London: Constable.

Rokeach, Milton, (1956), 'Political and religious dogmatism: an alternative to the Authoritarian Personality', Psychological Monographs General and Applied 70 (18).

Rokeach, Milton, (1960), The Open and Closed Mind, New York: Basic Books.

Roy, Ralph, (1953), Apostles of Discord: a study of organised bigotry and disruption on the fringes of Protestantism, Boston: Beacon Prss.

Russell, C. Alyn, (1976), Voices of American Fundamentalism: seven biographical studies, Philadelphia: Westminster Press.

Rutherford, James C., (1912), Life and Times of Reverend John Orr of Portaferry, Belfast: private publication.

Sandeen, Ernest R., (1970), 'Fundamentalism and religious identity', Annals of American Academy of Politics and Social Science, 387.

Sargant, William, (1957), The Battle for the Mind, London: Heinemann.

Scholes, Jerry, (1979) <u>Give Me that Prime-Time Religion</u>, New York: Hawthorn Books.

Schwarz, Paul A. and McBride, J., (1981), 'God's plan for America: the Christian new right and the battle with secular humanism' mimeo, New Religions Research Collection, Centre for the Study of New Religious Movements, Berkeley.

Shibutani, Tamotsu, (1955), 'Reference grops as perspectives', <u>American Journal of Sociology</u> 60, pp 562-9.

Shupe, Anson D. and Bromley, D.G., (1979), '"Just a few years seem like a lifetime": a role theory approach to participation in religious movements', in L. Kreisberg, <u>Research in Social Movements, Conflicts and Change</u>, 2, New York: JAI Press.

Sizer, Sandra, (1979), 'Politics and apolitical religion: the great urban revivals of the late 19th century', <u>Church History</u> 48 (1), pp 81-.

Smith, George Adam, (1902), <u>The Life of Henry Drummond</u>, London: Hodder and Stoughton.

Smith, Timothy L., (1965), <u>Revivalism and Social Reform</u>, New York: Harper (Torch Books).

Smyth, W. Martin, (1972), <u>The Battle for Northern Ireland</u>, Belfast: County Grand Orange Lodge of Belfast.

Spring, D., (1961), 'The Clapham Sect', <u>Victorian Studies</u> 5 (1).

Stark, Rodney, (1963), 'On the incompatibility of religion and science: a survey of American graduate students', <u>Journal for the Scientific Study of Religion</u> 3 (1), pp 3-20.

Stookey, Noel P., (1979), 'Interview', <u>Life of Faith</u>, May, 1979.

Storkey, Alan, (1979), <u>A Christian Social Perspective</u>, Leicester: Inter-Varsity Press.

Strauss, Roger, (1976), 'Changing oneself: seekers and the creative transformation of life experience' pp 252-272 in John Lofland, <u>Doing Social Life</u>, New York: Wiley.

Strauss, Roger, (1979), 'Religious conversion as a personal and collective accomplishment', Sociological Analysis 40 (2), pp 158-165.

Summers, J.E., (1972), 'Strict Baptists in the 1970's', Baptist Quarterly 24 (5).

Sundermeier, Theo, (1975), Church and Nationalism in South Africa, Johannesburg: Ravan Press.

Symondson, A., (1970), The Victorian Crisis of Faith, London: SPCK.

Szasz, Thomas, (1974), Ideology and Insanity, Harmondsworth, Middx.: Penguin.

Szasz, Thomas, (1979), Schizophrenia, Oxford: Basil Blackwell.

Target, G.W., (1968), Evangelism Inc., London: Allen Lane.

Tatlow, Tissington, (1933), The Story of the Student Christian Movement, London: SCM Press.

Thompson, D.P., (1966), Dr Billy Graham and the Pattern of Modern Evangelism, Crieff, Perthshire: St. Ninians.

Thouless, Robert H., (1971), An Introduction to the Psychology of Religion (3rd Ed.), London: Cambridge University Press.

Thurman, Joyce C., (1979), New Wineskins: a study of the House Church Movement, MA thesis, Birmingham University.

Toon, Peter, (1965), 'English Strict Baptists', Baptist Quarterly 21 (1).

Towler, Robert and Coxon, A.P.M., (1979), The Fate of the Anglical Clergy: a sociological study, London: Macmillan.

Vaughan, Ted R., Smith, D.H. and Sjoberg, G., (1966), 'The religious orientations of American natural scientists', Social Forces 44 (4), pp 519-526.

Vaus, Jim, (1961), Why I Quit Syndicated Crime, London: Marshall, Morgan and Scott.

Wallace, Robert, (1870), 'Church tendencies in Scotland' in Sir Alexander Grant, Recess Studies, Edinburgh: Edmonston and Douglas.

Wallis, Roy, (1980), 'Sociological reflections on the demise of the Irish Humanist Association', Scottish Journal of Sociology 4 (2), pp 125-139.

Wallis, Roy, (1981), Charisma, commitment and control in a new religious movement' in Roy Wallis (ed) Millennialism and Charisma, forthcoming.

Wallis, Roy and Bruce, S., (1981), 'Accounting for action: the commonsense heresy', Sociology 17 (1), pp 97-110.

Warburton, T. Rennie, (1969), 'The Faith Mission: a study in inter-denominationalism', in David Martin, Sociological Yearbook of Religion, 2, London: SCM Press.

Watt, Lauchlan Maclean, (n.d.), The Scottish Covenanters, London: James Clarke.

Weber, Max, (1970), From Max Weber (eds. H.H. Gerth and C.W. Mills), London: Routledge Kegan Paul.

Weber, Max, (1976), The Protestant Ethic and the Spirit of Capitalism (2nd Ed.), London: George Allen and Unwin.

Weber, Timothy P., (1979), Living in the Shadow of the Second Coming: American pre-millennialism, 1875-1925, London: Oxford University Press.

Wells, David F. and Woodbridge, J.D., (1975), The Evangelicals: what they believe, who they are, where they are changing, Nashville: Abingdon Press.

Weisberger, Bernard A., (1958), They Gathered at the River, Boston: Little Brown.

Whittam, Fred L., (1968), 'Revivalism as institutionalised behaviour', Southwestern Social Science Quarterly June, pp 115-127.

White, J.W., (1963), The influence of North American evangelism in Great Britain between 1830 and 1914 on the origin and development of the ecumenical movement, D.Phil thesis, Oxford University.

Whitlow, Maurice, (1938), J. Taylor Smith: everybody's bishop, London: Lutterworth/Religious Tract Society.

Wilkinson, Rupert, (1972), The Broken Rebel, London: Croom Helm.

Williams, Paul, (1980), <u>Dylan - what happened?</u>, South Bend, Ind. and Glen Ellen, Cal.: and Books/Entwhistle Books.

William, William H., (1976), 'Oral Roberts goes legitimate', <u>Theology Today</u> 33, pp 279-282.

Wilson, Bryan, (1970), <u>Religious Sects</u>, London: World University Library.

Wilson, Bryan, (1976), <u>Contemporary Transformations of Religion</u>, London: Oxford University Press.

Wilson, G.D., (1973), <u>The Psychology of Conservatism</u>, New York: Academic Press.

Wright, Frank, (1973), 'Protestant ideology and politics in Ulster', <u>European Journal of Sociology</u>, XIV.

Wuthnow, Robert, (1980), 'World order and religious movements', in Albert Bergeson, <u>Structures of Modern World System</u>, New York: Academic Press.

Zablocki, Benjamin, (1971), <u>The Joyful Commuity: an account of the Bruderhof</u>, Baltimore: Penguin Press.

Zipfel, Richard, (1974), 'Letting the scapegoat into the house', mimeo advertisement for SCM GOAT project, Bristol: SCM.